ANCIENT AUSTRALIAN LANDSCAPES

The Three Sisters is a well-known landmark located at Katoomba, in the Blue Mountains west of Sydney. The 'Sisters' are sandstone pinnacles, shaped by rainwater that percolated down and weathered the rock along the joints that separate the three. This took place beneath an ancient plain which has since been uplifted and a remnant of which can be seen on the skyline. The uplift caused rivers to cut into the high plain and carve deep narrow gorges. In the rock exposed in the walls of the narrow valleys the weathered rock adjacent to joints has been washed away leaving the pinnacles as prominent local features.

ANCIENT AUSTRALIAN LANDSCAPES

C.R. TWIDALE

School of Earth and Environmental Sciences, Geology and Geophysics,

University of Adelaide, Adelaide, South Australia 5005

ROSENBERG

Dedication

This book is dedicated to my long-time friend and colleague, Heli Wopfner. One of the last all-round geologists, scholarly, with eclectic interests and expertise in most of them, Heli is, like the author, happiest in the bush, preferably African or Australian.

Cover photographs
(Front) **Hamersley Range, Western Australia**

The smooth skyline is part of the Hamersley Surface, cut across Precambrian iron-rich sediments. During the later Mesozoic, 70-120 million years ago, the surface was weathered, producing a ferruginous soil cover. With the lowering of the then sea level, rivers incised their beds. The soil cover was largely stripped away from the upland and deposited in the floors of valleys radiating from the hills. The iron-rich deposits hardened on drying to form the Robe River Pisolite (which is now extensively mined). It was resistant to erosion, whereas the adjacent valley-side slopes were worn down, leaving the old valley floors as a series of upstanding, sinuous flat-topped mesas or table-topped hills, examples of which are seen in the foreground. This is an example of relief inversion, for what were valleys are now high points in the local landscape.

(Back) **Isa Highlands, Queensland**
The Isa Highlands is an uplifted block of folded Precambrian strata intruded by granite. During Early Cretaceous times the sea covered the area and was buried by marine sediments. With the withdrawal of the sea, rivers cut into and largely stripped the cover to re-expose the planate surface cut in Precambrian rocks on which the marine beds had been deposited. Here in the southern Isa Highlands weathered Cretaceous rocks rest on Precambrian granite, but where the sediments have been removed the unconformity between the older and younger rocks is exposed as an exhumed pre-Cretaceous landscape remnant. (CSIRO)

First published in Australia in 2007
by Rosenberg Publishing Pty Ltd
PO Box 6125, Dural Delivery Centre NSW 2158
Phone: 61 2 9654 1502 Fax: 61 2 9654 1338
Email: rosenbergpub@smartchat.net.au
Web: www.rosenbergpub.com.au

The National Library of Australia Cataloguing-in-Publication entry:

Twidale, C. R. (Charles Rowland).
Ancient Australian landscapes.

1st ed.
Bibliography.
Includes index.
ISBN 9781877058448.

1. Landscape - Australia. 2. Landforms - Australia.
I.
Title.

551.410994

Set in 12 on 14 pt Adobe Caslon Pro
Printed in China by Everbest Printing Co Limited

CONTENTS

FOREWORD

Australia is the continent of ancient landscapes. Younger landscapes dominate in Europe, Asia, and North America. Of the others, South America also has the relatively young Andes Mountains; Africa has its rift zones and the Atlas Mountains; and Antarctica mostly lies under currently active glacial ice. All of Australia, in contrast, is regionally characterised by various landscapes that date to at least the Tertiary, and, as argued in this book, to the Mesozoic. Of course, there are superimposed younger landforms, including coral reefs, shore platforms, and alluvial fans. However, Australia's regionally extensive plains and erosion surfaces all preserve indicators of their great geological antiquity.

Much of modern geomorphology has, until recently, moved away from the study of ancient landscapes. In the early part of the last century, great syntheses were developed to explain whole landscapes, many of which were first explored during the previous century. Unfortunately, these theories proved difficult to verify with the then-available quantitative tools appropriate to very large temporal and spatial scales. Partly in reaction to the perceived failure of this earlier thinking, the geomorphology of the later twentieth century progressively became more focused on physical-based mathematical treatments of processes. The 'new geomorphology' even developed into a kind of revolution, stipulating that the mathematical modelling of processes constitutes a more effective scientific approach than the explanatory description of whole landscapes. However, this process-based agenda had the partly unintended consequence that the temporal and spatial scales of geomorphological inquiry were diminished, simply because the time scales for measurement of active processes are limited to human scales, and large regions involve complex assemblages of processes. Of course, a Cartesian reductionistic metaphysics

presumes that, having effectively analysed the fine scale of things, one can then simply sum the fine-scaled components to generate what occurs at much larger scales of time and space. Presumption is not science, and it is now obvious that one cannot simply extrapolate the process measurements from fine scales of time and space. Landscapes, not unlike living organisms, display complexities of organisation at large scales that are not simply constituent of their fine scale parts.

I recall once reading that a question was put to the great evolutionary biologist, Ernst Mayr. Mayr was asked if there could possibly be anything more to a complex organism other than its molecular and physical components. Mayr quickly answered in the affirmative, stating that every known organism also has its own unique history. We probably won't have a definitive resolution on this issue unless and until the molecular biologists mix the right ingredients in the right way in a test tube to have something crawl out. Nevertheless, in regard to the landscapes of Australia, Twidale's approach is the geomorphological analogue to Mayr's historical viewpoint in evolutionary biology. In this spirit, the continent of ancient landscapes is dissected for our scientific appreciation. Each region is set in its geological context, and all the relevant arguments are mustered in regard to the evidence for antiquity.

Twidale's synthesis of ancient Australian landscapes is very timely. Geomorphology in the new century is beginning to rediscover its earlier intellectual excitement in regard to large scales and regional landscapes. This may well become another revolution, but not one that stipulates the proper methodologies for doing science. After all, the best methodology is not that which we stipulate in advance, but rather that which leads us on to important new discoveries. Thus, the new revolution will have to be 'adventitious', as the historian of geology, Rachel Laudan, once characterised plate tectonics. New tools have recently become available for exploring landscapes at large temporal and spatial scales. These include the use of cosmogenic nuclides for the dating of surface features, and improved tools for geochronology of rocks and sediments. Amounts of uplift and erosion can be specified over long time scales with thermochronology. High-resolution remote sensing and altimetry can now be applied to very large regions, combining various data sets with GIS technology. The latter tools are being applied to newly discovered landscapes on the ocean floor and on the rocky surfaces of extraterrestrial planets, moons, and asteroids in the solar system. Of course, there will be issues of how to interpret the new data, including how one can compare landscapes that form in very different environments, but these are all exciting questions associated with discovery. Because the fantastic ancient landscapes of Australia will figure prominently in this 'new geomorphology', it is very helpful to have this summary of Twidale's half century of research on the topic.

In developing the science of ancient Australian landscapes, Twidale introduces us to the key researchers who contributed to that science. His biographical notes provide a historical interlude to the descriptions of each region and the summary of current thinking about their origins. This approach is not without its critics. These critics sometimes cite the following quote (a favourite of some physicists), attributed to Alfred North Whitehead: 'A science which hesitates to forget its founders is lost'. The quote is used to imply that science, unlike the humanities, does not need history to get on with its task of developing new and better truths.

Indeed, Whitehead is saying that dwelling on past work can be counterproductive, since it is essential that science get beyond its previous paradigms and develop new, more effective theories. Science is not concerned with the past or even the present state of knowledge; science requires an attitude that propels inquiry to new levels of understanding.

I think it is quite wrongheaded to interpret the logic of Whitehead's quote as disparaging an important role for the history of science. Yes, outdated ideas of the past must be supplanted by the efforts of our ongoing inquiries. Nevertheless, the relation of our present-day science to the past state of knowledge (sometimes developed in so-called 'Whig history') is not what genuine history of science is all about. Nor is history of science a glorification of the past and its heroes. Its basic point is that science is an activity performed by and an attitude held by people. It is these special people, 'scientists' the mineralogist William Whewell first named them, who have the creative insights, do the first explorations, and make the tedious measurements. They write the manuscripts that convince their fellow scientists that some lines of inquiry are more productive than others for testing and new hypothesising. All this occurs in contexts of academic or government institutions, political agendas, professional rivalries, and colleagial collaborations. While such things are not the facts of science, they are absolutely essential to the processes of science happening. We can only learn about such processes by exploring the history of those engaged in science.

Victor R. Baker,
The University of Arizona

PREFACE

Anyone with half an eye for country and travelling with purpose cannot but notice the high plains and bevels preserved in most Australian uplands. Some workers suspected that these high plains are remnants of landscapes of great antiquity. Later geological mapping and technological advances in the dating of rocks have confirmed that they are indeed old but also revealed that they may be of an antiquity even greater than hitherto suspected.

It is said that A.W. Kinglake, traveller, author of *Eothen*, and historian of the Crimean War, would have liked to see on each church an inscription stating: 'Important if true'. His pithy and challenging implied query neatly summarises why this book was written. For if the surfaces discussed are as old as the evidence appears to suggest, they challenge several cherished geomorphological precepts concerning the processes at work at and near the Earth's surface. If they are as old as has been deduced — for no means directly of dating old surfaces has yet been devised — the implications for general geomorphological theory are several and fundamental. They could change the way landscapes are viewed. Obviously, I should not have recorded the evidence for the great antiquity of some surfaces had I not considered it compelling or at least plausible. Others, however, may see the landscapes under review in a different light and interpret them in other ways. Some already do. But the topic is sufficiently important to have the evidence presented and the arguments aired: 'there can be no debate, and no formal judgement, unless there is publication' (Rice 2005, p. 28).

In this account the conventional wisdom concerning the age of land surfaces is first explained. Types of surface and methods of dating them are outlined. The evidence for the antiquity of land surfaces in various parts of Australia is presented. Accepting the evidence and argument that very old surfaces exist, the factors conducive to their survival are suggested. The evidence pointing to long-term increases in relief amplitude are outlined. Consequences for general theory discussed.

Interspersed with these geological and geomorphological accounts are brief biographies of some of the early workers involved in the investigation and interpretation of some of these old land surfaces: this by way of a modest tribute to their perspicacity and tenacity, and to their courage in advancing what were even then outlandish ideas; for the way of the nonconformist has never been easy. To qualify for inclusion they had to have made notable contributions and no longer to be with us. Fortunately and happily several who have distinguished themselves in this field have not yet met the second of these conditions and are readily identified from the references to their work in the text.

The topics considered here have been described as 'dry', that is, dull or uninteresting. That may be true for some, but just as beauty is in the eye of the beholder so are hobbies and interests. Some find roses and orchids fascinating. Others are devoted to postage stamps, wine labels, or model trains. The interest of students of landscape may be captured by glaciers or volcanoes. For the author and for many before him and at present, the antiquity of some parts of landscapes has engaged his interest for more than half a century; not to the exclusion of all else but significantly and in the long term. I make no excuses for having been puzzled and entranced by landscapes like those of the Yilgarn Craton, a region that was once described by my friend and colleague Edwin Hills (1961, p. 87) as 'a veteran scarred and buffeted over the millennia but always apparently recognizable'. It is a description applicable to many parts of the island continent.

C.R. Twidale,
September 2006

ACKNOWLEDGMENTS

Although as an undergraduate in England I was told of O.T. Jones' outrageous suggestion that the summit surface of the Welsh massif may be of Triassic age, nothing was made of its possible implications for general geomorphological theory. It was not until I encountered and mapped Australian landscapes, and was faced with the task of producing legends for those maps, that the problems of dating surfaces hit home. On finding evidence of what my background assured me was unreasonable antiquity I was fortunate in meeting and coming to know Edwin Hills and 'Doc' Öpik, both of whom were familiar with, and seemingly entertained no qualms about, very old landscapes which they recognised as common components of the contemporary scenery (Hills 1934, 1938; Öpik 1961). I am grateful to them for moral support and encouragement in pursuing old surfaces. Lester King (1962) was also supportive from a distance, and the late Bob Sharp was typically generous of spirit in recommending publication of an early essay on old landforms. He could understand the evidence and argument which pointed to antiquity but his instincts, training and experience caused him to hesitate. He could not accept that such old landscapes exist. Nevertheless, he recommended that this different viewpoint be aired. (He later *almost* came to accept that old surfaces have persisted!) Over the years I have enjoyed constructive discussions and exchanges on palaeoforms with several colleagues, especially Heli Wopfner, Bill Bradley, Rudi Horwitz, Bob Young, J.R. Vidal Romaní (Moncho) and Liz Campbell, and I thank them.

Above all, however, I record my gratitude for discussions in the field and in the office with Jennie Bourne whose good sense and tenacity have helped me see this project through to publication. Without her help and support the book would not have happened.

Photographs of the persons featured in biographical notes were kindly provided, as follows: Professor E.S. Hills (courtesy Mrs Doris Hills); Dr B. Daily (courtesy Geology and Geophysics, School of Earth and Environmental Sciences, University of Adelaide); Professor G.D. Woodard (courtesy Professor Tom Anderson, Geology, Sonoma State University, California); R. Lockhart Jack (courtesy PIRSA); Dr J.T. Jutson (courtesy Professor E.J. Brock, Bryn Athyn, Pennsylvania); Dr A.A. Öpik (A.A. Öpik); C.S. Christian (© 2004 CSIRO. Reproduced with the kind permission of CSIRO Land and Water; and with the concurrence of Barbara Christian representing the Christian family); and F.A. Craft (courtesy Geographical Society of New South Wales).

Chapter 1

CONVENTION AND REALITY

'Australia is the flattest, driest, ugliest place on earth. Only those who can be possessed by her can know what secret beauty she holds.' (E.P. Willmot 1987, p. 1)

One of the most intriguing of the many problems posed by the Australian landscape concerns the great age of many of its component parts. Areas like Kangaroo Island, the Flinders Ranges, the Gawler Ranges, Yilgarn Craton or Block, Kakadu, and many areas of the Eastern Uplands are evidently so old as to be impossible in terms of traditional theory. Thus, this book is about an unusual aspect of an unusual continent. Some elements of the Australian landscape may not be the oldest in the world but they are certainly amongst the oldest. Such possible great antiquity is of importance to geomorphological theory, for its implications are at odds with the conventional wisdom. It is also of interest to stratigraphers who are concerned with not only depositional but also erosional aspects of past chronologies, and to palaeobotanists, for remnants of older landscapes may well prove to be plant refuges (e.g. Hopper et al. 1996; Fay et al. 2001).

It is widely accepted that the Earth's land surfaces are youthful, a conclusion well founded in everyday observations of natural events, and in common sense. Rivers, wind and the waves are constantly at work wearing away the rock exposed at the land surface. After heavy rains, rivers are turbid, discoloured with mud and clay. When river levels fall and the surface flow slows or ceases, the cobbles and boulders they have carried during periods of high flow and flood are clearly visible. This sediment must have been picked up by the river upstream, implying that the land surface there has been eroded. In human terms the flow of rivers is variable, some being episodic and unpredictable, some intermittent or variable, but regularly so. Even those that run permanently experience periods of flood and low stand. But, in the context of geological time, rivers and streams can be regarded as being constantly at work: hence the conclusion that the Earth's surface is undergoing continuous change.

This was appreciated over 200 years ago by James Hutton (1788, 1795), a Scottish farmer and scientist who is considered by many to be the 'father' of modern geology. Hutton recognised that though interrupted by catastrophic events (see also Baker 1973; Hunt 1990; Ager 1993) there have been long periods of gradual change during which the land surface has been modified, with erosion here, and deposition there. Hills have been made low and sediments have been laid down to form new strata. If the Huttonian concept of constant change is correct, no part of the Earth's surface can long have survived modification by external agencies such as water, ice and wind. For this reason geologists and geomorphologists have long asserted that in geological terms (Table 1.1) all landscapes are youthful (e.g. Wooldridge 1951; Linton 1957). Some have suggested that no landscape is more than a couple of million years old (e.g. Ashley 1931; Thornbury 1954, p. 26), while others allow that some landscape remnants may have persisted for a few tens of millions of years, or even as long as 60 million years (e.g. Brown 1980).

And it is true that most parts of the continental surfaces including the great riverine and desert plains that occupy huge areas of the centre of Australia are relatively young and are only a few thousands or hundreds of thousands of years old. In keeping

GEOLOGICAL TIME SCALE AND MAJOR EVENTS

ERA	PERIOD	EPOCH	DATE AT BOUNDARY (MILLIONS OF YEARS)	LIFE FORMS	IMMENSITY OF TIME
PHANEROZOIC / CENOZOIC	Quaternary	Holocene		Modern humans	Less than the last 1/2 second of December 31
			0.01		
		Pleistocene		Stone-Age humans	
			1.4		
	Tertiary	Pliocene		Flowering plants common	
			5		
		Miocene			
			24		
		Oligocene	37	Ancestral apes	
		Eocene			Soon after 9.00am December 26
			58		
		Palaeocene		Ancestral horse, cattle	
			66		
PHANEROZOIC / MESOZOIC	Cretaceous			Dinosaurs extinct, flowering plants appear	Just after Midday December 21
			144		
	Jurassic			Birds, mammals appear	
			208		
	Triassic			Dinosaurs appear	
			245		
PHANEROZOIC / PALAEOZOIC	Permian				
			286		
	Carboniferous			First reptiles, winged insects	
			360		
	Devonian			First amphibians, trees	
			408		
	Silurian			First land plants	
			438		
	Ordovician				
			505		
	Cambrian			First shelly fossils	
			540		
PROTEROZOIC	*Oxygen rich atmosphere*			First multicellular animals	
			1000		
			1500		
	Red beds			Bacteria and filamentous blue-green algae	
	Some free oxygen				
	Banded iron formation		2000		
			2500		Late on May 31
ARCHAEAN	*Oxygen poor atmosphere*			Oldest stromatolites	
	Greenstone belts		3000	Photosynthesis Bacteria, unicellular blue-green algae	
			3500		
				Earliest evidence of life	
	Oldest preserved rocks				
	Origin of hydrosphere and atmosphere		4000	? Origin of life	
	Origin of Earth		4500		One second past Midnight January 1

Table 1.1   Geological time scale and major events in organic evolution. Comparison with calendar year (on right) indicates the immensity of the abyss of time.

with this, the models of landscape evolution introduced over the last hundred years or so took cognisance of constant change and implied that the resultant land surfaces are youthful. The Davisian model (Davis 1899, 1909) was based in the lowering of slopes, or downwearing (Fig. 1.1a). King (1942), building on the work of earlier workers such as Fisher (1866), Jutson (1914) and Holmes (1918), considered that valley-side slopes were worn back within close limits parallel to themselves (Fig. 1.1b), but achieved baselevelling, or the reduction of the landmass to lower relief, in the course of a few tens of millions of years.

Hack and Goodlett (1960; Hack 1960) suggested that a surface could attain a steady state with slope development adjusting to valley incision and undergoing constant erosion without significant

Uplift > Incision	Incision > Wasting	1 Increasing relief
	Incision = Wasting	2 Static relief
	Incision < Wasting	3 Decreasing relief (P)
Uplift = Incision	Incision > Wasting	4 Increasing relief
	Incision + Wasting	5 Static relief
	Incision < Wasting	6 Decreasing relief (P)
Uplift < Incision	Incision > Wasting	7 Increasing relief
	Incision = Wasting	8 Static relief
	Incision < Wasting	9 Decreasing relief (P)

Note P = peneplain or other surface of low relief.

Table 1.2 Landform development caused by interaction of uplift, incision and wasting (after Kennedy 1962). Kennedy uses the term 'erosion' for river incision and 'denudation' for wasting, i.e. weathering and mass movement.

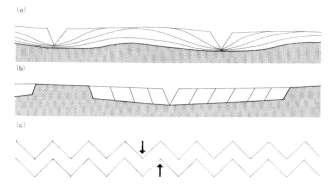

Fig. 1.1 Sections showing **(a)** Davisian downwearing of slopes, **(b)** backwearing as advocated by King, and **(c)** steady state development as suggested by Hack.

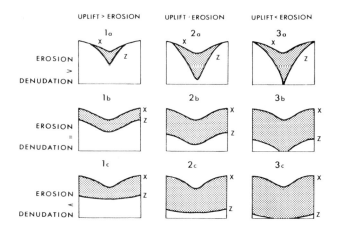

Fig. 1.2 Models of landscape evolution depending on variation in relative rates of uplift, stream incision and erosion of divides. (After Kennedy 1962)

change of shape (Fig. 1.1c). Others (e.g. Kennedy 1962) devised schemes of development in which various combinations of uplift, stream incision and valley-side development were considered (Fig. 1.2, Table 1.2). One of Kennedy's models involves pronounced river incision combined with minimal wasting of divides, but no spatial or temporal scales are indicated.

Walther Penck was primarily interested in the interplay between tectonics and exogenetic agencies and took this into account in his interpretation of slopes and planation surfaces (Penck 1924, 1953). Thus he suggested that convex valley-side slopes indicated increasing uplift, neglecting the controls exerted by regional and local baselevels. He advocated that slopes are regraded from the base upwards (see e.g. Bremer 1983). He recognised that plains could evolve in one of two ways, as a result of either lowering by streams (*Endrümpf*) or the interplay between a rising crust and incising rivers (*Primarrümpf*). Long-term survival is implied in neither.

Most of these models of landscape development assume baselevel control. Areas located on divides are older than those near the mouths of incised rivers, where younger surfaces are initiated and from which they gradually extend. This takes time, so that older landscape elements persist on divides, particularly if scarp retreat has been prevalent, for this allows remnants of the older, incised surface to persist until late in the sequence of events. In respect of an extensive continent such a sequence or 'cycle' (because the end result resembles the initial surface) lasts for 30–40 million years (e.g. Schumm 1963). This is still insufficient to accommodate the very old elements that persist in some contemporary landscapes.

That the youthful view of landscape was not universally applicable became clear when a few geologists, particularly, but not only, those working in the southern hemisphere concluded that some elements of the land surface are much older than is allowed by conventional theories and models. For example, O.T. Jones, a British geologist, in 1931 suggested that the upland surface of central Wales may be as old as Triassic, that is some 200–250 million years old. There, and in southern Africa, the evidence of antiquity, though suggestive, was inconclusive (e.g. Willis 1936; du Toit 1937, pp. 229–230; Wellington 1937; Dixey 1938, 1942; King 1942, 1962). Similarly, a Cretaceous age for the Schooley Surface of the Appalachians has been entertained for many years but conclusive evidence has not been forthcoming (e.g. Bascom 1921; Bliss Knopf 1924; but see Poag and Sevon 1989). In Australia, however, beginning in the 1920s and early 1930s, evidence was noted which points very clearly to landforms and landscapes more than 60 million years old (Hossfeld 1926; Craft 1932, 1933; Hills 1934, 1938).

Admittedly many of these old surfaces are of etch type for they have been largely stripped of any regolith developed during their planation. This is a crucial point, for there is more likelihood of a bare rock surface persisting than one covered by a soil or regolith that retains moisture. However, the etch concept, though of some antiquity (Twidale 2002), was not widely appreciated until the middle of the twentieth century or even later, and the geological world at large was not impressed by such evidence and argument and took little notice of these seemingly absurd suggestions. Yet in southern Africa (e.g. Partridge and Maud 1987), and in Australia (e.g. Twidale 1994), later geological mapping and technological advances in rock dating have together confirmed, and in some instances demonstrated afresh, that landscapes several scores and even a few hundreds of millions of years old survive in the contemporary scenery.

Such very old landscape elements raise questions as to why and how land surfaces have persisted. Also, the conventional models of landscape development involving either downwearing or backwearing imply a decrease in relief amplitude within the period of a cycle or sequence of change. Field evidence, however, suggests that relief amplitude — the vertical height between the highest and lowest points in a landscape — has increased through long periods of time because the plains and valleys have demonstrably been eroded faster than the uplands.

Thus three major conceptual problems arise from an analysis of Australian landscapes. First, some elements of the landscape are older than is feasible in terms of conventional models of landscape evolution. What is the evidence for their antiquity? Second, how have very old landscapes survived? Third, some landscapes have developed an increased relief amplitude through time. What is the evidence? Answers to all three problems bear on general geomorphological theory and the way landscapes are viewed. And implicitly they pose a fourth question, namely, how typical of the global picture is the surface of Australia?

These problems are explored in the following pages. Some general comments on the physical and geological characteristics of the Australian continent are followed by a discussion of what is meant by the age of a surface in various contexts: different types of erosional surface have been recognised and 'age' carries a different connotation for each. Because the procedures are later illustrated and explained in reference to specific examples, the justification of relevant methods used for dating land surfaces is brief and general. The regional sections contain accounts of old surfaces identified in various parts of the continent together with the evidence and argument concerning their age. If the earlier descriptions are longer and more detailed than some that come later, that is because, first, more is known about some regions than others, and second, the initial reviews of particular methods are necessarily longer than later references to the same procedure. How ancient landforms and landscapes have survived is then discussed. There follows an outline of the evidence and argument that points to increased relief amplitude at various scales of space and time. These several themes are drawn together in a final chapter. Biographical notes concerning investigators who contributed significantly to this story, but are now deceased, are included at appropriate points in the text, and a glossary is appended in order to clarify some of the terminology used.

Chapter 2

LAND OF SWEEPING PLAINS

Biographical note: E.S. Hills (1906–1986)
Edwin Sherbon Hills was born in Melbourne in 1906 and died there in 1986. Following a distinguished school career he entered the University of Melbourne in 1923. He intended reading chemistry but found he was colour blind, which was at that time a disadvantage in practical work. He switched to geology, taking First Class Honours. For his MSc he studied the geology of the Cathedral Range, some 50 km northeast of Melbourne, an investigation that caused the stratigraphy of that part of Victoria to be revised and also involved what were to become lifelong interests, including physiography (or geomorphology). He took his PhD in London (and met his future lifelong wife there), before returning to a lectureship in his alma mater, where he eventually (1944) became professor. He was a rounded, old-fashioned geologist with eclectic interests and several areas of acknowledged expertise including fossil fish, structural geology, igneous petrology and geomorphology.

During World War II Hills undertook the construction of a relief model of Australia. In theory this would provide a basis for making topographic maps, which were much in demand for military purposes. In reality it was not finished until after the end of the war, but it led Hills to the identification of lineaments which have proved to be important both in understanding landscape and in mineral exploration (e.g. O'Driscoll 1986). He coined the term 'morphotectonics' to describe the study of structural geomorphology at the regional scale. After his death his ashes were scattered on the Cathedral Range (Tattam 1972; Hill 1989; Twidale 2000a).

E.S. Hills

Physique

Australia is an extensive but low continent (Fig. 2.1a). Though some 7.66 million square kilometres in area, its mean altitude is only 330 m above present sea level. Forty per cent of the continent stands less than 200 m above sea level, and its highest point in Mt Kosciuszko rises to only 2227 m. By comparison Mt Cook (Aoraki), in the much less extensive New Zealand rises to a height of 3754

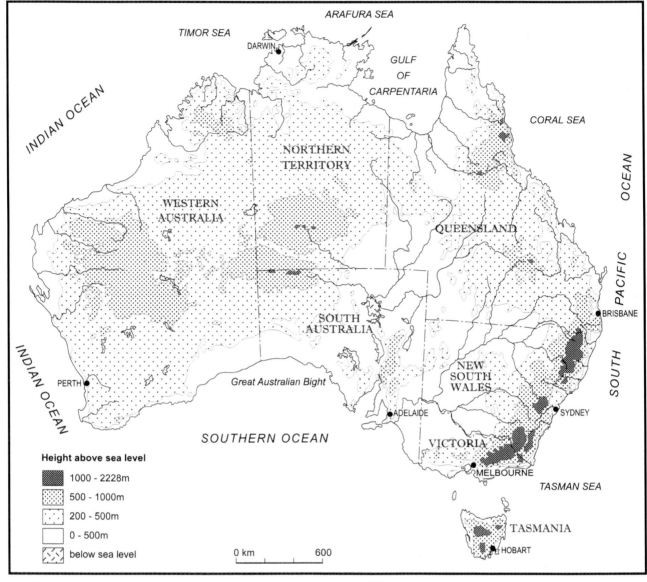

Fig. 2.1a Topography and major rivers of Australia. (After Jacobson & Lau 1987).

m. In North America, Mt McKinley stands 6194 m above sea level, yet is not amongst the world's highest mountains, at least 50 of which exceed the 7000-metre mark.

Australia is a compact continent with few major islands, inlets or embayments. Despite its large area, the coastline is just under 20,000 km long. The ratio of shore length to area of land mass is approximately one kilometre of coast for every 390 square kilometres of land. By comparison, the ratio for peninsular and insular Europe is 1:75. The only major indentations in the Australian coast are the Gulf of Carpentaria, Bonaparte Gulf, and King Sound on the north coast, Exmouth Gulf and Shark Bay on the west, and Port Phillip Bay and the gulfs St Vincent and Spencer on the south. The only major islands are Tasmania and Kangaroo

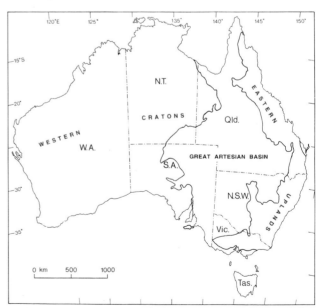

Fig. 2.1b Structural divisions of Australia. (After Palfreyman 1984).

Island in the south, Fraser Island on the east, and Groote Eylandt, Melville and Bathurst islands off the north coast. More than half of the area is served by endoreic streams flowing to basins of internal drainage. Of these, the Lake Eyre catchment accounts for 1.3 million square kilometres of central and northeastern Australia. Less than half of the continent is served by exoreic streams (i.e. by rivers that flow to the sea). Of these, only the River Murray is notably long, but it is of low discharge in terms of the catchment it serves.

Geological framework

Like all the other continents, Australia includes ancient massifs or *shields* built of crystalline rocks billions of years old (Fig. 2.1b). Many include zones of sedimentary rocks, some — surprisingly — still relatively undisturbed, but most of them more-or-less contorted in ancient fold belts or *orogens*. Several sedimentary basins of various ages, some at depth seriously deformed, underlie the Great Artesian Basin. This is a Mesozoic feature comprising the Eromanga, Surat and Carpentaria basins. Together with the Murray Basin they form a series of structural *platforms* or regions of relatively undisturbed strata, which extends from the northern to the southern coasts.

Remnants of old orogens and platforms occur as outliers within the shield areas. Taken together they constitute the various *cratons* (Fig. 2.1b). The terms 'craton' and 'block' are virtually synonymous, but following Trendall (1990, pp. 3–7), 'block' used in this context denotes an ancient relatively stable crustal unit that has evidently at all times been a tectonic high by contrast with adjacent, consistently depressed basins.

Australia is geologically an ancient continent. Physical datings show that the Earth is immensely, unimaginably old, having been formed 4.5–4.6 billion years ago (e.g. Dalrymple 1991; Table 1.1). Many meteorites are of that order of antiquity, while Moon rocks give ages around 3.5 billion years. Though not yet demonstrably the most ancient known, many of the rocks exposed in the western shield lands of Australia gave dates of more than 4 billion years old (Wilde et al. 2001; Laeter and Trendall 2002) and are amongst the oldest yet analysed from anywhere on Earth. The dates are derived from grains of zircon in quartzites exposed

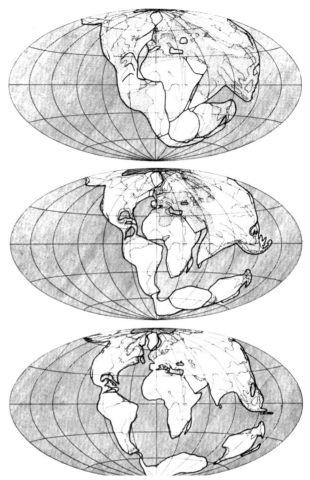

Fig. 2.2a The breakup of Pangaea, including Gondwana. (After Wegener 1924)

near Mt Narryer, in the Murchison River catchment of the northern Yilgarn Craton. The quartzite was produced by the weathering and erosion of an older rock, which has not been located. It may have been completely destroyed by the forces of nature, but there is here the possibility of finding rocks even older than the oldest yet dated.

In addition, alleged signs of former life — fossil bacteria or bacteria-like organisms (prokaryotes, some 3.4 billion years old) — have been discovered, again in the Mt Narryer area (Schopf and Packer 1987; Rasmussen 2000; but see also Brasier et al. 2002). Complex single-celled creatures (eukaryotes) from rocks in the same area date from some 3.1 billion years. Thus Australia can boast both rocks and organisms as old as any yet discovered.

Plates and lineaments

The present Australian continent was for maybe 1000 million years part of a super-supercontinent known as Rodinia. Later, after its breakup and migration, the various crustal blocks formed a

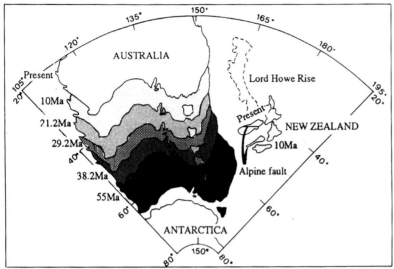

Fig. 2.2b Northerly migration of Australia during the Cenozoic. (After Ludbrook 1980)

supercontinent called Gondwana, which, with Laurasia, was a component of another super-supercontinent, Pangaea. It existed 300–200 million years ago. According to the now widely accepted theory of plate tectonics (Holmes 1931; Hess 1962; Vine and Matthews 1963; Morley and LaRochelle 1964; but also Meyerhoff and Meyerhoff 1974, and other chapters in Kahle 1974; also Larin 1993) about 200 million years ago Pangaea and with it Gondwana began to fragment. The component parts drifted apart, with what are now eastern South America, Africa (except for the younger Atlas Mountains), Antarctica and peninsular India going their separate ways (Fig. 2.2a); and those migrations continue. On separating from Antarctica, Australia

moved equatorwards (Fig. 2.2b). It is still moving at a rate of 65–70 mm per annum in a direction slightly east of north (e.g. Ludbrook 1980, p. 91; Parker 1993), and will eventually collide with the Indonesian Archipelago. These lateral migrations are but the most recent of a series of crustal motions that have had a profound effect on the structure of all of the continents, including Australia, for they have introduced into the crustal rocks and blocks stresses and strains most obviously manifested as fracture patterns.

As is apparent from the regional accounts that follow, structure is everywhere important in landscape analysis. Many sectors of the Australian coast as well as rivers and other large-scale topographic features are straight or linear. They are coincident with, and an expression of, long, straight or gently arcuate, deep-seated structures known as lineaments (Hobbs 1904, 1911; see also Hills 1946, 1956; O'Driscoll 1986, 1989; O'Driscoll and Campbell 1997). Many of them are fault zones (O'Leary et al. 1976), others, deep-seated linear zones of strain susceptible to weathering (e.g. Russell 1935; Turner and Verhoogen 1960, p. 476; Nabarro 1967, p. 4). Though they vary in age, some are of great antiquity, and formed as soon as the Earth's crust was cool, consolidated and brittle (see Skobelin 1992). They are due to torsion or shearing in the crust (e.g. Kalb 1990) related to plate migrations. They have been, and

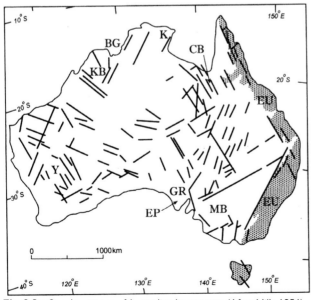

Fig. 2.3a Simple pattern of Australian lineaments. (After Hills 1956)

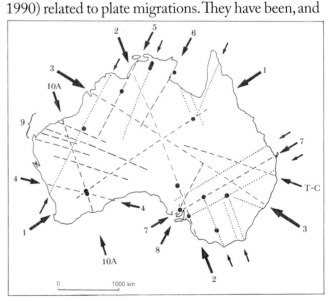

Fig. 2.3b Lineaments and associated corridors. (After O'Driscoll 1986)

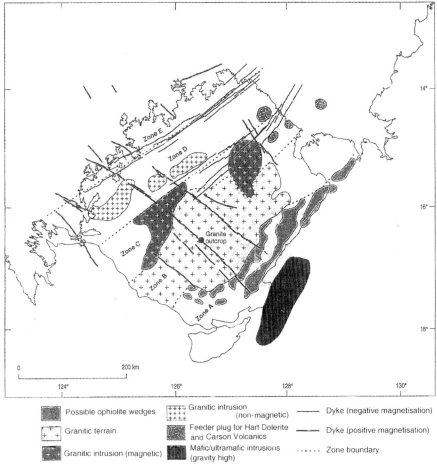

For the last 90 million years, at least, the Australian continent has been moving roughly northward and as it is made up of blocks of different compositions and strengths, the joggling induced by lateral movement caused, and continues to produce shearing, or deformation resulting from torsion, or excess transverse stress. Hence the many essentially orthogonal fracture patterns seen in outcrops of brittle rocks (Vening Meinesz 1947; Kalb 1990; O'Driscoll 1986). The many earthquakes and tremors recorded, if not felt (e.g. Gordon and Lewis 1980; McCue 1990; Bowman 1992; Greenhalgh et al. 1994; Twidale and Bourne 2000a; Bourne and Twidale 2005), attest continued and continuing differential migration of blocks as well as distortion within them. The resultant scarps and zones of

Fig. 2.4a Fracture patterns, Kimberley Block, Western Australia. (After Gunn and Meixner 1998)

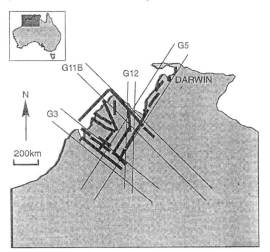

Fig. 2.4b Suggested lineaments of the Kimberley Block and Bonaparte Gulf, northern Australia. (After Elliott 1994, p. 76)

remain, recurrently active. They are part of a global network (e.g. Vening Meinesz 1947) and in Australia (Hills 1946, 1956), as elsewhere, are aligned roughly NE–SW and NW–SE. In addition, latitudinal trends associated with conjugate, or genetically and geometrically related, shears in the basement rocks, criss-cross the landmasses (Fig. 2.3).

Fig. 2.5 Outline of the structural or framed Murray Basin. (Hills 1956)

Morphotectonics

Despite their ancient origin, lineaments still find expression in the landscape. The study of the relationship between structure and surface at the regional or 'mega' scale is called morphotectonics (Hills 1961). Thus the alignment of several major coastal sectors, such as the west coast of Eyre Peninsula and of the Kimberley Block, the Bonaparte Gulf (Elliott 1994; Fig. 2.4) and the Gulf of Carpentaria, are coincident with lineaments or major fractures in the crust, as are the linear western margins of 'lakes' (actually salinas) Torrens and Eyre, and the outlines of the Murray (Fig. 2.5) and other structural or framed basins.

Several major river courses and sectors also are remarkably straight. The Darling is a prime example, but sectors of the Georgina, Diamantina, Lachlan, Thompson and Cooper are also remarkably linear (Fig. 2.6). Yet in all of these instances the rivers flow mostly through young alluvial sediments that are not brittle and lack regular systems and sets of fractures. These straight rivers have been attributed to underprinting or the imposition from below of fractures in the underlying basement on to the overlying sediments (Hills 1961; Firman 1974; Twidale 2006). Slight joggling of deep faults

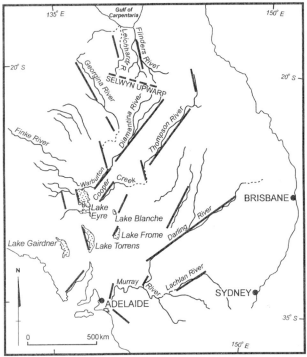

Fig. 2.6 Straight underprinted rivers in the Great Artesian Basin.

weakness are said to be of tectonic origin (i.e. due to deep-seated crustal movements). Those post-dating the Miocene are said to be neotectonic features.

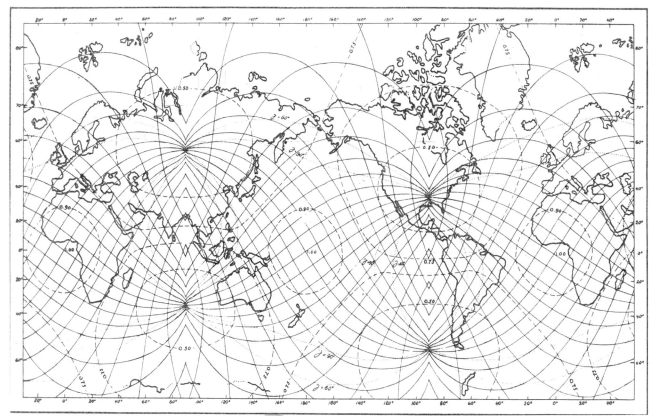

Fig. 2.7 The global pattern of shears or lineaments according to Vening Meinesz (1947).

may account for this. Alternatively, the underlying fracture zones may attract groundwater flow leading to weathering and subsidence (e.g. Twidale and Bourne 2000b). Whatever the mechanism, it is clear that even in geologically youthful terrains, ancient structures still find morphological expression, not only regionally but also at local and site scales (see Kalb 1990). Underprinting may also account for certain arcuate stream patterns (Saul 1976; Woodall 1994; O'Driscoll and Campbell 1997). It has been suggested that they are linked to meteorite craters in the primordial crust, which some consider may have been what is now termed the Mohorovicic discontinuity (Skobelin 1992; Twidale 2006).

Lineaments explain many salient features of the Australian landscape but they also pose a problem, for they developed at least 1000 million years ago, when Australia was part of Rodinia. The difficulty is that in every contemporary continent the lineaments form part of a global network (Fig. 2.7). This appears to imply that they have retained their original orientations, or have rotated through 90°, or multiples thereof, during lateral migration, which is unlikely. It may be that the pattern is more apparent than real, with random trends being subconsciously fitted into a preconceived pattern; but this also is unlikely, for the patterns as reported are statistically real.

Chapter 3

SURFACES AND THEIR AGES

'Age' and 'surface'

As with the age of a wine or of a sedimentary layer, the age of a surface refers to the time of its initiation or origin. The age of a wine refers to its vintage — the year of the season when the grapes from which it is produced were harvested. Similarly the age of, say, a sandstone stratum refers to the period when it was first laid down. The character of a wine changes in the years after its vintage as a result of chemical changes that occur in the vat or in the bottle. Likewise, a layer of sand buried and compressed under the weight of overlying strata becomes solid (lithified, *lithos* = rock). Later it may be folded, but regardless of its structure, the age by which it is known is that of the period during which it was deposited.

Similarly a landform — a specific individual feature, a hill, say, or a valley — or a surface or assemblage of features such as the low rises and broad valleys that together constitute a plain, is said to be *X* years old, *X* being the time span or period during which it developed. Some features are formed in an instant. The fault scarp (Fig. 3.1) appeared at 1137 hours CSST on 19 January 1999 (see Twidale and Bourne 2000a). But such forms are relatively rare. Most landscape features have evolved over a period of time and have an age-range rather than a date, but that age-range continues to identify the particular form, say, as of Miocene age, even when it persists as an integral part of the modern scenery. The time scales that apply to strata and landforms are, however, vastly different. Whereas sediments some four billion years old have been recognised, most of the land surfaces considered here are only scores, or a few hundreds, of millions of years old (Table 1.1).

Fig. 3.1   Fault scarp formed on Minnipa Hill, northwestern Eyre Peninsula, during an earth tremor at 1137 hours CSST on 19 January 1999.

The term 'surface' is ambiguous. Literally it means the shape or form (in this context, of a landform or landscape). Thus the word embraces hills and plains, blocks and boulders — any form that is part of the Earth's surface. But convention now dictates another more limited connotation, for when discussing planation and chronology, and unless otherwise stated, the word implies a surface of low relief, a planation surface.

Surfaces are either erosional or destructional, or depositional or constructional in type. Most carry a weathered mantle with more-or-less substantial additions of transported detritus, together forming a regolith. Some surfaces are protected by a regolith, which includes or consists of a concentration of minerals which is resistant to weathering and erosion and is known generally as a duricrust.

Depositional or constructional landforms

Most depositional surfaces, whatever their origin — volcanic, marine, alluvial — can be dated by

22

either stratigraphic or absolute means. Fossils — any sign of former life — may be preserved in sediments and they provide an indication of the relative age of the materials in which they occur. The age of the youngest bed is taken as the age of the surface and of the form, the time when the deposition of the alluvial fan, say, or flood plain was completed. But absolute dating procedures have provided numerical dates for geological or stratigraphic periods (Table 1.1). Thus stratigraphic relations have become more useful. For instance, the minimum ages of desert dunes in the Parana Basin of southern South America (Almeida 1953) and central Namibia (Jerram et al. 2000) have been provided by the numerically dated volcanic lavas that buried them. Similarly, palaeomagnetic dating has confirmed the Neoproterozoic age of a regolith and associated surface in northwest Scotland (Williams 1969; Williams and Schmidt 1997).

Physical or radiometric analyses can give direct numerical estimates of the age of deposits. Consider three examples: first, a pristine basalt flow; second a sand dune, whether desert or coastal; and third, an alluvial deposit. The age of the basalt flow (Fig. 3.2a) can be determined using potassium/argon (K/Ar) ratios, the dune sand using luminescence

dating (Fig. 3.2b), and the alluvium by the analysis of any contained organic material, using carbon dating.

Most depositional surfaces are readily eroded. There are, however, exceptions. Well-jointed and therefore pervious volcanic rocks have proved durable, and some regoliths and alluvia, for example, have formed caprocks because they carry a duricrust such as calcrete or travertine (e.g. Miller 1937).

Duricrusts

Duricrusts occupy a large part — possibly as much as 25% of the total area — of the Australian continent (see Milnes and Hutton 1983; Twidale 1983). They are of pedogenic or depositional origin. They are of various compositions, some being predominantly ferruginous, some aluminous, others siliceous, and yet others gypseous or calcareous (Fig. 3.3). Some have suggested (e.g. Goudie 1973) that the various mineralogical types of duricrust be named according to composition, with the dominant element indicated by a prefix attached to the suffix 'crete' (Latin *concretus*, to grow together or hardened) to indicate a resistant material, as in con*crete*: thus ferricrete, alcrete, silcrete, gypcrete, calcrete. The suggestion has merit, yet implies unfortunate historical oversights and at least one missed opportunity. For it would surely be a pity to overlook that the alumina-rich duricrust called bauxite takes its name from Les Baux de Provence, near Arles, in southern France. It would be unforgivable to abandon the term 'laterite', because it was so called by Buchanan (1807) after the Latin *later*, a brick, while Babington (1821) referred to it as brickstone. Both had witnessed Indian workers digging this reddish soil, trimming it into shapes suitable for building purposes and using the blocks so formed in various constructions. They noted the remarkable transformation of the malleable and easily dug 'soil' into durable bricks, resulting from drying on exposure to air. For the laterite hardens irreversibly on desiccation as a result of the development of a crystalline continuity (Alexander and Cady 1962).

There is also a practical advantage in distinguishing between laterite, which is of pedogenic origin and has well-developed horizons, and 'ferricrete', which term can be applied to any iron-rich encrustation whether of pedogenic or sedimentological origin (Lamplugh 1902;

Fig. 3.2a Ropy or *pahoehoe* surface of basalt flow in north Queensland. Such materials are susceptible of K/Ar dating.

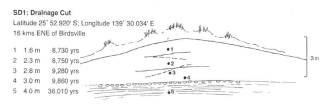

SD1: Drainage Cut
Latitude 25° 52.920' S; Longitude 139° 30.034' E
16 kms ENE of Birdsville

1 1.6 m 8,730 yrs
2 2.3 m 8,750 yrs
3 2.8 m 9,280 yrs
4 3.0 m 9,860 yrs
5 4.0 m 36,010 yrs

Fig. 3.2b Section though desert dune east of Birdsville, Queensland: luminescence dating indicated the base of the dune is about 10,000 years old. (Twidale et al. 2001)

Fig. 3.3a Laterite-capped surface at Buckleys Breakaway, south of Hyden, Western Australia. A thin ferruginous capping is underlain by kaolinised granite, semi-cohesive remnants of which can be seen low in the profile.

Fig. 3.3b Plateau and mesas capped by silcrete of probable Eocene age near Innamincka, northeastern South Australia.

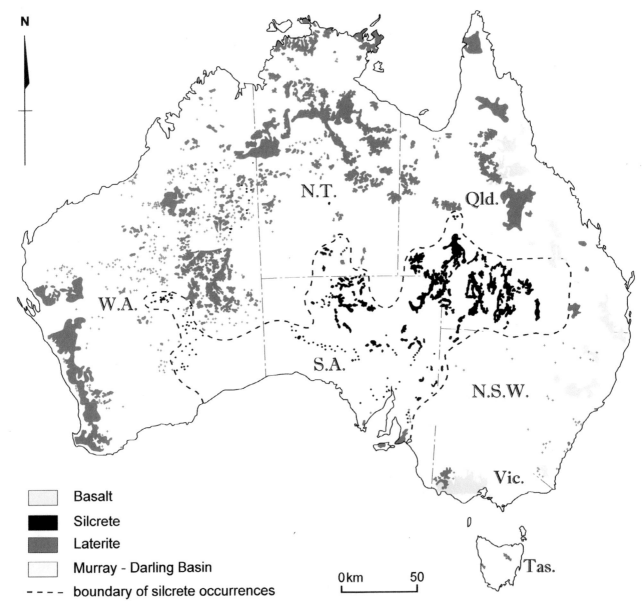

Basalt

Silcrete

Laterite

Murray - Darling Basin

- - - - boundary of silcrete occurrences

0 km   50

Fig. 3.4 Map showing distribution in Australia of laterite and silcrete.

Twidale 1976a, pp. 196–197). To abandon the term 'laterite' and call all ferruginous regolithic materials ferricretes is to associate regoliths that differ in morphology, origin and age.

In Australia, lateritic duricrusts occur in every state but have a marginal distribution (Fig. 3.4). Silcrete also is widespread but is most common in the interior of the continent (Twidale 1983). Though calcrete is found in northern monsoon lands developed on limestone outcrops, the main calcrete sheets are in the south, and particularly the semi-arid lowlands of the south and southeast (Milnes and Hutton 1983). Gypcrete is confined to the southwest of the Lake Eyre basin, though gypsiferous soils are more widely distributed and some major salinas such as lakes Gregory, Torrens, Amadeus, MacDonald and Gilles carry gypsiferous crusts (as opposed to the more common halite crusts of lakes Eyre, Frome, and so on).

Whatever their composition, all the duricrusts form caprocks on plateau forms. Laterite and silcrete are the most common, but calcrete-capped mesas are prominent in the southwestern Lake Eyre basin and in the Ashburton catchment of northern Western Australia, where the calcrete is commonly associated with opaline silica. Gypcrete underlies the plain between lakes Eyre and Torrens and caps the cliffs that border the Lake Eyre salina on its western side. Though dissected, the scarp is tectonic and the gypcrete crust, some two metres thick, consists of gypsum crystals which in the prevailing hyperarid climate impart a cohesion and resistance that contrast with the friable gypsiferous silts that underlie it.

Unlike the 'cornstones' or calcareous accumulations of the Old and the New Red Sandstone in Britain, which are of Devonian and Triassic ages respectively, both the calcareous and the gypseous duricrusts of Australia are of later Cenozoic ages and are therefore not germane to the present discussion. The same comment applies to some, though by no means all, encrustations of ferruginous, aluminous or siliceous composition.

Laterite is a weathered mantle consisting of an A-horizon which is usually sandy but in places consists of silt, and is underlain by a ferruginous (commonly haematitic, goethitic) zone, which may be pisolitic and vesicular. Beneath this is the mottled and pallid kaolinitic C-horizon that grades into the country rock. Bauxite is a laterite rich in hydrated alumina. Today laterite is forming in the humid tropics and particularly in monsoon lands (Sivarajasingham et al. 1962; Maignien 1966). The aluminous laterite is also associated with tropical climates. On the other hand, Pleistocene lateritic regoliths associated with cool temperate conditions have been reported from southeastern Australia (Taylor et al. 1992; Young et al. 1994). Thus, though many laterites developed during former periods of torrid climates, that association cannot be assumed.

Laterites preserved in northern Australia appear to be of Miocene age (e.g. Twidale 1956), but some in the southeast are, as mentioned, of later Cenozoic age and younger pisolitic regoliths are also reported from the southwest of Western Australia (e.g. Playford et al. 1975, p. 457). In the Darling Range and other parts of the Yilgarn the lateritic and bauxitic duricrusts are of Mesozoic, and probably Early Mesozoic, age (Jutson 1934; Clarke 1994a; Twidale and Bourne 1998a). The laterite of Kangaroo Island and other areas bordering the South Australian gulfs predates the Middle Jurassic and is younger than Permian, with Triassic as a likely age (Sprigg et al. 1954; Daily et al. 1974, 1979).

Silcrete differs from orthoquartzite in its texture for it typically includes porphyroclasts of quartz set in a siliceous matrix. In the older silcretes the matrix is crystalline but younger opaline accumulations, like those that underlie the plains southwest of Lake Eyre (the Warrina Surface of Wopfner 1978), are of Pleistocene age (Wopfner and Twidale 1967). In places, silcrete also occurs in skins plastered on host blocks or boulders (Hutton et al. 1972). More commonly it occurs as cappings to plateaux, which have been assumed formerly, before dissection, to have been extensive plains carrying a siliceous pedogenic horizon.

These assumptions may be in error. The detailed chemistry of silcretes (and especially rare earth elements) shows that some of their constituents are introduced or allochthonous, for they are not present in the country rock and cannot have been derived from the weathering of that material. An outstanding example can be seen in the southern Flinders Ranges where silcrete rests on limestone. Many silcretes contain cobbles and rounded gravels of exotic rocks. Though the plateau form is common, the remnants frequently together form a narrow winding pattern in plan. Some plateaux are slightly basin-shaped in cross-section. Thus, there is strong suggestion that some of the so-called sheet silcretes are valley fills, some of which display topographic inversion (e.g. Young 1985; Twidale 1985).

Stratigraphic evidence suggests that though preserved in aridity, silcrete was formed in humid warm climates. Its origin is still debated (see contributions to Langford-Smith 1978) but biota are almost certainly involved (e.g. Lovering 1959). A riverine connection is also significant, for rivers carry large volumes of silica in solution (Davis 1964; Douglas 1978). Streams flowing from humid to an arid internal drainage sump, such as the Lake Eyre basin, deliver their loads which include a siliceous fraction that could have precipitated out in the shallow subsurface or in stream channels (as is found in some contemporary stream beds).

Stephens (1964) suggested that the crystalline silcretes of central Australia are derived from the leaching by groundwaters of the headwater zones of catchments in which are exposed laterites of Miocene age. Silica and other solutes were transported in rivers and precipitated as the waters evaporated in the arid interior. This theory implies that the silcrete is of Miocene age. However, silcretes of various ages have been recognised. A Jurassic occurrence is preserved in stratigraphic section (Wopfner 1978). Some of the widely distributed crystalline form is attributed to the Early Tertiary, with Eocene and Oligocene periods of silicification indicated by the field evidence (e.g. Wopfner 1978; Young and McDougall 1982; Firman 1983; Hou et al. 2003). A later Tertiary (Miocene or even Pliocene) age has been suggested for occurrences in the Mid North region and the Arckaringa area of northern South Australia (McGowran et al. 1971; McNally and Wilson 1995).

But of all these duricrusts only the older laterites of the Yilgarn Block of southwestern Western Australia and of the Gulfs region of South Australia enter into consideration as conservative factors involving very old palaeosurfaces.

Erosional or destructional surfaces

Erosional surfaces are shaped by weathering and erosional processes active at and near the land

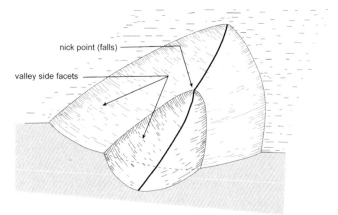

Fig. 3.5a Nick point and valley-side facets.

Fig. 3.5b Diachronic surface associated with retreat of scarp bordering capped plateau, Ooraminna Ranges, southeast of Alice Springs, Northern Territory. The plain at the base of the scarp (X) is younger than the plain near the valley axis (Y).

surface. These plains are classified as subaerial or epigene, etch and exhumed (Twidale 1985).

Epigene surfaces are shaped by rivers, glaciers, wind or waves, but overwhelmingly by rivers and wash. Fluvial plains develop over a period of time and have an age-range (Twidale 1956; King 1962). Thus the lowering of baselevel or the uplift of the land causes stream incision. A rejuvenation head or nickpoint marking the upstream limit of the new stream profile migrates upstream. It may be marked by a waterfall or rapids or merely a sector of steeper gradient. The slopes adjacent to the incised sector are graded to a new lower and local baselevel. They too are regraded and form distinct valley-side facets (Fig. 3.5a). Just as the nickpoint migrates inland so do the valley-side facets extend upslope. The landscape is said to be revived. But these migrations of stream and slope take time to develop, so that the resultant new land surface has an age-range. It is said to be diachronic. Similarly, a plain produced by the wearing back of scarps (King 1942; Twidale and Milnes 1983) is older near the stream lines where incision produced the initial scarps, and youngest at the present scarp foot, so that its development spans a period of time

(Fig. 3.5b): it too has an age-range and again is diachronic.

Etch surfaces are initiated below the land surface at the base of the regolith. Some of the rain falling on land surfaces percolates into the rocks beneath. These shallow groundwaters cause the rocks to be weathered. Where the rate of weathering exceeds the rate of erosion, a mantle of disintegrated and altered rock is formed. Whatever its thickness, the junction between the base of the regolith and the intrinsically fresh bedrock is frequently quite sharp and is known as the weathering front (Mabbutt 1961a; Fig. 3.6).

Most commonly the regolith is friable, in contrast with the still cohesive, intrinsically fresh rock below. Elsewhere, however, a duricrust may have formed. The resistant horizon is in many instances underlain by a clay (commonly kaolin) that is susceptible to attack (see Fig. 3.3). Such regoliths are readily eroded, for the capping is commonly undermined, causing it to collapse. Thus, many uplifted and dissected plains have been stripped of the former cover of weathered rock to expose what was the weathering front. Such exposed fronts are called etch (meaning to gnaw or eat away chemically) surfaces (Wayland 1934; Willis 1936; Twidale 2002). They are also known as two-stage forms because they have evolved in two phases, namely subsurface weathering, followed by the stripping of the regolith and the exposure

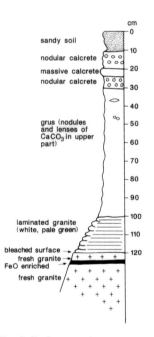

Fig. 3.6a Weathering front (W) in granite exposed in Yarwondutta Quarry, near Minnipa, northwestern Eyre Peninsula, South Australia. C – calcrete, introduced as calcareous dust on the wind.

Fig. 3.6b Section showing compositional changes in regolith at Yarwondutta Quarry.

Fig. 3.6c Weathering front in dacite exposed in Mt Cooper Quarry, also on northwestern Eyre Peninsula.

of the weathering front. The gross morphology of such surfaces broadly mimics that of the original low relief feature (Fig. 3.7a). In places, however, the weathering front is irregular. In particular, water has penetrated along joints and altered the rock leaving rounded masses of still fresh rock either projecting as incipient bornhardts or as kernels, or corestones, isolated within the regolith. After the stripping of the altered rock these remnants are exposed as landforms (Figs 3.7b–d).

In addition to these obviously erosional forms, structural surfaces or benches must needs be

Fig. 3.7a The Meekatharra Plain, an etch surface in granite and gneiss, in the central Yilgarn Craton. Duricrusted remnants underlain by kaolinised rock occur all around.

Fig. 3.7b Nascent bornhardt exposed north of Minnipa, northwestern Eyre Peninsula.

Fig. 3.7d Corestones and boulders near Pine Creek, Northern Territory. The intrusive sill shows that the exposure consists of weathered rock in situ: the boulders have not been transported by rivers or glaciers, as was suggested by some early workers in consideration of corestones exposed in the Rio de Janeiro area of Brazil, and on the Malay Peninsula.

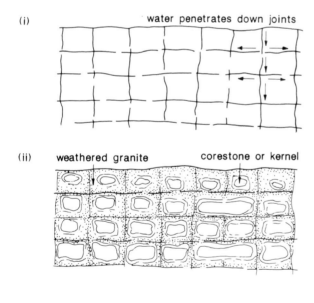

Fig. 3.7c Two-stage or etch development of corestone boulders, (i) orthogonal fractures, (ii) fracture-controlled weathering, and (iii) exposure of corestones as boulders.

Fig. 3.8a Granite hill partly buried by Late Pleistocene basalt, near Einasleigh, north Queensland. The granite hill clearly predates the lava flow.

mentioned. Structural benches stand at various heights in the landscape and are unlikely to have any chronological significance. More extensive surfaces coincident with a resistant outcrop pose problems. The discontinuity between, say, a flat-lying sandstone below and a conformable argillaceous sequence above may be exploited by weathering and erosion, yet in detail transect bedding, cross-bedding, and so on. Such an essentially structural

Fig. 3.8b Unconformity between the flat-lying Permian sandstone over dipping Devonian rocks, Ettrema Gorge, Shoalhaven region of New South Wales. (J. Roberts)

Fig. 3.8c Unconformity between weathered (lateritised) Jurassic or early Cretaceous mudstone above and Proterozoic granite below, southern Isa Highlands. Where the strata have been eroded, the unconformity, the surface on which the sediments were deposited, has been re-exposed as an exhumed surface on the crest of the ridge. Clearly it represents a huge time gap for the granite was emplaced at a depth of some kilometres about 1500 million years ago and the overlying rocks were eroded before the Mesozoic (ca 100 million years) beds were deposited. (CSIRO)

surface may be coincident with and be part of an erosional plain, and be of the same age. It may stand higher and still be of the same age. Or it may be inherited from a much older surface.

Epigene and etch surfaces may be buried by sediments or lavas (Fig. 3.8a). Where this has happened the discontinuity between the older and newer rock is called an unconformity. It implies a hiatus or time-gap for the older series of rocks was perhaps folded or weathered or eroded before the younger rocks were introduced. But there is frequently a contrast in rock type above and below the unconformity (Fig. 3.8b) and it is not uncommon for the old surface, that on which the marine beds or the lavas, or whatever, were laid down, to be re-exposed, as a resurrected or *exhumed* form or surface (Fig. 3.8c).

Burial does not preclude change. Being inundated by the sea most likely results in the stripping of any earlier formed regolith. But where the cover material is of volcanic or wind-blown (aeolian) origin, old regoliths and forms are preserved (e.g. Almeida 1953; Molina Ballesteros et al. 1995; Jerram et al. 2000). Also, weathering by moisture may take place at the unconformity. However, though bedrock surfaces may be weathered after being covered, lowering or erosion of the buried rock surface is physically impossible unless the bedrock is susceptible to solution.

Exhumed forms are younger than the youngest rocks cut across by the surface or unconformity, but older than the oldest rocks laid down on the unconformity. The age-range of such a surface or form is provided by the age of the rocks in which the surface is cut and that of the basal rocks that cover the surface. Both formations may be dated

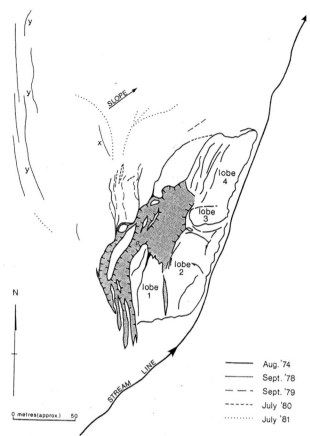

Fig. 3.9a Map of the Lochiel Landslip with stages in development following the initial failure in 1974.

Fig 3.9b–c View from the air, from the southeast, and (below) looking along the tension scar or headwall of the Landslip.

physically as well as stratigraphically. Like etch forms, exhumed surfaces can be regarded as having two ages, one referring to the time of burial and the other to the date of re-exposure. The age of an exhumed form is referred to as sub Y or pre Y, Y being the age of the cover rock. The implied hiatus may be of long duration but the age of the exhumed surface can be taken as immediately preceding the cover. In the context of the persistence of the surface, however, it is the age of exposure of the unconformity that is significant.

Value of dating

Dating a surface or form can greatly assist in pinpointing its origin. To consider a minor example first, mass movements of rock and soil such as landslides, landslips and earthflows can be caused in various ways. The soil may become saturated and unstable following heavy rains. The rock and soil may be destabilised by an earth tremor or earthquake. Clearance of woodland may deprive the soil of essential root binding. Cutting a road at the base of the slope may destabilise the soil uphill from the road. Knowing when, say, a landslip developed can indicate likely causation.

For example, the Lochiel Landslip (Fig. 3.9), about 115 km north of Adelaide, formed overnight on 8–9 August 1974. Enquiries revealed that no earth tremor had been recorded during that period at the nearest seismic or earthquake recording station. This does not preclude this factor, for a very small tremor may not have been recorded by the instrumentation available, yet have been sufficient to destabilise the slope which was cleared of most woodland for pastoral use almost a century earlier. On the other hand, records showed that the winter had been particularly wet. A long deep fissure several centimetres wide developed during

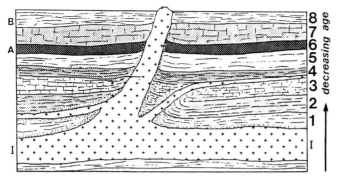

Fig. 3.10 Diagram showing relative ages of strata and intrusions. The age of strata is indicated by numbers (1 – oldest, 8 – youngest) and the intrusion (I) is more recent than the youngest stratum.

the previous May. This was to become a tension crack at the head of the Landslip. It allowed water readily to penetrate into and destabilise the rock mass. Saturated thin clay layers interbedded with the quartzite lubricated a large mass of rock and a sector of the slope, 150m x 75 m and at least 11 m thick and involving about a quarter of a million tonnes of rock and soil, slid downslope along bedding planes (Twidale 1984a, 2000b).

At a broader scale, dating a surface raises the possibility of its being placed in its environmental context. Does the fossil evidence indicate that the dated period was one of humid tropical climate, or did desert conditions prevail? Is there evidence of glaciation or cold conditions that ought to be considered? For example, analysis of infillings rich in potassium and manganese from a regolith at Mt Tabor in central Queensland indicated an Early Miocene age for the weathering. The type of weathering suggests a climate more humid than that presently experienced (Li and Vasconcelos 2002; see also Vasconcelos 1999).

Thus, dating provides a useful background for the understanding of landforms and landscape. It allows a realistic chronology of events to be constructed. It provides an essential time scale when, for instance, rates of activity of weathering processes and their possible climatic connections are considered (e.g. Vasconcelos and Conroy 2003).

Relevant dating methods

In the preceding discussion, reference is made to a surface being of a particular geological age (Table 1.1). How was this age discovered and how were the limits of the geological periods determined? Dating methods are either numerical or physical, or stratigraphic and topographic. 'Absolute' is a

misnomer. 'A close approximation' is a better term, for it implies a margin of error of a very small percentage, but nevertheless involving a latitude of many millions of years in some instances.

Numerical dating of rocks

The sedimentary rocks derived from igneous rocks can be dated relatively from geological evidence such as the position of strata (law of superposition), fossil assemblages, and composition (contained cobbles of older rocks). But until numerical ages were obtained for rocks that could be dated according to radioactive decay ratios, the order of magnitude and the duration of the various geological periods could not be determined. The ages assigned to surfaces eroded in them remained speculative. Once numerical ages had been derived for igneous bodies (batholiths, lava flows, sills and dikes), however, the absolute age of stratigraphic units was deduced from their relationship with the igneous intrusive bodies (Fig. 3.10). Later, sedimentary strata were dated by the numerical dating of contained minerals, especially durable zircons. Using such procedures, dates were gradually established for all the periods of the stratigraphic time scale. The refinement of the time scale continues and more, and more reliable dates become available.

How are numerical ages obtained? Late in the nineteenth century and early in the twentieth, it was recognised that many elements are unstable and shed particles through time, and in this way new substances are produced. During decomposition energy is emitted. Radioactive decay leads to the formation of an isotope either of the same element or of a different element. Radioactive disintegration of an atom implies emission of subatomic alpha and beta particles and gamma photons. The decay products are known as daughters. Continued radioactivity leads to a series of new daughter products. Thus the radioactive decay of the common isotope of uranium (^{238}U) leads to a loss of eight alpha or six beta particles, producing a series of daughters and eventually the stable lead (^{206}Pb):

$$^{238}\text{U} \rightarrow {}^{206}\text{Pb} + 8\,{}^4\text{He (or }\alpha) + 6\beta + \text{energy (see}$$
e.g. Dalrymple 1991, pp. 99-102).

The rate of decay is constant for all known conditions of pressure and temperature, with the 'half-life' describing the period during which half the original has been transformed into the daughter product. Thus by measuring the ratio of ^{238}U to ^{206}Pb the time which has elapsed since decay began can be established. This gives the age of the uranium-bearing mineral which, if original to the rock, gives the age of the host. Other pairs of elements linked by decay chains include potassium-argon, rubidium-strontium and thorium-actinium.

Very old land surfaces or palaeosurfaces are preserved on consolidated rocks and are of erosional origin. The surface may be the original surface of a basalt flow when a potassium-argon age of the rock will approximate the age of the surface. Otherwise such surfaces are probably well beyond the range of any known physical or numerical dating method: direct dating of such surfaces is not yet possible (Watchman and Twidale 2002). Nevertheless, some radiometric procedures used to date rocks, as opposed to surfaces, are vital to the dating of surfaces and forms in two ways. First, erosional surfaces are of various origins but they can be no older than the youngest rocks they transect. Radiometric dating has given closer approximations of ages than was previously possible. Thus a surface cut across rocks of, say, Permian and Eocene ages would at one time be dated as post-Eocene. But rocks determined as of Eocene age from their contained fossil assemblages may later have been dated as, say, 40–55 million years old: the surface can now be labelled as younger than 40–55 million years depending on to what part of the Eocene the youngest stratum transected belongs. Second, rocks susceptible to radiometric dating in some areas provide stratigraphic markers. Thus a regolith dated by physical methods (say, ^{40}Ar/^{39}Ar) provides an age for surfaces carrying that particular regolith within a given district. Any valleys cut into it are younger, and any hills standing above it, older.

In addition, palaeomagnetism and oxygen isotope ratios have been used to provide estimates of the age of old surfaces. The migration paths of magnetic poles have been dated by geologic and numerical methods, and comparison of palaeomagnetic determinations of magnetic components of regolithic profiles with apparent polar wandering paths have provided age estimates of those profiles. Regoliths, including laterites, in Australia and in India have been successfully dated using techniques that remove post-formational magnetic aberrations. But in many instances the relationship between time of magnetisation and the time of weathering remains ambiguous. The same comment applies to dates derived from fission track chronologies (e.g. Bishop and Goldrick 2000).

Oxygen isotope ratios can provide both checks on palaeomagnetic age estimates and independent age determinations. Fractionation of oxygen isotopes (^{16}O/^{18}O) in oxygen-bearing geologic materials is a function of temperature, as is oxygen isotope enrichment: thus, in both processes the oxygen isotope ratio acts as a geological thermometer. As such the ratio is useful in palaeoclimatology, but because of the behaviour of the Australian Plate since the rifting of Gondwana and the constant, essentially equatorwards, migration of its several parts, it has been used also as a means of dating regoliths and the surfaces on which they developed.

For the past 100 million years or so Australia has been migrating across a strong latitudinal gradient. Though such factors as climatic change and altitude of the land surface must also be taken into account, latitude is a major control of surface temperature. As palaeomagnetism has provided a chronology of the migration of the continent, temperature can be linked to time (Bird and Chivas 1988, 1989, see especially p. 3240).

Stratigraphy and topography

Various stratigraphic and geomorphological or topographic arguments can be used to provide a geological or stratigraphic age for a surface. In many instances, by using physical procedures to date the rocks involved, this can be translated to a numerical age-range. Given the nature of most surfaces and forms, this is more appropriate than a single or specific age. These stratigraphic and topographic arguments are illustrated in the chapters concerned with particular regions and landscapes. Only a brief summary of the principles involved is given here.

The geological-topographical dating methods are most conveniently considered in relation to surfaces of the various types — epigene, etch and exhumed. It has been said that science is nothing but trained and organised common sense, and this is certainly true of the relative stratigraphic or geological, and geomorphological dating methods. And as the numerical or 'absolute' methods must perforce be compatible with stratigraphy, the

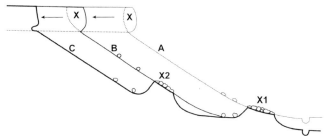

Fig. 3.11a Section showing how a younger scarp remnant may stand higher in the local relief than an older. (A) Collapse of the bluff (X) produces a rock avalanche and a patch of coarse detritus (X1) low on the debris slope. The valley floor is lowered and the scarp is worn back (B), but X1 protects that part of the footslope and a mesa is formed. Meantime the bluff again collapses (either in roughly the same sector or in an adjacent site) and another patch of coarse blocks (X2) accumulates but at a slightly higher level on the slope. Further recession of the scarp (C) leaves this patch upstanding as a capping to another mesa that, although younger, stands slightly higher than X1.

Fig. 3.11b Diagrammatic section of lava flow in valley with relative ages of forms indicated. As the lava can be numerically dated minimum ages of the valley and surface can be derived. 1 – old planation surface, 2 – younger valley, 3 – lava flow, the most recent event.

Fig. 3.11c Stepped northwestern slope of Yarwondutta Rock, near Minnipa, northwestern Eyre Peninsula. The lower concave or flared slope is younger than the higher because weathering and erosion work mainly downwards, but also laterally.

comment applies indirectly to them also.

Dating of plains, that are epigene, etch and exhumed types, is facilitated by marine transgressions, dated volcanic extrusions and duricrusts, the ages or age-ranges of which are known. In Australia, the extensive Late Palaeozoic glaciation (see e.g. BMR Palaeogeographic Group 1992) provides a back marker for the evolution of many of the old surfaces and forms, for the ice sheets as it were 'wiped the slate clean': apart from older exhumed forms, the evolution of the modern landscape began with the retreat of the glaciers.

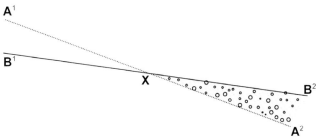

Fig. 3.12 Relation of sedimentary sequence and surface from which it is derived. Weathering and erosion of the surface A^1-X produces a weathered mantle or regolith some of which is stripped to expose B^1-X. The eroded material is deposited in the wedge X-A^2-B^2 so that the surface X-A^2 is built up to X-B^2. The age-range of the surface B^1-X is given by dating the deposits and particularly the youngest of these materials.

Fig. 3.13 Island protruding from the bed of a salt lake south of Woomera, South Australia.

Epigene and etch surfaces

(a) The law of superposition is a fundamental rule in geology: in an undisturbed rock sequence the lower strata are older than those nearer the surface. It is simply common sense. Similarly if one igneous rock is seen to intrude another, then clearly the intrusive member is younger than the host.

In landscapes a similar concept can be formulated, for position in the landscape is a useful indication of relative age. In an undisturbed fluvial landscape — and most landscapes have been shaped by rivers — and leaving exhumed forms out of consideration, a higher surface is older than a lower. Again it is a matter of common sense, for rivers cut down and as they do so create lower and lower surfaces. This was appreciated by Rütimeyer (1769) who pointed out that in valleys where a river has migrated laterally during incision a flight of flood plain remnants or river terraces is left behind. The terraces alternate in elevation on opposed sides of the valley and Rütimeyer realised that the higher its position in the flight, the greater the age of the terrace. At a broader, regional scale, the idea was succinctly expressed by Davies who, commenting on the Tasmanian scenery, stated that it developed through 'the successive inward transgression of landscapes formed at progressively lower levels' (Davies 1959, p. 20). The rationale in both instances is that erosion works downwards. This reasoning might be termed the principle of topographic position whereby the lower in an undisturbed erosional landscape, the younger the feature. Local exceptions involving preserved scarp-foot remnants may occur (Fig. 3.11a), though even there lower usually means younger. Exhumed surfaces and forms also call for separate consideration. Viewed generally, however, the logic behind this concept is sound.

Rütimeyer's and Davies' conclusions concerned relative ages; no absolute dating was implied. A dated lava flow in a valley floor (Fig. 3.11b) provides a minimum age for the valley and for the surface into which the valley is incised. Similarly, on stepped inselbergs (Fig. 3.11c) the higher step can, in the absence of evidence to the contrary, be taken as predating the lower (Twidale 1982a; see also Bierman and Caffee 2002).

By and large, weathering and erosion work downwards under the influence of gravity, and in a stable landmass the higher sectors are older than those preserved at lower levels in the landscape. Just as tectonism introduces departures from the principle of superposition, so it complicates topographic guidelines. Exhumed surfaces also call for a different interpretation (see below); but overall the elevational principle is useful at a variety of scales.

(b) Erosion or wearing away of rock implies deposition downstream or downslope, either in the sea, a lake or valley floor. Dating of such correlative deposits provides an age for the related period of erosion. The first problem is to ensure that a particular sedimentary sequence is genetically or causally related to a particular erosional surface (Fig. 3.12). This can be done by comparing composition of rock and sediment and particularly by examination of coarse materials. The second is to date the sediment, and this is frequently made possible by the preservation of fossils.

(c) Where fossiliferous sediments are laid down in basins or valleys the covered or buried surfaces predate the strata. To take a contemporary example, sandstone islands protrude from salinas or salt lakes (Fig. 3.13; see also Fig. 3.8a) that from time to time carry water. Clearly, the islands are older than even the oldest muds and sands laid down in the adjacent lake basin.

(d) Faulting can be dated and used to provide a minimum age for the dislocated surface. The minimum age of faulting and of the surface dislocated by the earth movement is provided by the age of the youngest stratum laid down on the downfaulted block.

(e) Though weathering is destructive, in some environments it is constructive. Weathering has caused various minerals (iron oxides, silica, carbonates, gypsum) to be concentrated in the B-horizon, minerals that later form the hard cappings collectively known as duricrusts. They are widely preserved and have been used as morphostratigraphic markers. Not only do the various duricrusts vary in age, but representatives of the same type also differ. Nevertheless, local correlation between surfaces carrying similar encrustations seems reasonable, as it does also where topographic relationships between different types are consistent (Twidale 1983; Twidale and Bourne 1975, 1999).

Exhumed surfaces and forms

Exhumed surfaces are exposed unconformities, resurrected, or disinterred landscapes. Surfaces with long and complex, but as yet undetermined, chronologies are typical of shield lands, areas that have been appropriately termed 'oldlands' (Wilson 1903; Hills 1955; Twidale 1999). They are difficult to interpret, for in many areas the ages and extents of marine transgressions have not been documented.

On the other hand, many exhumed surfaces are readily dated by bracketing: the surface is younger than the youngest rocks it transects, but older than the basal member of the cover sequence. In practice, the interval indicated may be enormous. Thus, on the west coast of Eyre Peninsula, a regolith developed on Middle Proterozoic granite, gneiss and sandstone is widely preserved beneath dune calcarenite of Middle-Late Pleistocene age. Clearly on the available evidence, the regolith is younger than Middle Proterozoic, but older than Middle Pleistocene in age, an interval of some 1600 million years. Common sense and long-distance correlation and general argument, however, suggest that it immediately predates the calcarenite, and is of Pliocene or even early Pleistocene age (Molina Ballesteros et al. 1995). And, in general, surfaces (and any preserved regolith) can be taken as immediately predating the oldest cover deposit.

Chapter 4

UPLAND BACKBONE OF SOUTH AUSTRALIA

Introduction

The distinguished academic and author A.J.P. Taylor has written: 'the historian can never speak with first hand authority; he can only piece together the accounts of others'. (Taylor 1950, p. 19). Geological analysis is similar. Time is the central concern of geologists for they aim to reconstruct the history of the Earth, or strictly speaking, as history is based in written records, its chronology or development through time. Yet rarely have geologists witnessed geological events. They must needs construct their chronologies through the interpretation of the rocks and land surfaces.

Occasionally, a geologist is in the right place at the right time. For instance, George Taylor was close to Mt Lamington, in northern Papua New Guinea, when it erupted at 1040 hours local time on 21 January 1951, and was able to give a first-hand account of the event and subsequent developments (Taylor 1958). Nowadays, the behaviour of many volcanoes, as well as rivers, coasts and glaciers, is monitored. But even if an event is witnessed, it is frequently difficult or impossible to absorb all that occurs, much less measure or understand what has

happened. Overwhelmingly, the reconstruction of ancient forms involves interpretation.

It has been said that, 'the interpretation of field work is often a strictly personal affair, depending on the observer's character, training and experience'(Read 1957, p. i). Moreover, that interpretation is influenced not only by the earlier conclusions reached by others and as recorded in the literature, but also involves reasoning from the observed evidence. And there is more than one logic (Kant 1781/1998). If a dozen geologists examine a road-cutting in which rocks are exposed, several interpretations will be offered in explanation of what each has observed. Furthermore, not only is the evidence flawed or incomplete but not everything that seems impossible is untrue (de Retz 1613–1679/1903; Namier 1955, p. 5; Crick 1988). Thus, interpretation is subjective and may be changed or modified, rejected and replaced, as new inform-ation or concepts becomes available. Any explanation must be perceived as offering the most likely answer based in the available evidence at a particular time and the considered opinion of a particular person: it is in the nature of a progress report.

Biographical note: P.S. Hossfeld (1897–1967)

Paul Samuel Hossfeld was born in South Australia, in the small Mid North town of Dutton, on the edge of the Barossa Valley, in 1897. After a period of school teaching he enrolled in the University of Adelaide. He graduated BSc in Geology in 1921, and MSc in 1926. After geological experience in New Guinea, he was appointed leader of the Aerial Geological and Geophysical Survey of Northern Australia. He saw war service as an industrial chemist but then returned to the University of Adelaide first to read for his PhD, and then as a member of staff. He retired in 1961 and died in 1967: one might almost add 'on schedule' for Hossfeld had predicted the end of his earthly span by totalling the age at death of his

parents, and dividing by two, the answer being 70!

Though perhaps best remembered for his work on the stranded coastal dunes of the South East district of South Australia (Hossfeld 1950), Hossfeld's greatest contribution arose from his Master's research on the geology of the northern Mt Lofty Ranges (Hossfeld 1926). Almost incidentally to his main theme, he concluded that the prominent planation surface preserved throughout the upland must be of Cretaceous or greater age because Early Tertiary strata are preserved in adjacent downfaulted basins. This deduction has been confirmed by later workers, such as Miles (1952) and Campana (1958a), though it is still not accepted by some.

Fig. 4.1 Southern Australian geological regions (after Palfreyman 1984) showing also major structural units. Similar maps are reproduced in the regional chapters, and serve as location maps for regions referred to in the text.

Mt Lofty Ranges

In Australia, the first inkling that landscapes are not necessarily youthful arose from work in the Mt Lofty Ranges, in southern South Australia (Hossfeld 1926; Miles 1952; Campana 1958a). Thus it is appropriate to consider that region first (Figs 2.1, 4.1). Adjacent areas are then discussed in roughly clockwise sequence, from the starting point in South Australia.

Adelaide Geosyncline

Both the Mt Lofty Ranges and Kangaroo Island are part of a fold mountain belt, or orogen, known as the Adelaide Geosyncline (Preiss 1987). As was appreciated by Benson (1909, 1911), the dominant landform is an upfaulted block of Proterozoic, Cambrian and Permian rocks (Table 1.1). It is a horst, or relatively long, narrow block of rocks, aligned roughly north–south, that has been uplifted along fractures or faults that run in parallel and are straight or only gently arcuate in plan. Post-Eocene, post-Pliocene and post-Pleistocene as well as contemporary dislocations are

Fig. 4.2a Reverse fault (f) exposed in river valley near Cambrai in the eastern Mt Lofty Ranges. Dark areas, to right, Cambrian schist; grey, to left, Pleistocene fanglomerate; light, Pliocene limestone involved in faulting, marked M. (J.A. Bourne)

recorded (e.g. Grant 1956; Glaessner and Wade 1958; Bourman and Lindsay 1989; see Fig. 4.2a). A prominent high plain, in places with an ironstone or lateritic crust, is preserved on it (Fenner 1930; Sprigg 1945; Miles 1952; Campana 1958a; Fig. 4.2b, c).

Geological framework

The faulting responsible for the horst block occurred over a considerable period 500–550 million years ago. Recent and contemporary earthquakes indicate that the faults that define the Mt Lofty Ranges remain active (Greenhalgh et al. 1994; Love et al. 1995). The entire area was affected by the Late Palaeozoic glaciation, and striated pavements and erratic blocks are well known from several sites such as Hallett Cove and Glacier Rock (Selwyn 1860; Tate 1879; Howchin 1895; David and Howchin

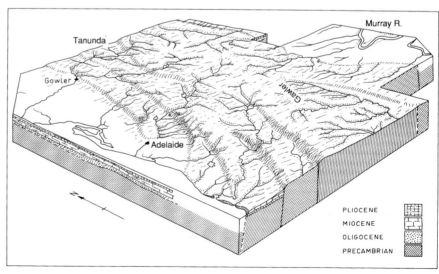

Fig. 4.2b Block diagram of part of the Mt Lofty Ranges. (After Sprigg 1945)

Fig. 4.2c   View of the summit plain of the Mt Lofty Ranges in the vicinity of the Torrens Gorge. (R.L. Oliver)

Fig. 4.2d   Summit surface, eastern Mt Lofty Ranges.

Fig. 4.3   Glaciated pavement of Permian age, Hallett Cove, near Adelaide, South Australia. (J.A Bourne)

1897; Fig. 4.3). The area was then reduced to low relief and deeply weathered. A lateritic crust developed prior to the Late Cretaceous–earliest Tertiary renewal of major faulting (Miles 1952; Campana 1958a; Glaessner and Wade 1958).

Age of the summit surface

When Hossfeld investigated part of the northern Mt Lofty Ranges in the early 1920s he realised that the lateritised summit plain must be of considerable antiquity. The horst on which it stands is bounded on the east by the Miocene marine beds of the Murray Basin, well exposed in the bluffs bordering the gorge excavated by the river during Pleistocene glacial periods of low sea level (Twidale et al. 1978), and displaced by recurrent faulting of the eastern scarp of the Ranges. On the west marine strata of Middle Eocene and younger ages (Reynolds 1953; Glaessner and Wade 1958) were deposited in embayments that occupied fault-angle valleys, or half-grabens, bordering Gulf St Vincent. The faulting that caused the ferruginised surface to be uplifted therefore probably predates

the oldest of the basin sediments and, in part at least, occurred prior to the Early Tertiary (Middle Eocene). The summit surface, and the ironstone carapace developed on it, must be at least as old.

If the lateritic surface had been disrupted by faulting in the earliest Tertiary, it might be expected that remnants would be preserved in basins as well as on the uplifted block. Lateritic debris has been reported from the basal Tertiary sediments (Glaessner and Wade 1958) but the lateritised surface as such has not yet been encountered in bores that penetrate through the Tertiary rocks and into the older strata. On the backslope of the Para Block northeast of Adelaide, for example, quarries excavated through the unconformity between Eocene sand and weathered Precambrian shale and mudstone encountered kaolinised rock but no ironstone horizon. The explanation may be that the ironstone has been dissolved in groundwaters. This process could have been facilitated by chemicals produced by the decay of eucalypt and other plant litter and some of which (the polyphenols) facilitate the dissolution of ferruginous compounds

(Bloomfield 1957; Hingston 1962). Eucalypt forests had become dominant in Australia by the Miocene.

However, taking into account the geological evidence then available to him, Hossfeld concluded that the summit surface of the Mt Lofty Ranges was probably of at least Cretaceous age. Startling though it was, it was an underestimate, as will be seen when Kangaroo Island is considered. Hossfeld was guided by two principles. First, because the summit surface stood higher in the landscape than the Tertiary rocks deposited in the downfaulted marginal basins, he concluded that the surface was older. In this instance the topographic difference was due to faulting or earth movements but the same principle would have applied if the discrepancy had been due to erosion.

Second, in adjudging the minimum age of the

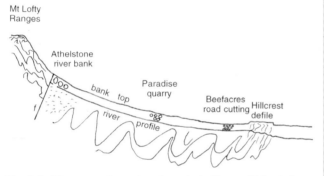

Fig. 4.4 Diagrammatic section through the Torrens Valley below the Gorge mouth, where it debouches on to the plains.

faulting responsible for the Mt Lofty Ranges horst he considered the age of the basal beds laid down in the adjacent basins, for in an undisturbed sequence the oldest beds occur at the base of the sequence and the youngest on top: the law of superposition. As marine Middle Eocene beds were deposited in the downfaulted basins flanking the western scarp, the fracturing and subsidence, as well as the surface that was disrupted, must predate those basin deposits.

The deduced great age of the summit surface of the Mt Lofty Ranges implies that the rivers that drained and shaped it are also very old. The Mt Lofty Ranges are drained by several major rivers, prominent amongst which is the Torrens. On debouching from its Gorge, the River Torrens has deposited alluvium derived from the rocks exposed in the Ranges on a surface cut in Proterozoic rocks.

The surface declines in altitude to the west, and the sediments become finer in the same direction (Fig. 4.4). In the northeastern suburbs of Adelaide the gravels grade laterally into fossiliferous sands of Eocene age (Twidale 1968a, pp. 389-390). Thus the River Torrens is at least of Early Tertiary age and as it is cut into the lateritic high plain, can be tentatively dated as Late Mesozoic or Early Eocene: as such it is one of the oldest extant rivers in the world.

Biographical note: Brian Daily (1931–1986)

Brian Daily was educated in the University of Adelaide, graduating BSc (Hons) in 1953, and PhD in 1957. From 1955 to 1961 he worked as a palaeontologist in the South Australian Museum but then accepted an appointment as Lecturer (later Senior Lecturer and Reader) in the Department of Geology. He specialised in palaeontology and in Cambrian stratigraphy, in which area he achieved an enviable distinction. He was a fine field geologist, seen to great advantage on Kangaroo Island where he tenaciously established the relationships of volcanics and sediments. His early death robbed the geological community of a dedicated and respected colleague.

Brian Daily

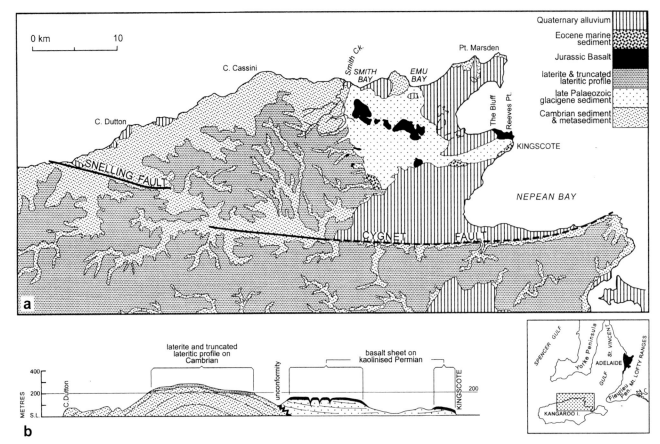

Fig. 4.5 (a) Geological map, and (b) section of part of Kangaroo Island.

Kangaroo Island and numerical dating

Lateritic surface

Though dissected and stripped, remnants of the weathered or lateritic land surface that dominate the Fleurieu Peninsula or southern Mt Lofty Ranges are also prominent on southern Eyre Peninsula (see below) and on Kangaroo Island (Daily et al. 1974; Daily et al. 1979). In this last-named area the laterite caps the plateau that forms the upland backbone of the Island. It is developed on rocks of Precambrian, Cambrian and Permian ages (Fig. 4.5). It is therefore younger than the Permian. It is also overlain by, and is therefore older than, a basalt.

When it was first mapped in the 1950s, the basalt was, and not unreasonably in view of its apparent freshness, correlated with the Pleistocene and Holocene volcanic rocks of the South East district of South Australia and western Victoria (Sprigg et al. 1954). This conclusion was seemingly consistent with the Pliocene age attributed to the laterite on the basis of long-distance correlation from northern Australia (Northcote 1946; see also Whitehouse 1940, though the age of the Queensland laterite

Fig. 4.6 Basalt exposed in quarry north of Kingscote, Kangaroo Island, showing closely spaced, steeply dipping fractures. These many partings allow ready water transmission. They contribute to the preservation of the rock and to any surfaces developed on it.

was later adjusted to Miocene). Physical dating using K/Ar ratios, however, showed the basalt to be of Middle Jurassic age, about 175 million years old (Wellman 1971; McDougall and Wellman 1976). Thus the laterite and the surface on which it is developed is younger than Permian and as it is overlain by a 175 million years old basalt it must be older than Middle Jurassic.

At present, laterite is well developed in the humid tropics (e.g. Maignien 1966). During the Triassic period, 250–210 million years ago, such conditions obtained in what is now South Australia. It was then that the brown coals of the Leigh Creek and other small depositional basins within the Flinders Ranges, and elsewhere, were formed (Parkin 1953; Wopfner 1969; Kwitco 1995). For these reasons it has been suggested that the laterite of Kangaroo Island is a remnant of a Triassic land surface, which appears to have been widely developed in what is now southern South Australia (Twidale 2000c) and elsewhere in Australia.

Thus, physical dating taken in conjunction with its well-established geological relationships suggests that the upfaulted lateritic surface of the Gulfs region is older than was at first thought. The Jurassic age of the basalt has been confirmed by repeated physical analyses. Also, oxygen isotopes point to a Mesozoic age for the clays beneath the basalt (Bird and Chivas 1988, 1989). Nevertheless, the suggested age is so old that many have queried the conclusion. Some have suggested that the basalt west of Kingscote rests not on laterite but on kaolinised clays unrelated to laterite. Certainly in road cuttings no ferruginised zone is exposed: it may have been dissolved by groundwater (see earlier). But in 1921 Tilley described from west of Penneshaw an exposure of basalt similar to that exposed west of Kingscote. Though the base of the basalt cannot be seen in contact with the ferruginous zone of the laterite, it stands higher in the local landscape than lateritised Proterozoic beds which here include a pisolitic ferruginous zone. As to why the basalt appears so fresh, it is suggested that because it is so

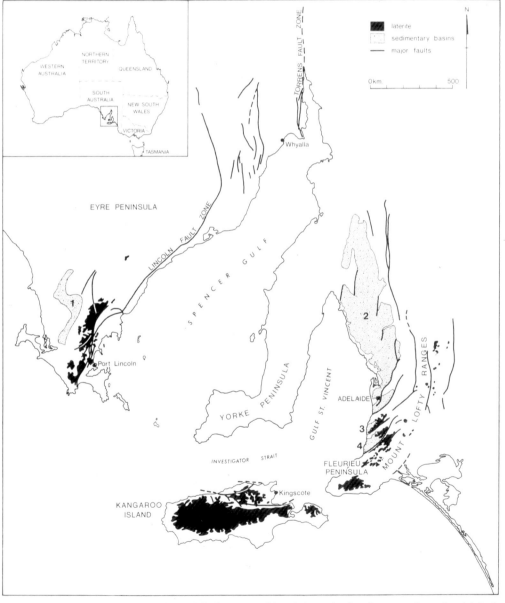

Fig. 4.7 Lateritic plateaux of the faulted Gulfs region of South Australia. I – Cummins Basin, 2 – Adelaide Plains Sub-basin, 3 – Clarendon Basin, 4 – Willunga Basin.

densely fractured (Fig. 4.6) meteoric waters falling on the surface readily percolate into and through the rock until they reach the water table, so that there is minimal contact and reaction with the country rock.

Gulfs region

Lateritic high plains are preserved not only on Kangaroo Island and in the southern Mt Lofty Ranges (Fleurieu Peninsula), but also on eastern Eyre Peninsula (Fig. 4.7), where the lateritic surface was assumed to be of Pliocene age (Johns 1961). On balance, however, the evidence points to the summit high plain preserved on various uplands bordering Gulf St Vincent and Spencer Gulf being comparable to and correlated with the Kangaroo Island occurrence, and thus being of great antiquity.

Fig. 4.8 Low oblique air photo of a planation surface cut and preserved in folded quartzite, The Battery, an asymmetric basin located in the western front of the Flinders Ranges west of Melrose. (Mapland DENR, South Australia)

Biographical note: G.D. Woodard (1930–1985)

In 1955 G.D. Woodard demonstrated that the prominent planation surface preserved in the northernmost Flinders Ranges, around Mt Babbage, is of exhumed type and pre-Cretaceous age (Woodard 1955). Geoff. Woodard (or 'Woody' as he was known) was born in Adelaide in 1930. He graduated in 1952 from the University of Adelaide, and took his MSc specialising in palaeontology. Working under the guidance of Martin Glaessner, Woody studied the Cretaceous marine beds preserved in Mt Babbage in the northern Flinders Ranges. From Adelaide he went to Berkeley to take his PhD and then was appointed to Sonoma State University, California, where, after a distinguished teaching career, he died in 1985.

G.D. Woodard

Flinders Ranges

The Flinders Ranges and Mid North regions are part of the same geosynclinal belt as the Mt Lofty Ranges. It is crossed by two major lineament corridors (4A and 8 *in* O'Driscoll 1986, 1989), which find expression in the Norwest-Macdonald fracture zone trending NW–SE and the Paralana fault system running NE–SW.

The folds are generally simple and open, though steeply inclined and even slightly overturned strata are evident in places. The uplands have been dissected to a much greater degree than have the Mt Lofty Ranges (Preiss 1987; Twidale and Bourne 1996), possibly because they lack a protective lateritic capping such as remains prominent to the south. Nevertheless, remnants of a summit high plain are preserved in many areas (Fig. 4.8), though ridge and valley topography (Figs 4.9a, b) is dominant, with small plateaux (mesas, or table-like mountains) standing where the strata in the crests of arches and troughs of basins are locally flat-lying (Fig. 4.9c). By and large the pattern of folds is reflected in the topography, but in some areas it is disturbed or interrupted by the occurrence of diapirs or emplacements of mudstone or shale that

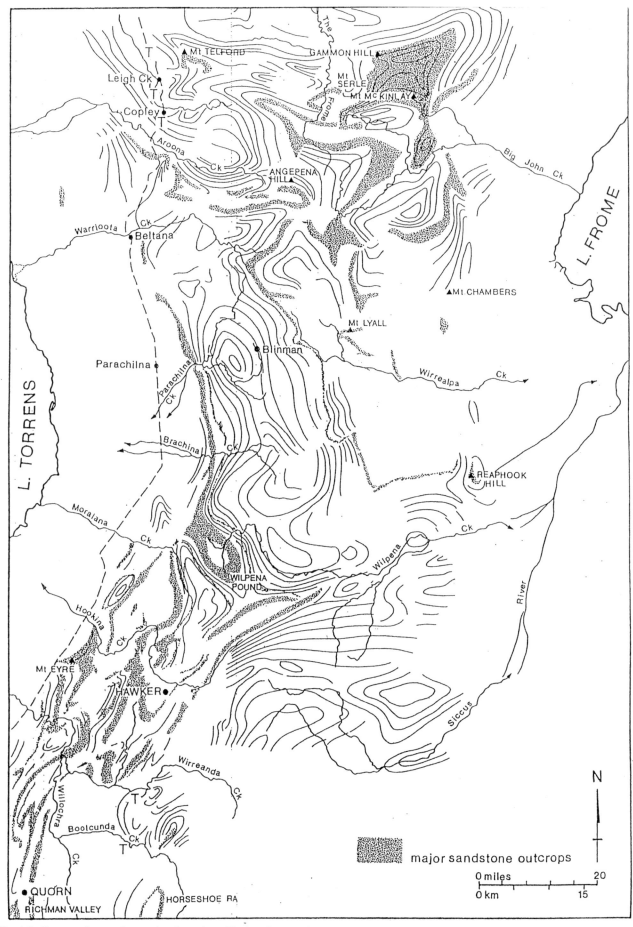

Fig. 4.9a Structural map of central and southern Flinders Ranges showing strike, major quartzite ridges and Triassic basins (T).

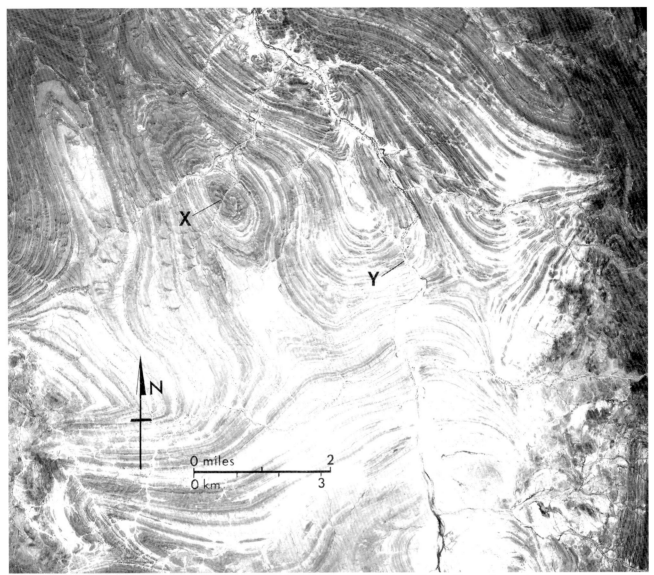

Fig. 4.9b Ridge and valley topography, as depicted on vertical air photograph of the Willouran Range, the northwestern extremity of the Flinders Ranges upland (S.A. Lands Department). X and Y – indicate transverse streams.

Fig. 4.9c Mesa in flat-lying strata in crest of anticlinal fold, central Flinders Ranges.

Fig. 4.10a Sketch map of part of the central Flinders Ranges showing diapiric intrusion located in the dome between Elder and Chace ranges, and...

Fig. 4.10b ...associated landscape. The conical hill known locally and for obvious reasons as 'Fuji Yama' is of shale. The gullies formed during a heavy rainstorm in February 1955.

have been injected from below, most of them in the cores of domes and anticlines (Fig. 4.10).

Ridge and valley topography

Ridge and valley landscapes owe their development to two factors — variations in lithology or composition of strata and tectonism, namely folding. The sequences of strata that were deposited in the Adelaide Geosyncline offshore from and between the Gawler and Curnamona cratons (Fig. 4.11) consisted of thick layers of sandstone,

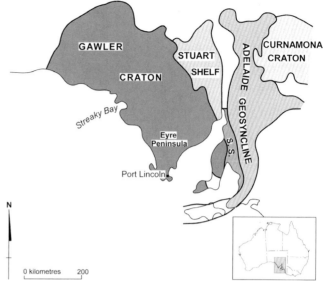

Fig. 4.11 The Flinders Ranges occupies the northern part of the Adelaide Geosyncline between the Gawler and Curnamona cratons. S.S. – Spencer Shelf.

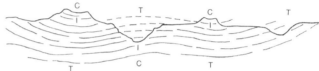

Fig. 4.12a Distribution of stress in folded sedimentary sequence. Dashed lines – strain lines, C – compression, T – tension, I – topographic inversion.

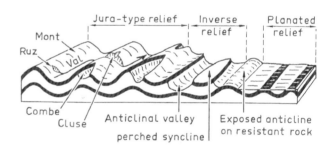

Fig. 4.12b Inversion of relief in folded sedimentary sequence. (After Derruau 1965)

limestone, clays and muds. Just as modern shorelines consist variously of shingle beaches, sands and mudflats, so at any given time 1000–600 million years ago the sedimentary layers being laid down offshore from the then continent varied in character. Also, the position of the shoreline varied in time with fluctuations in sea level, and according to earth movements that changed the level of the land. After burial and lithification, a given sedimentary stratum, although of the same age, may have varied laterally in composition or lithology. It may have consisted of sandstone here, mudstone there, conglomerate or puddingstone elsewhere, and so on. When subsequently uncovered and exposed to weathering, the stratum was, if only because of its varied composition, of varied resistance to attack by moisture and rivers. This is one reason for differential weathering and erosion, and for the development of valleys and, hence, ridges.

In addition, however, the folding that affected the area about 550 million years ago introduced local stresses. In particular the crests of arches (anticlines, domes) were stretched or in tension, high in the structure, but compressed at depth (Fig. 4.12a). Troughs (synclines, basins), on the other hand, were in compression high in the structure but in tension at depth. Stretching or tension opens fractures and leads to water penetration, to weathering and to erosion. Compression closes fractures, inhibits water penetration and thus protects the rocks involved.

Fig. 4.13a–b Inversion showing structural lows now located high in the local relief in (a) Mainwater Pound, northern Flinders Ranges, and (b) Wilpena Pound from the northwest. (Mapland DENR, South Australia)

For this reason relief inversion is commonplace in fold mountain belts (e.g. Derruau 1965, p. 320; Fig. 4.12b), with structural lows (synclines, basins) frequently standing high in the topography and structural highs (domes, anticlines or arches) reduced to valleys and plains. This occurs at various scales (Fig. 4.13; see also Fig. 4.8). Wilpena and Mainwater pounds or natural amphitheatres

are structural basins and the Dutchmans Stern, Gammon and Angepena ranges are pitching or tilted sync-lines that underlie positive relief features. On the other hand, the Willochra Plain, an intermontane plain of regional extent, occupies a denuded regional anticline (really an anticlinorium, for it consists of several minor arches and troughs within the overall structure; Fig. 4.13c). Like many other similar structures the Willochra anticline is also faulted, with a graben, rift valley or downfaulted block developed in the stretched crest of the fold (Milton and Twidale 1977).

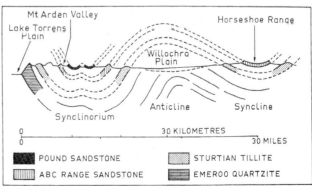

Fig. 4.13c Diagrammatic east–west section through the Willochra Basin showing plain developed on structural high (arch or anticline).

Mt Babbage

Notwithstanding the dominance of ridge and valley topography, a prominent summit surface is preserved throughout the Flinders Ranges (Fig. 4.14; see also Fig. 4.8). In the northernmost part of the upland, both the character and the age of the surface are indicated by the strata preserved in Mt Babbage (Woodard 1955), a small mesa standing prominently on the high plain cut across various sedimentary, metamorphic and igneous rocks (Fig. 4.15).

The strata are sandstones of Early Cretaceous age (about 130 million years old) and were laid down in the margins of the seas which then, and on several later occasions during the Cretaceous, inundated much of Australia (Frakes 1987; Fig. 4.16).

Cretaceous marine transgressions are frequently mentioned in later pages. They are crucial to the dating of large parts of the Australian landscape, for associated sediments buried and preserved many surfaces and forms that have been later re-exposed. Also, Cretaceous strata remain in valleys and basins, thus indicating a minimum age for the adjacent topography. Further, many old plains arguably were eroded by rivers flowing and graded to a Cretaceous shoreline.

Fig. 4.14a Exhumed summit surface in granitic rocks in the northern Flinders Ranges.

Fig. 4.14b Summit surface of probable exhumed origin cut across sedimentary and metamorphic rocks, northern Flinders Ranges. (B.P. Webb)

Fig. 4.15a Close view of Mt Babbage, an outlier of Cretaceous strata resting unconformably on older rocks. A palaeosol, the Bopeechee Regolith, is present at the base of the marine strata.

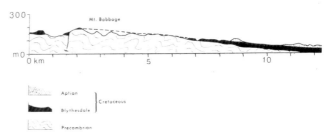

Fig. 4.15b Section showing Mt Babbage in relation to associated exhumed land surface. (After Woodard 1955)

At Mt Babbage the Cretaceous beds rest unconformably on a remnant of the Bopeechee Regolith (Sheard 2001) and were silicified after exposure. Given the marine cover, the preservation of a regolith is unusual. Nevertheless, Mt Babbage is an outlier of younger rocks and the only one preserved within the upland though there are equivalent beds beneath the adjacent plains (Fig. 4.15b). The Mt Babbage remnant demonstrates, first, that the upland surface predated the Early Cretaceous. Second, the unconformity between the Cretaceous and Precambrian at the base of Mt Babbage is level with the surrounding plain. The high plain has been re-exposed as a result of the erosion of the Cretaceous strata that formerly covered the whole surface in the northernmost Flinders (Fig. 4.15c). Thus it is an exhumed surface from which a pre-Cretaceous regolith was stripped by wave action. The surface predates the Early Cretaceous, and originated more than 130 million years ago.

Riverine planation surface

The strata preserved in Mt Babbage contain plant fossils of littoral or shoreline type (Alley and Lemon 1988). This suggests that the present Mt Babbage was close to the former southern limit of the Cretaceous sea and that

Fig. 4.15c Mt Babbage seen from a distance and showing its relationship with the surrounding terrain, in particular the correlation of the unconformity and high summit surface.

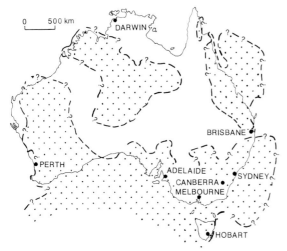

Fig. 4.16 The extent of seas and land in the Australian region in Early Cretaceous times. (After Frakes 1987)

the summit high plain to the south is of a different age and character. It was most likely eroded by rivers which flowed to the Early Cretaceous shoreline and is thus 130–120 million years old. It is preserved mostly on the crests of quartzite or sandstone ridges and at some sites clearly cuts across tilted strata. In the central Flinders Ranges, however, it is developed on shale and mudstone. These are easily erodible rocks, but they vary in resistance so that several bevels at different but closely related elevations occur even in the same area, as for instance around the Stokes Hill Lookout, in the central part of the upland (Fig. 4.17a).

The conservation of this surface in argillites may be another effect of deep erosion. The central Flinders Ranges is essentially a regional anticline. The crest of the structure was in tension and it has been weathered and eroded. Consideration of stratigraphic sections suggests that several

Fig. 4.17a Planation surfaces cut in shale and mudstone, around and to the north of Stokes Hill Lookout, central Flinders Ranges.

Fig. 4.17b Concordant summits of multiple quartzitic ridges which form the western ramparts of the Flinders Ranges near Brachina, north of Wilpena Pound. Note pediment apron fronting the limestone ridge (light colour).

Fig. 4.18b   Cross-bedded and cemented gravel and sands of ?Middle Eocene age, exposed in bank of Wirreanda Creek, near Gordon, northern Willochra Plain.

Fig. 4.18a   World War II (1942) air photo of the northern Willochra Plain (RAAF), taken from the north.

Fig. 4.18c (below) Map showing distribution of ?Middle Eocene lake sediments around northern Willochra Basin. The probable limits of the Eocene Willochra Lake are indicated by a dashed line.

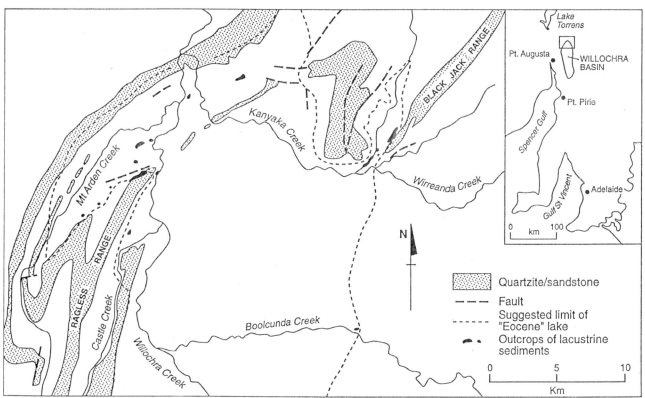

kilometres of rock have been worn away. Thus, erosion may have been so deep that the lower compressional zone of the structure is exposed. This central region has also been protected by the buttressing effect of quartzite and sandstone ridges exposed to both east and west of the core area. Such protection and strata in compressive stress exposed by deep erosion, together go some way to explaining why a high plain is preserved between Wilpena Pound and Blinman, even though it is developed in weak rocks (Fig. 4.17).

Ghost of an earlier landscape

As has been mentioned, basins of Triassic sediment, including brown coal, are preserved in the south at Boolcunda and at Springfield, and to the north around Leigh Creek and Copley (Fig. 4.9a). The sediments of the Springfield Basin (Johnson 1960) are fine-grained and become finer higher in the sequence (they display upward-fining), suggesting derivation from a terrain of diminishing relief. It has been suggested that they were derived from a surface of low relief 250–210 million years ago. No remnants of a surface of such a demonstrated Triassic age have been located in the Flinders Ranges. This does not, however, rule out the possibility that some of the bevelled ridge crests within the ridge and valley topography are remnants of such a landscape. If so, they can be correlated with the lateritic surface of the Gulfs area (Twidale 2000c). It is suggested that this implied Triassic landscape be referred to as the Webb Surface after Bruce P. Webb (1926–2000), who investigated and mapped many parts of the Flinders Ranges while serving with the Geological Survey of South Australia.

The Willochra Lake

After the planation that resulted in the reduction of the area to low relief, with only low rises where quartzite and other resistant rocks cropped out, there was a period of deep dissection with outcrops of weaker rocks (shale, mudstone) worn down, leaving quartzite and sandstone standing as ridges and ranges. This stream incision was induced partly by a lowering of baselevel following the withdrawal of the Cretaceous seas, partly by renewed faulting and uplift. It was then, in later Cretaceous and earliest Tertiary times, that the present ridge and valley landscape was produced as rivers carved deep valleys in weaker strata, leaving sandstone and quartzite formations as ridges. In the southern Flinders Ranges, this dissection took place prior to the Middle Eocene, about 60 million years ago, as is demonstrated at the northern margin of the Willochra Plain.

The rivers draining this plain were blocked in Early Tertiary times, probably as a result of the upfaulting of the western margin of the upland (see e.g. Williams 1973; Quigley et al. 2006). The blockage of drainage caused a lake to be formed in the northern part of the Willochra

Basin. Sediments deposited in the Basin tongue up adjacent valleys (Fig. 4.18). They have been dated by fragmentary plant fossils as ?Middle Eocene in age (Harris 1970), showing that in this part of the Ranges at any rate the ridge and valley topography was developed by that time. Silicified old valley floor remnants capped by coarse introduced debris, and graded to the lake margin, are common in the Kanyaka and Mt Arden valleys.

The Kanyaka, Wirreanda and the Mt Arden creeks, which still flow from time to time, eroded the valleys in which they now run and up which, in Middle Eocene times, arms of the Willochra Lake extended. Like the River Torrens which drains the central part of the Mt Lofty Ranges, they are very old streams (Twidale 1997). Remnants of a surface cut across Cambrian strata and on which lake beds were laid down have been re-exposed in the Mt Arden Creek valley close to the junction of that Creek with the Willochra.

Can the age of the ridge and valley topography adjacent to the northern Willochra Basin and Plain be taken as characteristic of the entire fold mountain belt? Stratigraphic evidence is missing, yet bevelled ridge crests of putative Cretaceous age are well preserved and like old valley floor remnants, occur throughout the upland. Erosion low in the landscape is indicated by abandoned pediments, and by mesas that occupy the sites where coarse debris fallen from the nearby bluffs preserves the old piedmont. These old valley floors stand 5–10 m higher than the present valley plains

Fig. 4.19a Low oblique aerial view of part of Wilpena Pound showing the distinct platform in the scarp-foot zone. It is correlated with the mesa.

Fig. 4.19b Perched platform (P) and matching pediment remnants, Brachina Gorge area, western piedmont of the Flinders Ranges.

(Fig. 4.19a) and in many instances can be correlated with fragments of platforms perched on adjacent scarps (Fig. 4.19b). Weathering beneath the former valley floors resulted in the formation of kaolinised regoliths that have in places been stripped to give local etch plains (Figs 4.19c, d). In addition, the advent of humans and especially European settlers has resulted in widespread accelerated soil erosion, most obviously in the form of gullying (Twidale

and Bourne 1996).

In the overall view these recent changes are minor, though significant in terms of models of landscape development, for the modern Flinders landscapes are basically those that were in existence in Cretaceous and earliest Tertiary times. The planation surfaces date from the Early Cretaceous (130–120 million years) and the high plains of the central southern region from the Late Cretaceous (100–70 million years). The ridge and valley assemblages are some 60 million years old.

Deep erosion and river patterns

The present Flinders Ranges landscape includes elements of several ages and has involved the erosion of at least 6 km of rock. This is not to suggest that at any time the ancient Ranges ever attained any great altitude, for as soon as the marine sediments were folded and appeared above the then sea level they would have been subjected to weathering and erosion, and worn down.

The ridge and valley topography has been

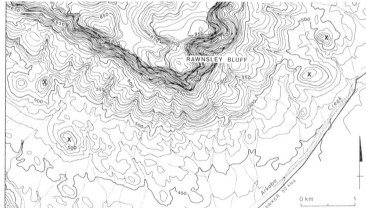

Fig. 4.19c Map of Rawnsley Bluff area. X – mesas or debris-capped remnants of old valley floor.

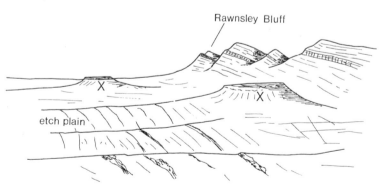

Fig. 4.19d Sketch from northeast showing mesas (X) east of the Bluff capped by coarse debris fallen from the outward-facing scarp of Wilpena Pound, and underlain by kaolinised rock, near Rawnsley Bluff. Note the associated etch plain exposed by the stripping of the clay zone which formerly covered the entire plain and the associated lowering of the valley floor.

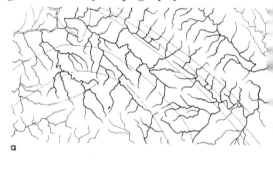

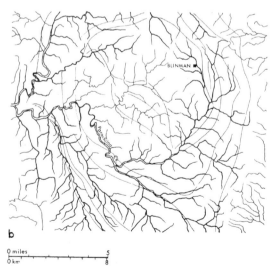

Fig. 4.20 (a) Trellis, and **(b)** annular drainage patterns, Flinders Ranges.

shaped by rivers and streams, the patterns of which largely reflect natural selection. A stream rising in a weak (i.e. non-resistant) layer such as shale develops more rapidly than one flowing on, say, sandstone, and becomes the dominant or master stream. Once it has cut lower it attracts more runoff and becomes even more prominent. For this reason stream patterns are usually adjusted to the occurrences of weak and resistant rocks, or to the arrangement of fractures that may be planes of weakness. Thus in the Flinders Ranges and in other fold mountain belts trellis and annular patterns are dominant (Fig. 4.20). Long streams developed in weak beds are called strike streams because they follow the strike or bedding of the strata and are linked by shorter dip or antidip streams that have extended back into and through ridges by headward (or regressive) erosion. Such headward erosion is achieved by seepage and slumping, most commonly along fractures.

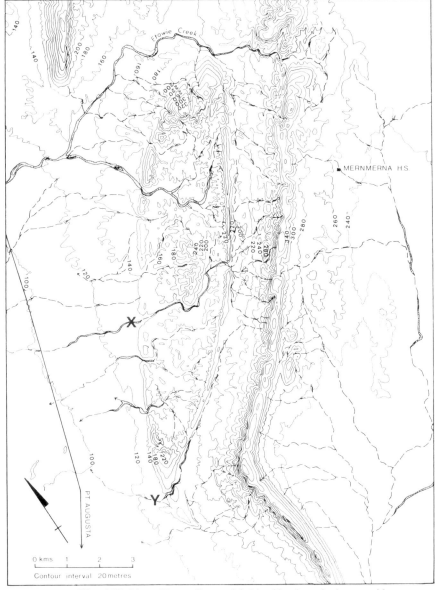

Fig. 4.22 Mern Merna Dome **(a)** Map, Y – breached snout, X – stream running across the core of the dome, and

(b) low oblique photo of dome from the south. The breached snout, Y in (a), seen in foreground. (J.A. Bourne)

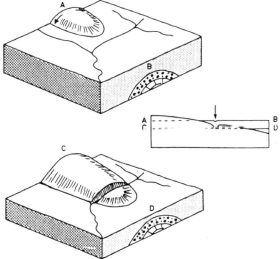

Fig. 4.21 Development of breached snout of fold by stream which maintains course while lowering its bed. Initial position also given by A-B (in section), and after erosion, C-D, with gorge cut through exposed resistant rock in fold.

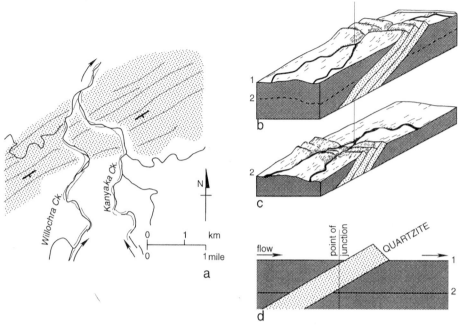

Fig. 4.23 (a) Plan view, **(b–d)** suggested developmental sequence, Partacoona drainage.

Fig. 4.23e Low oblique photo of Partacoona drainage (D. Beng).

on to a resistant formation. If it had sufficient energy, it could have carved a gorge, which is anomalous in terms of the present structural pattern (Fig. 4.21).

Erosion deep into rocks of contrasted character and structure may explain odd drainage patterns such as those seen on the Mern Merna Dome where a stream has cut a gorge in quartzite despite being only a few hundred metres from a plain eroded in weak rocks (Fig. 4.22). Moreover, a small river flows directly across the domal structure cutting through two quartzite ridges in doing so. Still more curious is the development of the two gorges cut by the Kanyaka and Wirreanda creeks where they pass through a quartzite ridge near Partacoona Homestead in the southern Flinders Ranges. Having both cut gorges, they converge before flowing on to the Lake Torrens plains (Fig. 4.23). They too and many other anomalous patterns can be explained in terms of the local disposition of strata, the changing distribution of strata with depth and deep erosion.

Mid North region

Remnants of laterite stand high in the relief in the southern Mid North region. Silcrete-capped remnants, possibly of Early-Middle Tertiary age, are also present (Alley 1973). So far, however, there has been no suggestion that these duricrusted remnants predate the Tertiary, though the ridges and valleys that form the framework of the relief (Fig. 4.24) and stand higher than the duricrusts may be of an antiquity similar to those of the Flinders Ranges. Certainly, Preiss (1995) assigns the planation and deep weathering of the region, the landscape from which the present topography has been shaped, to the Mesozoic. Thus, it is suggested that this area as well as being a structural extension of the Flinders Ranges, but with open folds, is also comparable in its morphological evolution.

But some river patterns, far from being adjusted to structure, cut across hard strata and across folds: they are said to be transverse or anomalous. There are several notable examples in the Flinders Ranges. Explanations of anomalous stream sectors include diversion by faulting, glaciation, volcanism, antecedence, superimposition and inheritance (see Twidale 1976a, 2004). Many, however, can be explained in terms of the deep erosion that is known to have taken place in the Flinders (Twidale 1966a, 1972, 2004; Twidale and Bourne 1996). The distribution and geometry of folds varies in depth as well as plan. The distribution of weaker strata that determined early river patterns differed from that at the present land surface. Where there has been deep erosion, a stream adjusted to a weak layer exposed in a higher surface could have been let down

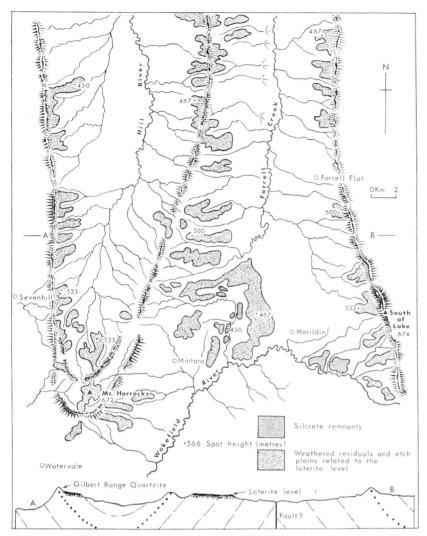

Fig. 4.24a Ridge and valley, and duricrusts in the Mid North region. (After Alley 1973)

Fig. 4.24b Dissected ridge preserved in gently dipping shale (dip down to right), Spalding area of the Mid North. (J.A. Bourne)

Chapter 5

SOUTH AUSTRALIAN CRATONS AND BASINS

Biographical note: R. Lockhart Jack (1878–1964)

The exhumed sub-Cretaceous surface of the northern Flinders Ranges is only part of an extensive resurrected surface, the existence of which at the southwestern margin of the Eromanga Basin was recognised in 1931 by R. Lockhart Jack, the son of R. Logan Jack, also a well-known and widely travelled geologist. Lockhart Jack spent most of his working life in the South Australian Geological Survey. He accomplished intrepid journeys by camel into the northwest of the State and made observations that are still pertinent. He, and later Woodard (1955) and Wopfner (1964), noted the unconformity between the Mesozoic strata (later Jurassic and Early Cretaceous) and the Precambrian and Palaeozoic rocks beneath (Jack 1931). It extends without obvious topographic discontinuity to the west. How far to the west, however, is yet to be determined. The extent of the unconformity is of economic interest because groundwaters rich in silica evidently accumulated at the base of the Mesozoic cover and on and in the older rocks: hence the opal of gem quality worked at Mintabie.

R. Lockhart Jack

Arcoona Plateau and the Tent Hills

Geological framework

To the north and west of the upland spine based in the Adelaide Geosyncline desert conditions prevail over the Stuart Shelf, the Gawler Craton, and various basins and older structural remnants of South Australia (Fig. 4.10). The Stuart Shelf is a region of essentially undisturbed Neoproterozoic strata laid down on, and underlain by, the crystalline basement of the Craton (Johns 1968). The Shelf sediments find expression in the Arcoona Plateau and the Tent Hill region, west and north of Port Augusta (Twidale et al. 1970; Twidale 1994).

Age of the landscape

The sedimentary sequence consists of interbedded siltstones and quartzites that dip gently down to the north. The dip is so gentle that when dissected they give rise to plateaux and mesas. Yet a dip of only 1° implies a change in elevation of 17–18 m per km, and over a distance of several scores of kilometres, successive quartzite layers are exposed, each forming a capping to plateaux and high plains, but clearly bevelled, with the summit surface cutting across bedding (Figs 5.1a, b). Many of the plateaux, however, are domed because thin remnants of weaker sediments survive above the caprock (Figs 5.1b–d). The Arcoona Plateau and

Fig. 5.1a Diagrammatic north–south section through the Arcoona Plateau.

Fig. 5.1b Domed plateau in the southern Arcoona Plateau. The form is clearly erosional because it cuts across strata.

Fig. 5.1c Plateau with scarp-foot depression and false cuesta, southern Arcoona Plateau.

Fig. 5.1d Detail of scarp-foot depression and false cuesta, Tent Hill region near Lincoln Gap.

its composite summit surface were delineated on the east by movement along the Torrens Fault. In the downfaulted basin to the east, which is now occupied mainly by Lake Torrens, was deposited a sequence of freshwater sediments, the basal members of which are of Eocene age. Thus, the faulting is at least of that age, and the dislocated high plain surface of the Arcoona Plateau is at least as old (Johns 1968).

As with the Mt Lofty Ranges, however, a much greater age than that suggested by the date of the faulting is indicated by other palaeogeographic evidence. In the Woomera area and elsewhere, the valley floors cut below the plateau are underlain by Early Cretaceous marine strata (Johns et al. 1981). The valleys in which these beds were laid down must have been in existence prior to the Early Cretaceous marine transgression and the surface into which they were incised is even older — Jurassic and possibly Triassic.

Again, then, geological methods and common sense permit the sequence of landscape development to be established. The landscape — plateaux and valleys — predates the Early Cretaceous. The summit surface or plateau is even older for it had developed before rivers incised valleys and the Cretaceous sea advanced into the area (Twidale 1994). Silcrete of Early Tertiary age occurs in valley floors located to the west of the Plateau (e.g. Hou et al. 2003; Fig. 5.1e). It is also preserved in old valley floors and as skins on blocks and boulders in piedmont zones in the southeast of the Plateau (Twidale et al. 1970; Hutton et al. 1972). The age of silicification is difficult to determine, but given the Eocene age of the faulting that delineates the

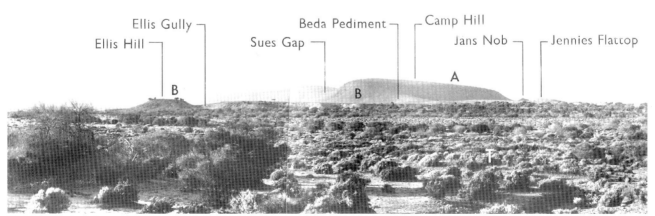

Fig. 5.1e Typical plateau (A) with silcrete, (B) preserved in the old valley floor, and present Beda Valley (T), southern Arcoona Plateau.

Plateau on its eastern side, appears to be of younger rather than older Tertiary age.

Adjacent plateaux and high plains

Probable remnants of this old surface survive in the Tent Hills and Baxter Range, west and

Fig. 5.2 Summit surface of Baxter Hills seen from the east. The valley at left is the site of one of Eyre's 1839 camps. (J.A. Bourne)

southwest of Port Augusta, and probably also on the Baxter Hills, an outcrop of folded Proterozoic conglomerate located further to the west (Bourne and Twidale 2003; Fig. 5.2). Silcrete again occurs in the plateau piedmonts.

Gawler Ranges

The Gawler Ranges is a massif of ancient volcanic rocks (Fig. 5.3; see also Fig. 4.1) of Mesoproterozoic age. The volcanics are silicic (i.e. they exhibit free silica in the form of quartz). They may have been deposited as ash-flows during effusive eruptions and later welded to form the present rock formations (dacite, rhyolite and rhyodacite). Other explanations for this puzzling rock sequence have, however, been suggested (see Blissett et al. 1993; Allen et al. 2003).

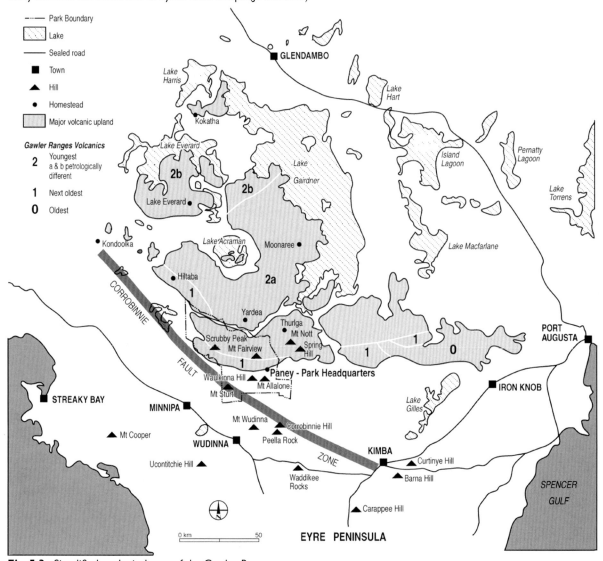

Fig. 5.3 Simplified geological map of the Gawler Ranges.

Fractures

The Gawler Range Volcanics were formed some 1592 million years ago and columnar or cooling joints developed soon afterwards. Granites were intruded later, about 1585 million years ago (Fig. 5.4). Orthogonal fractures, or systems of partings

Fig. 5.4 Granite intrusive into Volcanics **(a)** near Hiltaba Homestead, and **(b)** (below) near Kondoolka Homestead (g – granite, v – volcanics), western Gawler Ranges. (After Campbell & Twidale 1991a)

arranged at right angles to one another, were formed in both the volcanics and granites, probably as a result of shear stresses some time later than 1585 million years ago and prior to 1400 million years ago when dolerite sills were injected along some members of the orthogonal fracture system. Sheet structures that are arcuate-upward occur within the orthogonal blocks. They formed before the deposition of physically dated riverine sediments, some 1424 million years old, in the area that is now east of Lake Gairdner (Campbell and Twidale 1991a). The surface on which they were laid down has been partly exhumed (Twidale et al. 1976).

Neoproterozoic and Palaeozoic events

About 600 million years ago the Acraman bolide or meteorite impacted on the western Gawler Ranges (Williams 1994). The salina known as Lake Acraman marks the weathered and eroded disturbed zone but the impact also imposed a set of

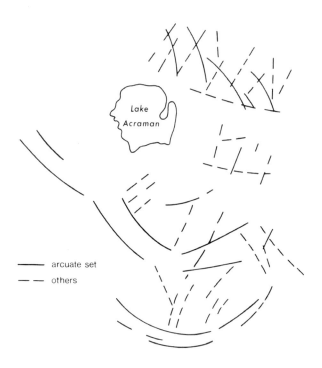

Fig. 5.5 Fracture patterns, concentric imposed on orthogonal, around the Acraman impact site, western Gawler Ranges.

concentric fractures on the pre-existing orthogonal (slightly rhomboidal) systems of fractures (Fig. 5.5).

Ice sheets overrode the region about 330 million years ago, in Permo-Carboniferous times (BMR Palaeogeographic Group 1992). The ice sheets stripped previously developed regoliths and in many places left behind scoured bedrock surfaces and deposits of ill-sorted debris. In the Gawler Ranges, and in many other areas, this glacial event provides a valuable marker in landscape chronology, for, with the exception of the minor exhumed forms of Neoproterozoic age located southeast of Lake Gairdner and features associated with the Acraman bolide impact, the development of the present landscape began with the melting and disintegration of the Late Palaeozoic ice sheets.

Landscape development

The Gawler Ranges massif is higher in the south than in the north. It comprises ordered rows of dome-shaped hills or bornhardts, each of which is developed on a fracture-defined block which is orthogonal or rhomboidal in plan-shape (Fig. 5.6a). The sheet fractures determine the rounded form of the hills (Fig. 5.6b). The domical hills (bornhardts) are bevelled, and the flattish crests

Fig. 5.6a Landsat image showing bornhardts developed in fracture-controlled blocks, west and east of Lake Gairdner. Lake Acraman is the roughly circular lake to the southwest.

Fig. 5.6b Sheet structure and columnar joints exposed east of Yardea Homestead, Gawler Ranges.

together form a prominent summit surface sloping down to the north (Campbell and Twidale 1991b; Fig. 5.7). This is the Nott Surface, which includes both bornhardts and bevelled crests.

The hills are bald and rocky, with little or no soil cover. Yet there was once a regolith. This is evidenced far to the north, in the Eromanga Basin (Wopfner 1969, pp. 152–156; Wopfner et al. 1970). There, the Mt Anna Sandstone, which is of Early Cretaceous (Neocomian–Aptian) age and 130–120 million years old, contains cobbles and small boulders of Gawler Range Volcanics (Fig. 5.8a). Sedimentological evidence (current bedding, thickness of strata) suggests that these fragments have been carried by rivers draining the

Fig. 5.7   The prominent summit surface and component bornhardts (a) seen from Spring Hill, near Mt Nott, southern Gawler Ranges, with sheet structure exposed on near slope,

Fig. 5.7b near Hiltaba Homestead, Gawler Ranges, where granite intrusive into the volcanics is exposed (boulders) in left foreground and on the lower slopes (pale outcrops) in the middle distance, and

Fig. 5.7c as seen from the air in the southern Ranges. (E.M. Campbell)

Fig. 5.8a Creek section with cobbles and small boulders of Gawler Range Volcanics, near Mt Anna, western Eromanga Basin. (H. Wopfner)

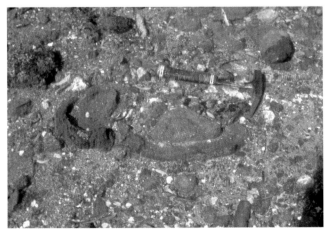

Fig. 5.8b Patch of regolith formed on the Gawler Range Volcanics with corestones set in a matrix of granular clayey weathered rock, between Thurlga and Yardea.

upland at that time. Thus, prior to some 130 million years ago the present massif carried a weathered mantle developed in association with a plain which is known as the Beck Surface, named after Lance Beck (1907–1997), a well-known amateur geologist with a long-standing interest in the Gawler Ranges. No remnant of the Beck Surface has been recognised in the present landscape. Like many regoliths developed in well-jointed but impermeable rocks (e.g. granite, basalt), the mantle consisted of corestones or boulders embedded in a finer clayey grit or sand. Only one patch of regolith with spherical corestones set in weathered country rock (Fig. 5.8b) has been noted from hillslopes in the Ranges, though others, of kaolinised dacite,

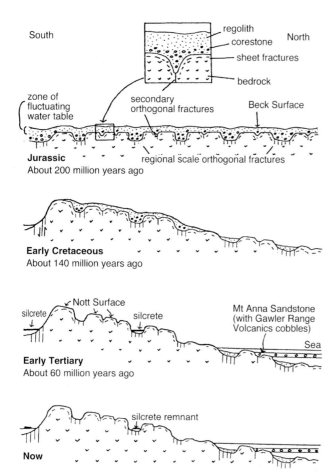

Fig. 5.9 Sections showing suggested stages in development of Gawler Ranges landscape.

and preserved east of Nonning Homestead and to the north, occur near the eastern shore of Lake Gairdner.

This evidence suggests that the Beck Surface predates the Early Cretaceous but developed after the withdrawal of the ice sheets which covered the area during the Permian. The stripping of the Beck regolith occurred during the Early Cretaceous, possibly as a result of river rejuvenation that resulted from the upfaulting of the southern margin of the present upland along the Corrobinnie Fault Zone. The Corrobinnie Depression (Bourne et al. 1974; Binks and Hooper 1984) is developed along the fracture zone. It was eroded and drained by the Narlaby drainage during the Eocene and Pliocene. Like the Early Tertiary faulting reported from the Mt Lofty and Flinders ranges, the dislocation along the Corrobinnie Fault Zone may have been related to the separation of Antarctica and Australia.

The Gawler Ranges massif has remained virtually unchanged since the Early Cretaceous. This is suggested by the preservation at the margins of the

upland of siliceous duricrusts of Early Tertiary age — Eocene according to Firman (1983); Eocene or Oligocene in Hou et al. (2003). The occurrence of Eocene alluvia in the Corrobinnie Depression corroborates the Cretaceous age of the upland. Stability is also suggested by the absence of any significant volume of Tertiary sediments in adjacent basins to the east and north.

Also, although the Gawler Ranges drainage has been affected by tectonism and climatic changes, rejuvenation and associated landscape revival has influenced the margins of the massif but not the interior. Early Tertiary silcrete surfaces are dissected at the eastern margin but not elsewhere. Minor flared slopes and associated rock platforms occur only in the southern piedmont. Remnants of a pre-Cretaceous regolith are preserved only in interior locations and only at a few sites there. The development of the upland is shown diagrammatically in a series of sections (Fig. 5.9).

Eyre Peninsula

Eyre Peninsula lies to the south of the Gawler Ranges and the Corrobinnie Depression. The region consists mainly of plains, with old dunefields and a calcrete crust prominent in the northern areas. In the east and south, however, remnants of higher ground occur in the Lincoln Uplands and in the Cleve Hills, where very old gneisses and other igneous and metamorphic rocks are exposed (Johns 1961; Parker 1993). They were weathered and lateritised during the Early Mesozoic, probably at the same time as the Mt Lofty Ranges and Kangaroo Island were duricrusted, though in the Cleve Hills (Fig. 5.10) only pockets of pisolitic iron oxide associated with deeply kaolinised and mottled bedrock occur beneath the summit surface. To the west of the

Fig. 5.10 Summit surface of the Cleve Hills, eastern Eyre Peninsula.

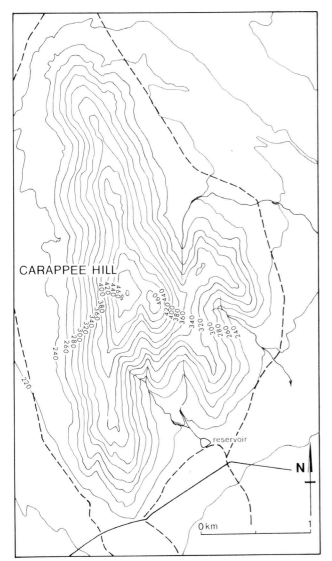

Fig. 5.11c Crest of Ucontitchie Hill, northwestern Eyre Peninsula, with bevel transecting massive sheet structure.

Fig. 5.12 Silcrete-capped mesa near Coober Pedy, north of Port Augusta, South Australia.

Fig. 5.11a Topographic map of Carappee Hill, northern Eyre Peninsula, an example of a stepped inselberg. A prominent shoulder or surface stands below the peak of the gneissic remnant.

Lincoln Uplands the lateritised surface appears to dip beneath the Eocene strata of the Cummins Basin (Johns 1958).

Granitic terrain

Granitic rocks underlie most of the north and northwest of the Peninsula. Most of these old igneous rocks have been weathered and eroded to form rolling plains, but especially massive compartments of rock have resisted weathering and erosion to form prominent rounded hills known as inselbergs or bornhardts (Twidale 1964, 1982a, 1982b). They were noted by E.J. Eyre in 1839 during his exploration of northern Eyre Peninsula and the southern Gawler Ranges (Eyre 1845, pp. 198–205). On 24 September 1839 he found himself west of the Baxter Range in a landscape with many isolated hills 'resembling so many islands in the level waste around them' (Eyre 1845,

Fig. 5.11b Platform or shoulder located high on western slope of Carappee Hill.

p. 203). Giles (1889, p. 158) remarked of some hills he encountered in central Australia: 'The mount, and all the others connected with it, rose simply like islands out of a vast sea of scrub'. These are but two of several uses of the 'island' analogy by early explorers for what are now generally known by the German equivalent, inselbergs.

Inselbergs were formed by differential subsurface weathering followed by the exposure of the compartments of still-fresh rock. Like the bornhardts of the Gawler Ranges, they are etch forms. Some of them are bevelled and stepped with breaks of slope, including flared sectors which mark pauses in weathering and erosion (see Chapter 11). The crests and high shoulders of major inselbergs, such as Mt Wudinna, Carappee Hill, and Ucontitchie Hill (Fig. 5.11), are possibly Mesozoic in age and can be correlated with the summit surface of the Gawler Ranges (Twidale 1994).

North and west of the Gawler Craton

To the north of the Gawler Craton several planation surfaces and palaeodrainage channels with siliceous fills have been recognised in the Officer Basin. The silicification has been variously attributed to earlier and later Tertiary (Wopfner 1967; Benbow et al. 1995a, 1995b; McNally and Wilson 1995; Hou et al. 2003). Silcrete plateaux are also prominent

in the Eromanga Basin (Figs 3.3b, 5.12). The plains southwest of Lake Eyre, however, carry a Pleistocene silcrete with an opaline matrix, which contrasts with the microcrystalline matrices of older siliceous duricrusts (Wopfner and Twidale 1967).

To the southwest of the Basin, the Cretaceous and Upper Jurassic strata thin out and disappear. To the west is a plain that is eroded in various Proterozoic and Palaeozoic rocks and that was long ago identified as an exhumed sub-Cretaceous (or Late Jurassic) surface (Jack 1931; Wopfner 1964). The Peake and Denison (or Davenport) Ranges are isolated remnants of the Adelaide geosynclinal fold belt (Flint 1993). They are upfaulted on their eastern side and the prominent summit surface (Fig. 5.13) is most likely an uplifted part of the exhumed sub Late Jurassic surface that is so prominent at the southwestern margin of the Eromanga Basin (Jack 1931; Wopfner 1968).

To the west of the Gawler Craton, the Eucla Basin with its Eocene and Miocene limestones exposed in coastal cliffs is occupied by the Nullarbor Plain, a featureless plain best interpreted as an etch plain of Pliocene and Pleistocene age (Lowry 1970; Lowry and Jennings 1974; Twidale 1990). The Barton and Ooldea ranges, at the northeastern margin of the plain, are coastal dunes of ?Miocene age preserved by virtue of a capping of calcrete (Benbow 1990).

Fig. 5.13 Part of summit surface of Mt Margaret Plateau, in the Peake and Denison Ranges. (PIRSA)

Chapter 6

PALAEOSURFACES OF THE SOUTHWEST AND WEST

Biographical note: J.T. Jutson (1874–1959)

John Thomas Jutson was born in Richmond, Victoria, in 1874. After high school he became a law clerk but began formal geological studies at night school. He became an assistant to Professor E.W. Skeats in the Department of Geology, University of Melbourne, in 1908. Though not formally qualified he learned enough geology to be appointed Field Geologist in the Geological Survey of Western Australia in 1911. There he remained until 1918 when government financial stringencies led to his being retrenched. Undeterred, he enrolled as a mature-age student at the University of Western Australia and graduated BSc in 1920. He still hoped for a career in geology and applied for a survey post in West Africa, but failed the medical because he was, increasingly, afflicted with deafness and it was thought that the daily doses of quinine, necessary at that time to ward off the malaria prevalent in tropical Africa, would accentuate his problem. He returned to Melbourne, joined a legal firm as a solicitor, graduated LlB in 1925 (University of Melbourne) and retired in 1952. He died in 1959.

J.T. Jutson

While pursuing his legal career in Melbourne Jutson continued his geological researches, mainly concerned with shore platforms, as a hobby during weekends and vacations. In this as in all else, he was greatly aided by his wife. His most important legacy, however, is his 1914 review and synthesis of the physiography of Western Australia. Revised and republished in 1934 and again printed in 1950, it is replete with ideas, many of them discovered by others and given an appropriate name in later years. In particular, he noted that the New Plateau which occupies huge areas of the Yilgarn Craton was produced by the stripping, implicitly as the result of scarp recession of the lateritic regolith formed on the Old Plateau (Brock and Twidale 1984). The resultant New Plateau is essentially what later became known as a two-stage or etch surface (Mabbutt 1961a, 1961b). Others had earlier reached similar conclusions about certain landforms and landscapes in Europe and Africa (see Twidale 2002), but Jutson was the first in Australia to recognise the origin of this important type of feature.

Fig. 6.1 Location map for geological regions of southwestern Australia (after Palfreyman 1984) showing also major structural units.

Yilgarn Craton

Geological framework

The Yilgarn Craton is an extensive exposure of Archaean granite, gneiss and 'greenstone' (basic volcanic rock) located in the southwest of Western Australia (Geological Survey of Western Australia 1975, 1990; Fig. 6.1). Topographically, it is

Fig. 6.2b Laterite-capped mesa near Cue, Western Australia.

dominated by high plains and by plateaux capped and protected by duricrusts, most commonly laterite (Figs 3.3a, 6.2) or bauxite (as in the Darling Ranges), but siliceous in some valley fills, as at Buckleys Breakaway, between Norseman and Hyden, and in the Killara district of the northern Yilgarn. Dismembered remnants of an old drainage system, now represented by strings of salinas or salt lakes, form prominent features in the landscape (Van de Graaff et al. 1977; Commander 1989; Kern and Commander 1993; Clarke 1994a; Waterhouse et al. 1995; Fig. 6.3). The original channels were initiated in the Eocene and can be compared to the old rivers noted earlier in the Mt Lofty and Flinders ranges.

Fig. 6.2a Laterite-capped mesa of the Old Plateau surface with kaolinite zone exposed on scarp, at The Granites, Mt Magnet, Western Australia. Granite boulders and platforms indicate that bedrock is present at shallow depth beneath the surrounding plain.

Fig. 6.2c Piping and differential weathering have created these short-lived but spectacular lateritic columns at Althorpe Peaks, SSE of Quairading, Western Australia.

Fig. 6.2d Silcrete exposed at The Breakaway, between Norseman and Hyden. Note the readily eroded, kaolinised zone, above which the silcrete is preserved.

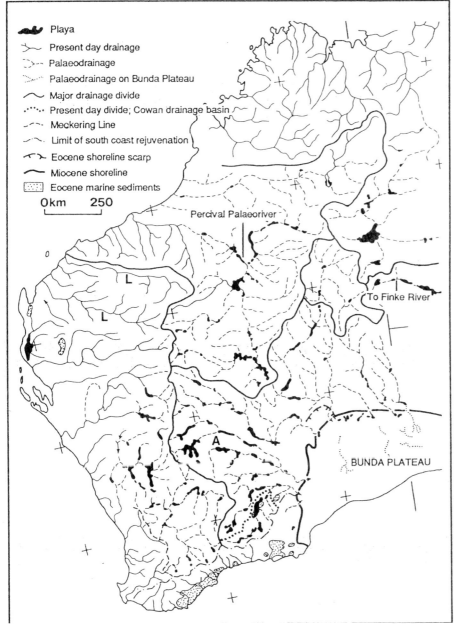

Fig. 6.3 Eocene drainage channels of the Yilgarn Craton (after Van de Graaff et al. 1977). The streams were rejuvenated in the Eocene which can be taken as the date of initiation of the New Plateau, but upstream incision did not begin until later and in places is still in train.

Old and New plateaux

The laterite-capped remnants of the Yilgarn were labelled the Old Plateau by Jutson (1914, 1934) in contrast with the present high plain above which they stand and which, rather misleadingly, for it is not entirely bounded by scarps, he called the New Plateau. The latter was formed by the dissection of the lateritic duricrust, recession of the valley-side slopes (scarp retreat),

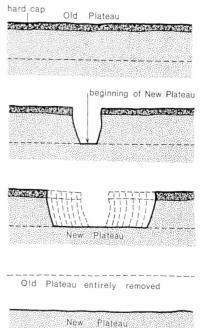

Fig. 6.4 Relationship of the Old and New plateaux. (after Jutson 1914, p. 143)

Fig. 6.5a The Humps, seen from the north, with a borrow pit in lateritic gravel in the foreground.

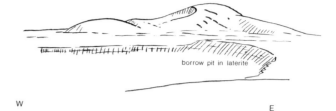

Fig. 6.5b Explanatory diagram of (a).

Fig. 6.5c Suggested relationship of The Humps to primary laterite and secondary ferruginous rubble.

Fig. 6.5d Flared slope about 12 m high on the inselberg but below crest level.

and the stripping of the associated soil or regolith that consisted of white kaolinitic clays. The clays were and are susceptible to erosion and stand in marked contrast to the cohesive intrinsically fresh granite below the regolith. In general terms, the New Plateau marks the lower limit of effective weathering, or weathering front, and is thus an etch surface (Jutson 1914, p. 143; Mabbutt 1961a, 1961b; see also Falconer 1911, p. 246; Fig. 6.4).

The Old Plateau and associated duricrusts are at least of Cretaceous age, for they were dissected by rivers in the lower reaches of which Eocene strata were deposited (Clarke 1994a, 1994b; Twidale and Bourne 1998a). The silcrete valley fills may be of the same age, with the silica derived from the weathering that resulted in the laterite (Stephens 1964). They could, however, be younger and be comparable to the valley fills of the western Gawler Craton. That the Old Plateau is of considerable antiquity finds corroboration in the volcanic episode evidenced at Bunbury on the southwestern coast (Playford et al. 1976, pp. 195–196). The basalts exposed are of Early Cretaceous age and were extruded when that section of the Australian continent broke away from the rest of Gondwana. The disruption triggered the uplift and dissection of the Old Plateau and the exposure of the New. Clarke (1994b) considers that the deep weathering profiles of the Old Plateau date from the Permian–Middle Jurassic, but they were largely stripped during the later Mesozoic and Early Tertiary.

Sectors of the New Plateau situated adjacent to major Eocene channels are Eocene in age but they become younger (Miocene, Pliocene) toward the headwater reaches (e.g. Salama 1997; Twidale et al. 1999) as the scarps have been worn back and a new, lower plain has been developed (Fig. 6.4). Thus the surface has an age-range; it is a diachronic surface, older near the river 'mouth' but younger and younger up-valley. In the headwater reaches of

Fig. 6.6 Wave Rock, a flared slope 14–15 m high and about 100 m long located in a fracture-defined embayment on the northern flank of Hyden Rock, near Hyden in the southern Yilgarn Craton about 320 km east of Perth, Western Australia. It was developed by differential subsurface weathering beneath a Cretaceous land surface.

the river and tributaries, where scarps flank the Old Plateau, the plain was formed only recently and is still extending.

When Australia and Antarctica separated, about 60 million years ago, the present southern margin of the Craton was uplifted, causing some stream courses to be disturbed and even reversed. Hence the short, south coast rivers. Others, like the Avon and Lefroy rivers, rise comparatively near to the south coast but run inland. The river systems were further modified in the Pleistocene when the climate changed. Aridity, which set in about 2 million years ago, caused the river systems to be dismembered, though they still flow in the channels below the surface (underflow), and locally, and from time to time, at the surface.

Older inselberg forms

The crests of inselbergs like The Humps stand

Fig. 6.7b Hamersley Surface with strong Banded Iron Formation producing a caprock and a structural bench. (Geological Survey of Western Australia)

above this duricrusted Mesozoic land surface (Figs 6.5a–c) and are therefore at least as old, for they were in existence when the surrounding plain was weathered. Pronounced flared slopes (Fig. 6.5d) argue a long-lasting scarp-foot weathering at the hill-plain junction. Similar evidence points to the great antiquity of the crestal areas of other inselbergs such as Boyagin Rock, and Jilakin Rock, in the southwest of the Yilgarn Craton, and of Disappointment Rock, in the southeast (e.g. Bourne and Twidale 2002). All stand higher than the adjacent laterite surface, which points to their being of at least Cretaceous age.

On the other hand, many well-known granite inselbergs of the Yilgarn region have been exposed as a result of the stripping of the weathered rock. They include Hyden Rock on the northern slope of which is developed Wave Rock, one of the best known of all Australian landforms (Twidale 1968b; Twidale and Bourne 1998a, 1998b, 2001; Fig. 6.6).

Hamersley Range

Geological framework

The upland known as the Hamersley Range is underlain by Proterozoic Banded Iron Formations (Macleod 1966). To the west and southwest the Carnarvon Basin was an embayment of the sea during the Early Cretaceous (Hocking et al. 1987) (Fig. 6.1).

Fig. 6.7a The Hamersley Surface developed on flat-lying strata but with prominent Banded Iron Formation capping.

Fig. 6.8a Dissected hill country eroded in dipping strata, Hamersley Range.

Fig. 6.8b The Hamersley Surface with ferruginous crust over dipping Banded Iron Formation strata in Wittenoom Gorge.

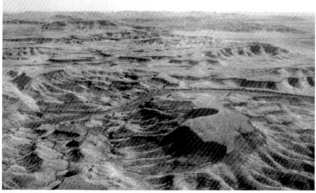

Fig. 6.9a Mesas capped by Robe River Pisolite, Hamersley Range. (Geological Survey of Western Australia)

Fig. 6.9b Sinuous mesa capped by Robe River Pisolite, southern piedmont of the Hamersley Range.

Fig. 6.9c Inversion mechanism. RRP – Robe River Pisolite, f – alluvial fill.

Hamersley Surface

The high plain or plateau known as the Hamersley Surface dominates the landscape. It is a picturesque landscape with white gums standing in stark contrast with the red-brown hills. Bedrock is widely exposed. The strata are mostly flat-lying (Fig. 6.7), though there are disturbed areas of dipping strata (Fig. 6.8). Shallow pockets of pisolitic iron are patchily preserved on the summit surface and are interpreted as remnants of a once more extensive regolith (Fig. 6.8b).

Most of the regolith has been stripped by rivers flowing radially from the high plain. Some of it was reconstituted in valley fills as the Robe River Pisolite (e.g. Macleod 1966; Ramanaidou et al. 2003). These old valley floors are now upstanding as sinuous mesas and provide clear examples of relief inversion (Fig. 6.9). The Pisolite in places overlies alluvium containing pollen and spores of Middle Eocene age. Thus, the erosion of the surface, the stripping of its regolith and its deposition as the Robe River Pisolite in adjacent valleys took place in the Middle Eocene some 45–50 million years ago. The high plain surface with its pisolitic mantle predates this event and is an etch surface of Middle Eocene age (Twidale et al. 1985). It may have been eroded by rivers graded to the Cretaceous shoreline of the sea that then occupied the Carnarvon Basin. Its stripping may have been initiated by rejuvenation of streams following the withdrawal of the Cretaceous sea. Thus the existence of a planation surface with a ferruginous capping, and of earliest Tertiary or later Mesozoic age, is implied. It predated the Hamersley Surface. It can appropriately be referred to as the Horwitz Surface after Rudi Horwitz (1924-1997), a geologist who contributed much to the knowledge of the geology of the Hamersley Range and adjacent areas.

Carnarvon Basin

The Carnarvon Basin is bordered on its eastern flank by Proterozoic and Archaean blocks and to

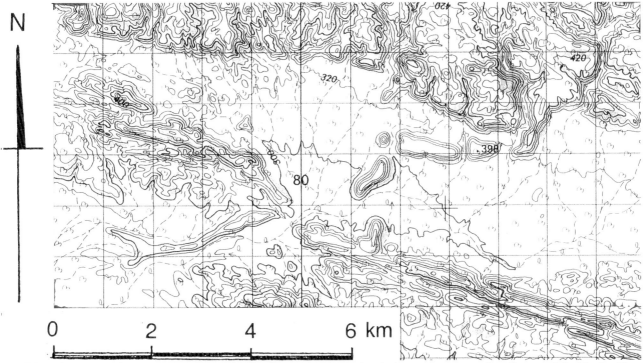

Fig. 6.9d Map extract showing sinuous inverted valley floor, now a mesa, in relation to the course of a tributary of the Hardey River, south of Mt Wall, Hamersley Range. Contour interval 20 m. (after Sheet 2252 *Hardey* National Topographic Map Series, 1977)

Fig. 6.10a In the northern Carnarvon Basin, Cretaceous strata are preserved in the plateau remnants. The plain is cut in Precambrian rocks and is essentially the surface over which the Cretaceous seas advanced, and on which marine sediments were deposited. Where exposed it is an exhumed sub-Cretaceous surface, and is at least of Jurassic age. (Geological Survey of Western Australia)

Fig. 6.10b Plateau, mesa and butte landscape of the Carnarvon Basin. The present plain is exhumed and of pre Early Cretaceous age. The plateau surface may equate with the Hamersley Surface and be an Eocene feature. (K.-H. Wyrwoll)

Fig. 6.11 'Beehives' in Permian limestone exhumed from beneath sandstone of later Permian age. (Geological Survey of Western Australia)

the south by the Phanerozoic Perth Basin. Strata ranging in age from the Silurian onwards are exposed (Hocking et al. 1987). An exhumed sub-Cretaceous surface preserved in Precambrian rocks has been identified (Fig. 6.10). A karst assemblage developed in earlier Permian strata, about 270 million years old and taking the form of a group of domes or beehives (Young 1986, 1987; Hocking et al. 1987), has been exhumed from beneath sediments of younger Permian age (Fig. 6.11).

In the Carnarvon region, the Murchison River is, both in broad view and in detail, fracture-controlled. Its course consists of linked NW–SE and NE–SW sectors, and where it flows across the Silurian sandstone of the Victoria Plateau in a gorge, control by orthogonal fractures is obvious. The gorge is of considerable antiquity, for patches of Early Cretaceous marine strata are preserved in the gorge it has eroded in the duricrusted Silurian sandstone of the Victoria Plateau (Fig. 6.12). Thus, the valley, and the river responsible for shaping it, were in existence prior to the Cretaceous.

Pilbara Craton

Geological framework

The Pilbara Craton or Block consists of an extensive outcrop of interbedded Archaean basic volcanic lavas and related sediments together with acid lavas and cherts and downfaulted troughs of Proterozoic Banded Iron Formation (Geological Survey of Western Australia 1975, 1990; Hickman 1983; Fig. 6.1).

Landforms

The regression of the Cretaceous seas and subsequent erosion have re-exposed a number of forms and surfaces in the Pilbara region. Sub-

Fig. 6.12 Murchison River gorge incised in the Victoria Plateau, duricrusted but eroded in Silurian strata, near Carnarvon. Note fracture-controlled rectangular pattern. Marine strata of probable Cretaceous age are preserved within the gorge, showing that it is even older. (Geological Survey of Western Australia)

Fig. 6.13a Granite bornhardts partly exhumed from beneath Cretaceous sediments, east of Karratha, in the northwest of Western Australia.

Fig. 6.13b ?Sub-Jurassic surface exposed near Shay Gap, western Pilbara Craton.

Fig. 6.13c Inselberg landscape, western Pilbara Craton.

Fig. 6.14a Sketch of bornhardts of Archaean granite in process of exposure from beneath a sequence of interbedded sediments and volcanics of latest Archaean or earliest Proterozoic age, headwaters of Yule River, central Pilbara Craton.

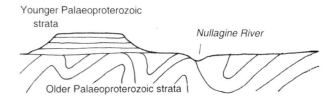

Fig. 6.14b Exhumed Palaeoproterozoic surface, Nullagine area, western Pilbara Craton. (After Jutson 1914, p. 168, based on Maitland 1911)

Cretaceous (and also sub-Tertiary) bornhardts have been exhumed at the northern margin of the Pilbara Craton, between Karratha and Shay Gap (Fig. 6.13a), as have remnants of an exhumed ?sub-Jurassic planation surface (Fig. 6.13b). The inselberg landscape of the Pilbara (Fig. 6.13c) is either of etch origin, or is exhumed from beneath a Cretaceous cover; or elements of both types of landform may be present. In addition, Archaean bornhardts are in process of exhumation in the central Pilbara, in the headwater region of the Yule River (Twidale 1986; Fig. 6.14a). Also, an extensive surface of Early Palaeoproterozoic age eroded in folded and cleaved beds has been exhumed from beneath flat-lying strata of younger, but still Early Palaeoproterozoic, age preserved in scattered mesas in the Nullagine area (e.g. Jutson 1914; Daniels 1975, p. 143-144; Fig. 6.14b).

Chapter 7

ANCIENT SURFACES OF NORTHERN AUSTRALIA

Biographical note: A.A. Öpik (1898–1983)

Armin Öpik was a man of outstanding intellect and character. Educated in Estonia, he was appointed Professor of Geology and Palaeontology at Tartu before the Second World War. Overtaken by that conflict, like many others he found his circumstances changed at war's end. From a displaced persons camp in Germany he and his family emigrated, by invitation, to Australia to join the Bureau of Mineral Resources. There he forged a brilliant new career.

A palaeontologist of distinction, 'Doc' Öpik was, like all good geologists of his generation, a scientist of eclectic interests. He had a marvellous eye for country. He established the age of the exhumed summit surface of the Isa Highlands by dating the remnants of overlying strata. He appreciated the importance of the Selwyn Upwarp and also proposed an innovative explanation for silcrete.

Öpik's indomitable fatalistic spirit was never seen to better advantage than after the disastrous fire which engulfed the BMR offices in Canberra City Centre in April 1953. It destroyed many of his specimens and manuscripts, but even in an hour of great loss he was already prepared and preparing for yet another start in life.

A.A. Öpik

Kimberley region

The Kimberley Plateau (Fig. 7.1) is developed in an essentially undisturbed sequence of interbedded Neoproterozoic sandstones and volcanics. They are subdivided by NW–SE and NE–SW trending fractures (Figs 2.4a, 7.2) and are intruded by kimberlites and lamproites of Proterozoic and Miocene ages. Dissection is most prominent along fractures. It has produced a plateau landscape (Fig. 7.3a), but pipes of injected materials give rise to prominent buttes or isolated residuals.

The flat-lying character of the strata, which include resistant sandstone and quartzite that support structural benches and surfaces (Fig. 7.3b), complicate interpretation, as does the absence of a useful and widespread marker horizon. Also, the Cretaceous shoreline which has proved so useful in dating surfaces in other parts of the continent was located well offshore from the Kimberley region.

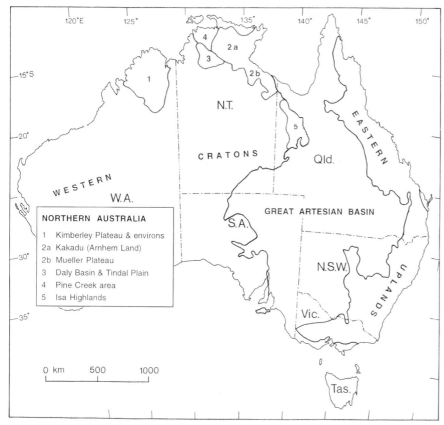

Fig. 7.1 Location map for geological regions of northern Australia (after Palfreyman 1984) showing also major structural units.

NORTHERN AUSTRALIA
1 Kimberley Plateau & environs
2a Kakadu (Arnhem Land)
2b Mueller Plateau
3 Daly Basin & Tindal Plain
4 Pine Creek area
5 Isa Highlands

Some prominent bevels and surfaces are most probably exhumed from beneath various sedimentary covers (see e.g. Young 1992). Paucity of evidence and the presence of surfaces of various origins probably accounts for various numbers of planation surfaces having been identified in the Kimberley and adjacent regions (Wright 1964; Hays 1967; Paterson 1970; Plumb and Gemuts 1976). For example, map interpretation led Young (1992) to suggest four surfaces standing higher than present valley floors. They stand higher than the Miocene deposits preserved in adjacent basins, suggesting that they are all at least of this age.

Wright (1964), on the other hand, identified only

Fig. 7.2 Vertical air photograph of Prince Regent River area, showing fracture patterns typical of the Kimberley Block. (Commonwealth of Australia)

Fig. 7.3 **(a)** Plateau with prominent bluffs (K. Kenneally), and **(b)** (below) structural benches, Kimberley region of Western Australia. (Geological Survey of Western Australia)

Fig. 7.4a King Leopold Range, western Kimberley Plateau, with remnant of planation surface. (Geological Survey of Western Australia)

Fig. 7.4b Escarpment with structural benches, Kimberley Plateau, near Wyndham, Western Australia. (K.-H. Wyrwoll)

two prominent epigene planation surfaces (Fig. 7.4). The lower surface, with duricrusts (lateritic on volcanics, siliceous on felsic igneous rocks), is of Miocene age, as suggested both by the duricrust and a physical dating of Miocene lamproites exposed on the surface (Wellman 1972; Jaques et al. 1984, 1986). The incised valleys are more prominent to the south where they are regarded as of Pliocene age (Plumb and Gemuts 1976). The higher surface is either older, or, if the intervening break of slope is structural, of similar age. If older, the high surface may be epigene and Cretaceous, for thick sequences of Cretaceous strata fill basins to the west and north.

Another possibility is that the higher surface is epigene, glaciated, and of Proterozoic age, as suggested by Ollier et al. (1988), who assert that there has never been a cover of any kind. But the former extent of the ice sheet to which the 700 million years old Welsh Tillite is related is indicated by striated pavements, which occur on the surface. Admittedly, most are preserved in valleys, but one striated site occurs on the crest of a ridge (Perry and Roberts 1968, p. 54). Clearly the Tillite was once widely distributed, and the associated surface is more likely to have been exhumed from beneath the glacial deposits. It is likely also to be an etch surface, for any former regolith would surely have been stripped by the ice sheet.

To the east of the Kimberley Plateau, a pronounced erosional bevel is preserved in the Osmond Ranges (Fig. 7.5), and a sub-Devonian surface is exhumed as a summit bevel in the Carr Boyd Range. In the Bandicoot Range a surface is in process of re-exposure from beneath Cambrian basalt (Plumb and Veevers 1971; Young 1992) though the crestal bevels are also equated with the Ashburton Surface, the age of which is disputed (Hays 1967; Plumb and Gemuts 1976; Mory and Beere 1988; see also below). Considered regionally, however, it appears likely to be of Mesozoic (Cretaceous) age.

Of special interest is the Bungle Bungle Range, a

Fig. 7.4c Bungle Bungle Range, with innumerable 'beehives' formed by fracture-controlled subsurface weathering beneath a planation surface represented by the accordant crests of the residuals. (D. Netoff)

Fig. 7.5 Bevelled crest developed on folded Palaeozoic strata, Osmond Ranges, northwest of Western Australia. (R.W. Young)

Fig. 7.6 Kakadu **(a)** general view of summit, **(b)** (below) the western scarp of the upland. This was a shoreline in Early Cretaceous times.

Fig. 7.7a Exhumed sub-Cretaceous surface at Bullocky Point, Darwin.

Fig. 7.7b Plateau capped by Cambrian basalt near Timber Creek, northwestern Northern Territory.

complex of gigantic sandstone 'beehives' formed by fracture-controlled subsurface weathering beneath a prominent planation surface, and subsequent stripping of the weathered rock (Young 1986, 1987; Fig. 7.4c).

Kakadu and the Top End

In the McArthur Basin, the Kakadu (Arnhem Land) massif is delineated in the east by lineaments and underlain by essentially undisturbed Proterozoic sandstone and quartzite (Fig. 7.6). Proterozoic metamorphic rocks and granite are exposed in the Pine Creek area and lateritised Cretaceous beds overlie Cambrian limestone in the Daly Basin.

Kakadu is a complex sandstone plateau with prominent summit towers (Jennings 1979). So striking are they, that they were initially identified from the air during World War II as limestone features. The massif was a land mass during the Early Cretaceous for seas lapped its borders, and the western escarpment probably formed sea cliffs at that time (Skwarko 1966; Needham 1982; Fig. 7.6b). On the eastern side of the massif the Cretaceous strata stand at about 75 m above present sea level (Frakes and Bolton 1984), whereas the high plateau surface stands at 200–250 m. The

Fig. 7.8a Exhumed sub-Cretaceous surface cut in granite north of Katherine. Note granite boulders at left.

Fig. 7.8b Katherine Plateau eroded in flat-lying Proterozoic sandstone. Note fracture-controlled gorges.

Fig. 7.9a Mueller Plateau eroded in flat-lying sandstone in northeastern Northern Territory. Note thin soil on the high plain, and joint-controlled blocks (X) exposed on the scarp. (RAAF)

Fig. 7.9b Sandstone towers, Keep River Nature Reserve, Northern Territory. (A. & R.W. Young)

1997), Cretaceous marine strata are preserved in valleys cut into the laterite surface. This situation has been taken to prove that the laterite predates the Cretaceous marine transgression (Nott 1994). It is a reasonable interpretation, and if correct, the Groote Eylandt laterite can be correlated with that of the southwestern Yilgarn Craton. Yet it poses a problem.

Two major periods of laterite formation have been identified in Australia, one Mesozoic, the other mid Tertiary (Twidale 1956, 1983). The difficulty with the Groote Eylandt laterite being as old as has been suggested is that all around, in the Pine Creek and Katherine areas, and to the east in north Queensland, laterite is developed on Cretaceous (and younger) strata and must therefore be younger than Cretaceous. It is usually assigned to the Miocene. To the west, in the Kimberleys, the laterite also has been assigned to the Miocene. How can an apparently old laterite appear in isolation surrounded by younger developments? Yet Nott's interpretation of the evidence is persuasive, and though apparently incompatible with the regional setting, may be correct.

dissected summit high plain is erosional and must be older than the Cretaceous, for it had already been planed off when the Cretaceous seas invaded the surrounding areas. Thus palaeogeography, the distribution of land and sea in Early Cretaceous times, provides an age for the Kakadu massif, and a minimum age or ages for the Kakadu summit surface or surfaces.

Partial planation may have occurred more than once, for several stands of the Cretaceous seas have been recognised, and several levels are discernible in the high plain. Whether they are related to structure, and in particular to the presence of resistant beds, or to separate phases of erosion, is not known.

To the east, on Groote Eylandt (Pietsch et al.

An alternative explanation could invoke the Cretaceous seas covering the entire area. Pre-existing valleys were filled with Cretaceous sediment. Planation and lateritisation then produced essentially the present landscape. Laterite was preserved on the resulting high plain strata, but any lateritic soil was removed as the weaker Cretaceous valley fill was preferentially eroded.

Daly Basin

An exhumed sub-Cretaceous surface is exposed on the coast at Darwin (e.g. Fig. 7.7a). To the west, toward Timber Creek and the Western Australian border, plateaux capped by Cambrian basalt are prominent (Fig. 7.7b). In places the basalt is unconformably overlain by Lower Cretaceous Mullaman beds (Traves 1955), suggesting that the upper surface of such mesas is exhumed and of Early Cretaceous age.

Inland, to the south of the Pine Creek area, laterite-capped plateaux of Early–Middle Tertiary age are prominent. Examples occur north of Katherine (Wright 1963), with exhumed sub-Cretaceous plains cut in granite revealed (Fig. 7.8a) where the Cretaceous strata have been eroded to expose the granitic rocks across which the seas advanced 120 or so million years ago (Stuart-Smith et al. 1987). The bare sandstone surface of the Katherine Plateau (Mulder and Whitehead 1988; Fig. 7.8b) is probably an etch surface graded to one or other of the Cretaceous shorelines. The sandstone plateau extends to the southeast in the Mueller Plateau (Fig. 7.9a), which in the lower Roper River valley has been so dissected that only fingers and slim towers of sandstone survive (Fig. 7.9b).

Tindal Plain

To the south of Katherine, the Tindal[1] area is occupied by an extensive karst or limestone plain with some caves (e.g. at Cutta Cutta). On the limestone plain are preserved numerous pinnacles and small towers, with surfaces that display typical solution patterns. The plain is eroded in the Cambrian Tindall Limestone, but has been

Fig. 7.10a The Tindal Plain: karst plain eroded in flat-lying Cambrian limestone,

exhumed from beneath a cover of Early Cretaceous Mullaman sandstone (Twidale 1984b; Fig. 7.10).

Many of the limestone residuals are smeared with a reddish iron-rich sandstone, which is also preserved in many joint clefts within the limestone (Fig. 7.11). This suggests that the pinnacles predate the Early Cretaceous marine transgression and the deposition of the associated sandstone. But if so the question arises as to how such fragile forms could have survived wave action and other processes of weathering and erosion during the Cretaceous marine transgression during which the Mullaman sandstone was deposited. The sea which inundated the area was shallow so that wave action would likely have been weak, and seawater is at most times saturated with lime, so that solution would not have been pronounced. Alternatively, the minor karst forms now exposed on the Tindal Plain could have been shaped by moisture retained in the rotted sandstone of the basal Mullaman beds (cf. Twidale et al. 2005).

Isa Highlands

In the Isa Highlands, folded Proterozoic strata and granite batholiths are exposed in a fold mountain belt. A prominent high plain surface is preserved as bevels on quartzite ridges (Fig. 7.12). Isolated remnants of ?later Jurassic and Early Cretaceous shale and sandstone are preserved, with the unconformity between them and the underlying Proterozoic rocks coincident with the high plain level (e.g. Twidale 1956; Carter 1959; Carter and Öpik 1959, 1961; Öpik et al. 1961). This shows that the latter predates the later Jurassic and the

---

1 The spelling of Tindal — one 'l' — Plain is correct, because it was named after the commanding officer of the World War II airbase. The name of the stratigraphic unit, however, was accidentally given an extra 'l' — hence the Tindall Limestone — and that error is perpetuated in the geological literature.

Fig. 7.10b–c (above and below) Sandstone hills, Tindal Plain, with the unconformity between Cretaceous and Cambrian coincident with plain level.

Fig. 7.11 Cretaceous sandstone — smears and thin beds of red materials — preserved **(a)** on limestone pinnacles, and (below) **(b)** in a joint in a limestone block.

Early Cretaceous and is exhumed (Fig. 7.13). The summit bevels occur high in the relief in the central parts of the upland (Fig. 3.8c) but the unconformity between the Mesozoic and Precambrian rocks stands at lower levels at the margins (Figs 7.12, 7.13), suggesting that the upland may have been warped. If so, the earth movements occurred in the later Cenozoic for lateritic weathering developed during the Miocene in this region. This is consistent with the regional setting, for the Selwyn Upwarp, an ancient structure which affects the southern Isa Highlands, has evidently been active relatively recently (Öpik 1961). Indeed, the curious pattern of the headwaters of the Diamantina River (Fig. 7.14) can be attributed to the structure. It has been suggested (Twidale 1966b) that the headwaters of the Flinders River, which flows to the Gulf of Carpentaria, have been diverted to the south by the Upwarp, causing them to join the Diamantina and to flow toward Lake Eyre. In this way what has been called a 'palm tree', or recurved, drainage pattern was produced (Taylor 1911, p. 10).

The sub-Cretaceous plan-ation surface extends

Fig. 7.12 Prominent summit high plain of the Isa Highland, **(a)** and (below) **(b)** view at ground level. (CSIRO)

Fig. 7.12 (c) and **(d)** summit bevel, Isa Highlands, seen from the air.

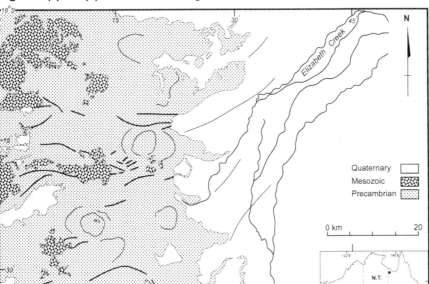

east in unconformity beneath the Carpentaria Basin and emerges to the east in the Einasleigh Uplands, part of the Eastern Uplands (Twidale 1956; Fig. 7.15).

Quaternary
Mesozoic
Precambrian

0 km   20

Fig. 7.12e Map showing distribution of Mesozoic beds on part of the northern Isa Highlands (after Carter and Öpik 1961). Heavy lines – faults, fine lines – strike, H.S. – Homestead.

Fig. 7.13 Unconformity low in the relief, southern Isa Highlands. The lateritised ?Late Jurassic strata overlie dipping Proterozoic rocks.

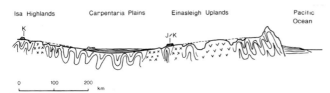

Fig. 7.15 Section across the Carpentaria Basin. J – Jurassic; K – Cretaceous.

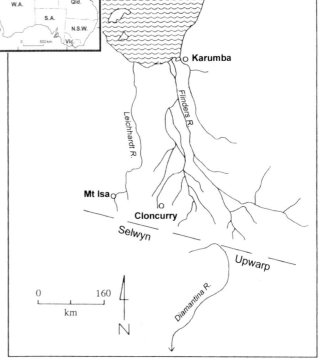

Fig. 7.14 Origin of the 'palm tree' pattern (so-called because in plan it resembles a palm tree bowed and bent in a strong wind) of the Diamantina headwaters.

Chapter 8

CENTRAL AUSTRALIAN PALAEOFORMS

Biographical note: C.S. Christian (1908–1996)

C.S. Christian was a scientist of vision, allied with a talent for leadership and friendship. After agricultural training in Queensland and Minnesota, he joined what is now the CSIRO and undertook research in plant breeding and pasture research. In 1946 he was invited to organise and lead the Northern Australia Regional Survey unit, which later became the Division of Land Research and Regional Survey. He appreciated that many factors influence the capacity of land. To this end he organised multidisciplinary survey units which produced integrated surveys of large areas of northern and central Australia, and later, Papua New Guinea. They formed the basis of research

C.S. Christian

stations at Katherine and on the Ord River. They provide a record of the land as it was at the time of survey. Also, the method developed (e.g. Christian 1952; Christian and Stewart 1953) was employed in many countries where integrated surveys had not then been accomplished.

'Chris' inspired his 'troops' ('Christian Soldiers') to produce a wealth of knowledge about hitherto uninvestigated areas. In particular, he encouraged a genetic and interrelated view of landscape, with emphasis on its evolution through time. He demonstrated the value of such surveys and showed them to be an investment in the future. Many have reason to be grateful for his vision and inspiration.

Fig. 8.1 Location map for geological regions of central Australia. (After Palfreyman 1984) showing also major structural units

CENTRAL AUSTRALIA
1a Ashburton-Davenport Ranges
1b Devils Marbles
2 Arunta Block & Macdonnell Ranges
3 Musgrave & Everard ranges
4 Uluru

Fig. 8.2a Bevelled quartzite ridge with ferruginised capping, Ashburton Range, near Powell Creek.

Fig. 8.2b Castle Rock, near Renner Springs, Northern Territory, with a siliceous-ferruginous capping showing well-developed columnar structure.

Ashburton Range to Barrow Creek

In the Ashburton and Tennant blocks (Fig. 8.1), prominent summit bevels are preserved on ridges of folded Neoproterozoic quartzite (Fig. 8.2a). The Cretaceous shoreline stood a little distance to the north and northeast and the summit surface, referred to as the Ashburton Surface, has been construed as part of the Cretaceous landscape (Hays 1967). Alternatively, it and remnants of terraces preserved on Cambrian valley fills have been interpreted (Stewart et al. 1986) as of possible Cambrian age but the evidence is equivocal. Any epigene form dating from the Cambrian would surely have been destroyed or modified by frost action during the Early Permian, when glaciers occupied the uplands of central Australia (BMR Palaeogeographic Group 1992). Also, there is no evidence that the terrace deposits mark the upper limit of deposition. The beds are described as being ferruginised and silicified, which argues periods of weathering resulting in duricrusts similar to those recognised from the Mesozoic and early Cenozoic.

Regional considerations suggest that the surface is more likely either to have been exhumed from beneath a Cretaceous cover, or be a remnant of a complex epigene surface graded to shorelines of the Cretaceous seas which extended over adjacent basins just to the east (Frakes 1987). No evidence pointing one way or the other has been preserved in the local area. Tertiary (Miocene) laterite and silcrete are known from adjacent regions (see e.g. Daly River, Macdonnell Ranges) and a ferruginised siliceous caprock with columnar structure is responsible for the preservation of the mesa known as Castle Rock, near Renner Springs (Fig. 8.2b).

On the basis of apatite fission track thermochronology (AFTT) and cosmogenic nuclide analysis Belton et al. (2004) consider the alleged Cambrian terraces described by Stewart et al. (1986) to be much younger than had been suggested. They also deny the postulated Cretaceous age for the Ashburton Surface (Twidale 1994).

Stewart et al. (1986) announced very low rates of erosion, but did not consider the possibility of a sedimentary or regolithic cover having been stripped from the surface. As to the age of the bevelled ranges, deep erosion is indicated by AFTT analysis, but when did it occur? Was there a substantial Cretaceous cover? The morphostratigraphic argument is suggestive rather then compelling. To extrapolate their conclusion to all central Australian high surfaces is unwarranted in light of the field evidence. The paper by Belton et al. is nevertheless welcome as a contribution to the debate between the physical and morphostratigraphic schools, but so far as the Ashburton terraces are concerned the question remains open.

In passing, it may be commented that AFTT dates are not uniformly reliable. In places AFTT analysis corroborates morphostratigraphic interpretation. Elsewhere in southeastern Australia and southern Africa, however, its findings, like cosmogenic nuclide dates, are at odds with the geological evidence (e.g. Partridge and Maud 1987; Twidale 1990; Birkenhauer 1991; Fleming et al. 1999; Bishop and Goldrick 2000).

Fig. 8.3a General view of typical partly rounded granite blocks of the Devils Marbles, with part of the bevelled quartzite ridge of the Davenport Ranges in the background.

Fig. 8.3b Split boulders, Devils Marbles. The split is probably not due to heat but rather to the weight of rock on either side of a secondary strain zone or parting causing the original rounded mass to pull apart.

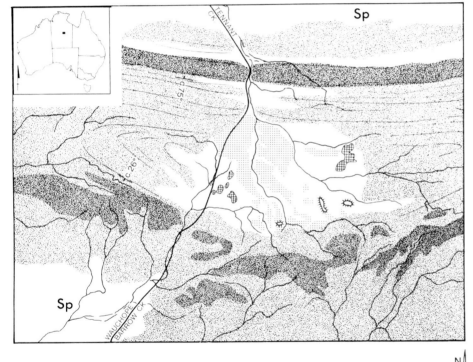

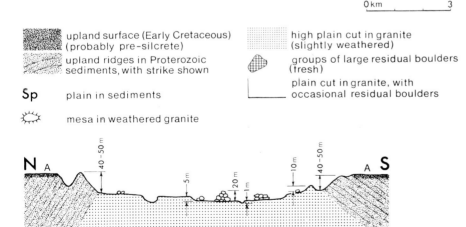

DIAGRAMMATIC SECTION

Fig. 8.3c Map and diagrammatic section through the Davenport Ranges and Devils Marbles. A – old land surface.

Devils Marbles and Barrow Creek

The spectacular granite blocks and boulders of the Devils Marbles (Figs 8.3a, b) are exposed in the floor of a valley eroded in an anticline and bordered by bevelled sandstone ridges of the Davenport Ranges. The bevels have been interpreted as of Cretaceous age, possibly Early Cretaceous (Mabbutt 1966; Hays 1967; Twidale 1980; Frakes 1987). The Marbles were probably produced by weathering beneath the then higher valley floor enclosed by the quartzite ridges (Figs 8.3c, d). Thus if the bevelled ridges are, as suggested, of Early Cretaceous age, then the Devils Marbles were initiated by differential weathering and their present general shapes formed beneath the land surface about 120–130 million years ago.

In the Barrow Creek area a gneissic and bouldery exhumed surface is exposed from beneath the flat-lying

Fig. 8.3d Weathered (ferruginised) valley floor remnants in the Devils Marbles, with bevelled quartzitic ranges in background. It was beneath this valley floor that the Marbles were shaped by fracture-controlled water weathering.

Fig. 8.5 Dissected metamorphics of the Arunta Block. (R.L. Oliver)

Fig. 8.4 Forster Range near Barrow Creek, Northern Territory, is a plateau formed in Proterozoic quartzite. The surrounding plains, cut in gneiss, are the surface on which the sandstone was laid down about 1000 million years ago. It is now exposed as an exhumed surface, seen in the foreground. That the Proterozoic beds remain essentially undisturbed despite 100 million years of earth movements is surprising.

Fig. 8.6a Ridge and valley, Macdonnell Ranges. Note the summit bevels on broader ridges. (Australian National Publicity Association, Melbourne)

Fig. 8.6b Flatirons developed on ridges in the James Range, southwest of Alice Springs. (BMR, Canberra)

Neoproterozoic sediments of the Forster Range (e.g. Haines et al. 1991). The plateau surface itself may be part of a Cretaceous or sub-Cretaceous surface, probably the former (Fig. 8.4).

Macdonnell Ranges and associated uplands

In the Arunta Block a Proterozoic batholith is exposed. Here jagged peaks, an all slopes topography, prevail (Fig. 8.5). To the south the Macdonnell and associated ranges (James, Krichauff, Waterhouse) are underlain by folded and faulted Middle Palaeozoic strata. Ridge and valley topography is well developed (Fig. 8.6). The Macdonnell Ranges have been described as 'the only known contemporary land surface that has persisted unburied since pre Tertiary times' (J.A. Mabbutt, cited in Brown et al.

1968, p. 304), a claim that, though reasonable at the time, cannot be maintained in light of later work, which demonstrates or at least strongly suggests that Mesozoic surfaces are quite widely preserved. Certainly the Ranges have stood as uplands for scores of millions of years and the bevelled crests may well be of Cretaceous age.

Fig. 8.7a Low bevelled quartzite ridge in the central Macdonnell Ranges just west of Alice Springs.

Fig. 8.8a Silcrete-capped mesas, in the southern piedmont of the Macdonnell Ranges.

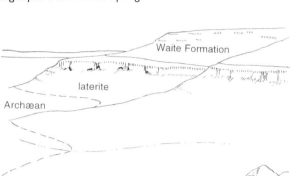

Fig. 8.7b Section with laterite exposed at Alcoota. The overlying lake and riverine sediments are of Upper Miocene age. The contained fossils indicate a wetter humid climate at that time. (after Woodburne 1967)

Fig. 8.8 Silcrete-capped mesas **(b)** southeast of Alice Springs in the Ooraminna Ranges developed on Miocene lake sediments, and (below) **(c)** near Rumbalara, southern Northern Territory (CSIRO). Note the kaolinised zone beneath the capping. The base of this clay zone is coincident with the plain level, suggesting that the latter is of etch type.

Fig. 8.7c Silcrete remnants in valley in the western Macdonnell Ranges near Glen Helen Homestead.

Prominent bevels are preserved at two levels, above the present valley floors. The lower summit bevels preserved on some quartzite ridges (Figs 8.6, 8.7a) may be part of a landscape represented in intervening valleys by duricrusted plateau remnants. They are lateritic and predate the Late Miocene in the north near Alcoota (Woodburne 1967), but silcrete-capped mesas are preserved near Glen Helen (Mabbutt 1966; Figs 8.7b, c) and in the southern piedmont of the Ranges. Silcrete cappings and associated kaolinitic weathering profiles extend far to the south and across the South Australian border into the Oodnadatta area on the western side of the Simpson Desert dunefield, and the Birdsville–Innamincka area (Sturts Stony Desert) on the east (Mabbutt 1965; Wopfner 1978). The age of silicification is difficult to establish but in

Fig. 8.8d Chambers Pillar was visited and sketched by Giles in 1872 (Giles 1889, p. 9). This photograph was taken during the Barclay–MacPherson Expedition of 1904–05. The Pillar is one of several buttes or narrow mesas preserved in Late Palaeozoic sandstone in the vicinity. The strata are duricrusted and kaolinised.

Fig. 8.8e Weathering has produced natural arches and caves in some of the residuals near Chambers Pillar.

the Lake Eyre region a Late Eocene date is most consistent with the stratigraphy of the basin deposits (Wopfner et al. 1974; Wopfner 1978; Benbow et al. 1995b). These valley-floor remnants imply that the ridge and valley topography of the Macdonnell Ranges was established by the early

Fig. 8.9 High bevels in the central Macdonnell Ranges **(a)** cutting across dipping strata, and (below) **(b)** across vertical beds, with cuesta developed in gently dipping sediments in middle distance.

Tertiary; by the Eocene if the silcrete is of that age. The Alcoota lateritised surface may indicate local stream rejuvenation or it too may be older than Miocene. The field evidence indicates an early Miocene or pre-Miocene age. Only a few metres of valley-floor erosion has taken place since that time. Silcrete-capped remnants also occur in the piedmont of the upland and on the plains to the south (Figs 8.8a, b). An etch plain related to a widespread silcreted regolith has been identified on the plains south of Alice Springs (Mabbutt 1965; Fig. 8.8c). The summit of Chambers Pillar (Figs 8.8d, e) and adjacent remnants may be part of this weathered land surface.

The summit bevel of the Macdonnell Ranges (Fig. 8.9) stands substantially higher and is therefore older than the duricrusted valley remnants and bevelled lower ridges. It may be part of the Cretaceous land surface drained by rivers running to the Cretaceous seas (Twidale 1994). That an older land surface of Cretaceous age existed in this region is demonstrated by the Gosses Bluff bolide

Fig. 8.10 Gosses Bluff meteorite crater, southwest of Alice Springs, Northern Territory. (BMR Geology & Geophysics, Canberra)

Fig. 8.11a Fracture-controlled stream and valley in the Gill Range, central Australia.

Fig. 8.11b Transverse drainage in the James Range. Many of the streams follow strike, but one river flows across the structural dome. (C. Wahrhaftig)

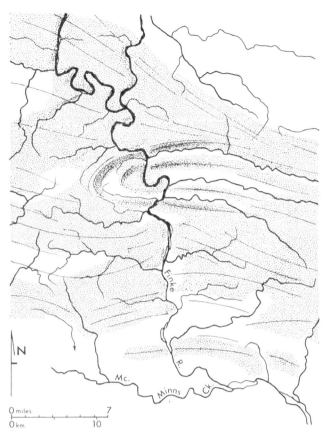

Fig. 8.11c Structural snout, Krichauff Range, breached by the Finke River.

Fig. 8.11d 'In-and-out' stream pattern near the Ormiston Gorge, western Macdonnell Ranges.

or meteorite, that impacted about 142.5 million years ago and created a crater and amphitheatre (Crook and Cook 1966; Milton and Sutter 1987; Fig. 8.10).

Though many stream courses are determined by structure (Fig. 8.11a), examples of transverse drainage, including breached snouts, abound in this region (Figs 8.11b, c). Explanations vary. Ward (1925) implied that the rivers are superimposed from a Cretaceous cover and also stated that the incised meanders of the Finke where it flows through the Krichauff Ranges are inherited from a former surface of low relief; an explanation which persisted (e.g. Campana 1958b, p. 42) for several years, though Mahard (1942) had pointed out that such features are authigenic and develop during incision (see also Twidale 1955).

Fig. 8.12 Sandstone 'beehives' in the Gill Range. Note the crests are all of similar height, suggesting that the domes formed by weathering along fractures beneath a summit surface.

Fig. 8.13a Summit bevel of Uluru, seen from the west.

Fig. 8.13b Mt Conner, a mesa capped by massive sandstone, the base of a structural basin.

Fig. 8.13c Profile showing projected Cambrian/Upper Cretaceous unconformity and projection into the upper surface of Uluru. K – uppermost Cretaceous or Maastrichtian.

Madigan (1931, 1932) attributed them to antecedence, that is, to their having been developed and then survived earth movements by cutting through rising blocks. There is no evidence of block-faulting or similar localised differential uplift, and Hills (1961, p. 82) may have been right to label some drainage elements as inherited, that is, deriving their pattern from an old weathered landscape such as the silcreted surface, which is still much in evidence in this part of central Australia (Mabbutt 1965). Some are, however, understandable in terms of deep erosion (as described in the Flinders Ranges) and imposition of drainage patterns from higher levels. Such an explanation also accounts for curious 'in-and-out' rivers and valleys — rivers which have carved meander loops in steep hillslopes, alternating with valley floor sectors (Fig. 8.11d). Despite these various possible explanations, some patterns such as those investigated on the Finke River (Pickup et al. 1988) remain puzzling.

The Gill Range, with Kings Canyon at the western end (Bagas 1988), is noted for its prominent beehive forms (Fig. 8.12) developed in Palaeozoic sandstone (cf. the Bungle Bungle Range: Fig. 7.4c). The summit bevel may be a remnant of the same high planation surface preserved in parts of the Macdonnell Ranges (Fig. 8.9). It stands higher in the landscape than the remnants of the silcreted surface (e.g. Fig. 8.8).

In the Amadeus Basin, the summit bevel of Uluru appears to be an etch form of Maastrichtian (latest Cretaceous) age, that is, it is about 70 million years old (Twidale 1978a; Twidale and Bourne 1978; Harris and Twidale 1991; Fig. 8.13a). The crests of some of the lower domes of Kata Tjuta and the bevelled summit of Mt Conner (Fig. 8.13b) can be correlated with the surface preserved on Uluru. The postulated age of the summit bevel of Uluru is speculative for it rests on the assumption that the unconformity — the former land surface between the latest Cretaceous beds above and Cambrian strata below — maintained a similar inclination throughout; and it may not have (Fig. 8.13c). On the other hand, Tertiary (Eocene) strata occur beneath the plains west of Uluru, and Tertiary rocks were also encountered in bores located just south of the southern face of the residual (Twidale 1978a). Various Tertiary rocks including duricrusted deposits and accumulations on the desert plains rest unconformably on Precambrian, Palaeozoic and Mesozoic rocks (Wells et al. 1970). Also, widespread remnants of a silcreted surface of probable Eocene age are preserved on the plains south of the Macdonnell Ranges (Mabbutt 1965).

Musgrave Block

The Musgrave Block is an exposure of Proterozoic plutonic rocks, with granites and gneisses prominent (Figs 8.14a, b). The varied composition of the hills gives an irregular skyline but remnants of what appears to be a summit surface of low relief can be detected. A prominent high plain which cuts across metamorphic and sedimentary rock in the Petermann Ranges (Fig. 8.14c) may be a clearer representative of this surface. If only because of its elevation above an extensive Miocene silcreted surface to the north and east, it is likely to be of considerable antiquity.

Fig. 8.14a Granite domes in the Musgrave Ranges.

Fig. 8.14b Mt Lindsay, a bald granite dome in the Birksgate Range, northwestern South Australia. (PIRSA)

Fig. 8.14c Planation surface, Petermann Ranges. (T. Flöttmann)

Fig. 8.15a Granite domes of the Everard Ranges.

Fig. 8.15b Mesa in Jurassic strata amongst bornhardts of the Kulgera Hills.

Fig. 8.15c Bevelled bornhardts in the eastern Everard Ranges.

To the south, the Everard Ranges consist of granite domes or bornhardts (Fig. 8.15a). In the east, in the Kulgera area, the bornhardts predate the Jurassic, for sedimentary remnants of that age stand as mesas amongst the bornhardts (Twidale 1994; Fig. 8.15b). As with the planation surface at the southwestern margin of the Eromanga Basin, south of the area under discussion (see Chapter 5), the western limit of the later Mesozoic marine transgressions, and hence of the exhumed surface, is not known in detail. The bevelled domes to the west (Fig. 8.15c), roughly to the west of the Stuart Highway, may be either exhumed or epigene Late Jurassic or Early Cretaceous landforms.

Chapter 9

EASTERN UPLANDS

Biographical note: F.A. Craft (1906–1973)
Frank Alfred Craft was a New South Welshman, born at Leura near Katoomba, in the Blue Mountains west of Sydney, in 1906. Despite difficult circumstances (Craft's father died when he was 11) he completed his high school education before proceeding to the University of Sydney on a teaching scholarship in 1926. There, inspired by Griffith Taylor, he enjoyed a distinguished academic career, emerging with First Class Honours. He had trained as a teacher and spent two years thus engaged in the Hunter Valley. He was then awarded a Linnaean Society of New South Wales Fellowship which enabled him to spend five years on research in the Shoalhaven and Monaro districts. His award terminated in 1935 and Craft returned to high school teaching, mainly in country areas, but later (1957) in Canberra. He was dogged by ill health, which forced him to retire from teaching and in the mid 1960s from a temporary public service position.

F.A. Craft

He died early in 1973, following an accident.

One is left with a strong feeling of talent unfulfilled, of 'what might have been' had Craft enjoyed better luck, backing or timing. Nevertheless, the five-year period spent in the Shoalhaven and Monaro districts was productive and of lasting significance for the interpretation of Australian landscapes. In particular, he noted the crucial evidence which led him to deduce that the high surfaces were of considerable antiquity.

Introduction

The Eastern Uplands is a major, and complex, geological and topographic region which occupies the eastern fifth of the continent and includes the island of Tasmania (Fig. 9.1). Its representation on older regional maps is somewhat misleading, for the words 'Great Dividing Range' were commonly placed along the length of the upland, giving the impression of a sharp crest separating the waters flowing to the Pacific and those running westwards towards the interior. Instead there is a broad watershed with an ill-defined separation of the waters between those flowing to the Tasman and Coral seas and those running to the inland and, in the north, to the Gulf of Carpentaria. Instead

of jagged peaks like those developed in the alpine ranges of Europe, the Rocky Mountains of the American West, and the Himalayas, for instance, the observer is presented with an even skyline interrupted only by the occasional peak standing above the general level of high plains that transect local structure (Fig. 9.2). Though their presence is obvious, the high-level planation surfaces of the Eastern Uplands still give rise to lively debate (see, for instance, Ollier and Pain 1994; and their reply to various responses in the 1996 *AGSO Journal*).

The complexity of the problems which bedevil the interpretation of surfaces in the Eastern Uplands is encapsulated in the Canberra landscape, where evidence of the age of surfaces is lacking, which

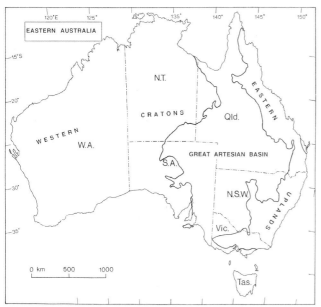

Fig. 9.1 Map of major structural regions of Australia including the Eastern Uplands. (After Palfreyman 1984)

Fig. 9.2a Even skyline of the Snowy Mountains, New South Wales and Victorian border, with a residual, The Pilot, upstanding.

has given rise to contrasted interpretations by distinguished investigators. Öpik (1958) regarded the framework of the landform assemblage as very old, originating more than 400 million years ago, and largely a function of structure. Jennings (1972), on the other hand, saw in the landscape evidence of several phases of erosion and fault dislocation and concluded it was youthful, though affected also by recurrent movements along old faults.

Geological framework

Geologically the Eastern Uplands comprise a complex series of fold belts involving Proterozoic and Palaeozoic rocks (e.g. Hodgkinson Fold Belt), Palaeozoic and Mesozoic strata (e.g. Lachlan and New England fold belts), together with numerous basins carrying Palaeozoic and Mesozoic strata (Fig. 9.1). Old shield remnants are exposed in the far north in the Georgetown, Coen and Yambo blocks. Structure is in places complicated, and the nature of topographic discontinuities located at the margins and within the Uplands is frequently contentious. Beginning in the Eocene but carrying through spasmodically

Fig. 9.2b Dissected summit surface, Snowy Mountains, New South Wales.

Fig. 9.2c The main range around Mt Kosciuszko, much dissected but with accordant crests.. (Geological Survey of Victoria)

Fig. 9.3a High plain with monadnock on horizon, Herbert River region, north Queensland. (J. Stephenson)

Fig. 9.3c High plain on Triassic sandstone in the Blue Mountains, west of Sydney, New South Wales. The pinnacles are the well-known 'Three Sisters' at Katoomba.

Fig. 9.3b Planation surface, New England plateau. (J. Roberts)

Fig. 9.3d Summit surface around Pigeon House Mountain, southeastern New South Wales. (J. Roberts)

Fig. 9.3e High plains in eastern Victoria, looking west from Mt Matlock to the Gregory Range. (Geological Survey of Victoria)

to the Holocene, hotspot volcanicity affected the entire region, with several plume centres involved (e.g. Sutherland 1991). Yet these volcanic events have proved invaluable for they have allowed landform developments to be dated.

The complexity of earth movements over eons of time is reflected in the many anomalous drainage patterns. Some stream courses are clearly structurally determined, but many appear to reflect capture of various kinds (Bishop 1995). Some are caused by volcanic and other tectonic diversions, whereas others remain the subject of debate and controversy.

Fig. 9.3f High plain, Cradle Mountain National Park, Tasmania. (J. & P. Davill)

Fig. 9.4 Summit surface preserved on **(a)** Permian porphyry, near Einasleigh, and (below) **(b)** folded Proterozoic metasedimentary rocks and granites near Forsayth, both in north Queensland.

Historical background

Examples of planation surfaces, some of extraordinary smoothness, that transect complex structures have been reported from north Queensland, in New England, from as far south as eastern Victoria and Tasmania, and from virtually all areas between (Figs 9.1, 9.2, 9.3). High-level planation surfaces were recognised by such early workers as David (1908), Dunn (1908), Baragwanath (1925), and others. Their geological settings are complex and their ages, origins, and hence correlation, are in many instances difficult to ascertain. Considering the region as a whole, are some surfaces related to cycles of scarp recession working westwards (inland) from the Pacific coast (e.g. Ollier 1982b); or, looking at regional and local landscapes, have they been shaped by rivers that have responded to changes in local baselevels?

Although it has long been recognised that the surface has been disrupted by earth movements, whether faulting or warping is involved is still frequently disputed (e.g. David 1908; Sussmilch 1909; Baragwanath 1925; Hills 1940; Wellman 1979a, 1979b, 1980; Crohn 1979; Bishop and Young 1980; Jones and Veevers 1982, 1983a, 1983b; Brown 1983). The amount of associated displacement also is difficult to ascertain. Are the scarps tectonic and due only to faulting, or are they structural fault-line forms? For these reasons alone, correlations between firmly dated surfaces and adjacent areas lacking independent evidence of age are unreliable.

Lithology also has influenced the mode of landscape development (downwearing or backwearing) as well as degree of lowering of outcrop. In addition, surfaces coincident with

bedding planes are prominent in some areas as, for instance, those developed on the Nowra Sandstone which are evident in the Sydney Basin. They can be regarded as having been exploited by erosional agencies but stabilised on structural planes. Thus, their ages relative to adjacent erosional bevels are suspect. In many places, surfaces of possibly similar ages stand at different elevations simply because they are developed on rocks of contrasted resistance to weathering and erosion. Frequently the question arises whether the difference in height between two

Fig. 9.5a Herbert River gorge cut into high plain, probably of epigene-etch type, north Queensland. (J. Stephenson)

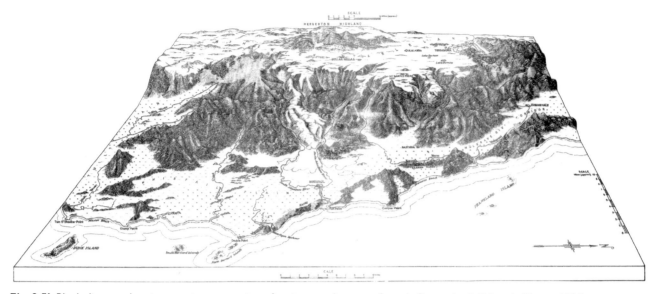

Fig. 9.5b Block diagram showing prominent summit surface in coastal ranges of north Queensland. (After de Keyser 1964)

planation surfaces is a reflection of age, or relative resistance to weathering and erosion, or is it due to faulting or warping?

Possible origins of the high planation surfaces

How were the various planation surfaces of the Eastern Uplands formed and what is the chronology of events to which they are related? In north Queensland, the western Einasleigh Uplands, a high plain exhumed from beneath a ?Jurassic-Cretaceous cover, and comparable to the summit surface described from the Isa Highlands on the western side of the Carpentaria Basin (see Fig. 7.15), has been identified. The remnants of ?Late Jurassic or Early Cretaceous strata indicative of the origin and age of the surface are preserved as far east as the Newcastle Range (Twidale 1956; Fig. 9.4).

Further east, however, the origin of the summit surface, like that on the Featherbed Ranges and in the coastal uplands where a planation surface is prominent (Fig. 9.5), is not known. There is no evidence that the area was covered by the Cretaceous seas and the surface or surfaces are probably of epigene type, having been eroded by rivers graded to the Cretaceous shore (cf. Flinders Ranges, in Chapter 4). The same pattern may hold for the western slope of the Eastern Uplands throughout their length, with some planation surfaces exhumed from beneath the cover of Mesozoic or younger strata preserved in the various components of the Great Artesian Basin, but others shaped by rivers

Fig. 9.6a Corestone boulders, Monaro district of southeastern New South Wales.

Fig. 9.6b Bouldery residual located high in the relief in northeastern Tasmania; note high plain on horizon represented by accordant crests.

Fig. 9.6c Large residual boulders on high plain adjacent to Herbert Falls, north Queensland. (CSIRO)

flowing to the then shorelines.

The evenness of some of these very old surfaces may be related to their origin. Hills had read Jutson's accounts of Western Australian physiography and appreciated that like the New Plateau, the high plains of eastern Victoria had been stripped of regolith: they are etch surfaces. Hills suggested that the older plains as represented in the Baw Baw Surface could have originated during the Jurassic or even the Triassic (Hills 1975, p. 302; Jenkin 1988, p. 408). Such prolonged weathering by moisture held in a regolithic cover could explain the regularity of the high plains, for over long eons of time most bedrock projections would be eliminated by preferential physico-chemical attack. Many of the high plains of the Eastern Uplands, several of them of extraordinary flatness (e.g. Keyser 1964; Ollier

Fig. 9.7 Basalt flow remnant, New England Plateau. (J. Roberts)

1982a, 1982b) appear to be of epigene-etch type.

That etch surfaces are widespread throughout the Eastern Uplands is suggested also by the occurrence of such etch or two-stage forms as boulders and nubbins (Fig. 9.6), which imply possible development beneath a regolith-covered surface (Twidale 1981a). Examples are reported from many areas including the boulder-strewn granitic landscape of the Monaro of New South Wales (Browne 1964), the New England plateau

(e.g. Ollier 1982a), northeastern Tasmania, and the high plains flanking the Herbert Gorge in north Queensland (Fig. 9.5a).

Ages of surfaces

As well as the Cretaceous marine transgression, the hotspot volcanic activity that affected the Eastern Uplands throughout the Cenozoic has been crucial in dating land surfaces, for volcanic rocks are susceptible to physical (numerical) dating. For instance, dating of lava flows in the southeastern highlands shows that many mid Tertiary and some Mesozoic elements survive in the landscape in that particular region (Young and McDougall 1993).

The problem of origin and dating of surfaces is eased where Cenozoic volcanism has produced constructional surfaces (Fig. 9.7), for the age of volcanic lavas and associated domes and plateaux is the same as the age of the extrusion, now commonly determined by radiometric means. Thus the Barrington Tops and the Mt Warning dome are constructional surfaces, and their ages are those of the volcanicity to which they are due, i.e. Eocene and ?Miocene, respectively (e.g. Ollier 1982b; Pain 1983). Similarly, the various volcanic provinces of north Queensland (Stephenson et al. 1980), though complex in detail and each comprising several individual lava flows, are little changed by weathering and erosion and are broadly of later Cenozoic age, with some like the McBride Province being of Late Pleistocene and Holocene derivation,

Fig. 9.8a The Nunniong (granitic) Plateau from Mt Seldom, eastern Victoria. Eocene-Oligocene basalt in valley. (Geological Survey of Victoria)

Fig. 9.8b Prominent summit surface of the Baw Baw Range, eastern Victoria, from Mt Skene. In the middle distance the Gregory Range is capped by Eocene-Oligocene basalts. Thus the higher surface is even older. (Geological Survey of Victoria)

Fig. 9.9 Planation surface in south central Tasmania. Dolerite is exposed in cliffs bordering The Acropolis and Mt Geryon, but the summit surface transects the beds. (Government Stills Photographic Section, Tasmania)

whereas the Toomba flow of the Nulla Province appears to be only some 13,000 years old.

The age or age-ranges of some lavas have been determined within close limits, and some of the earliest evidence of very old surfaces in the Eastern Uplands resulted from the linking of valley volcanics and adjacent high plains by Craft and Hills, working in uplands of southeastern Australia. Craft (1932, 1933) investigated the Shoalhaven and Monaro districts in the late 1920s and early 1930s. He noted basalt flows in the floors of valleys deeply incised into the sandstone plateaux. He deduced that the valleys and plateau surface into which they were cut must be older than the volcanics. Initially he considered the lavas to be of later Tertiary age. Subsequently he adopted the interpretation, based in Hills' stratigraphic work in Victoria, that they were earlier rather than later Tertiary and, thus, that the adjacent high surfaces were probably of Cretaceous or earlier origin.

Basalt flows occupy valleys and basins cut into a high plains surface in eastern Victoria. Some of the lavas are of Early Tertiary age, a conclusion initially based in the regional stratigraphy of east Gippsland and the Bogong High Plains. There the basalts both rest on and are overlain by fossiliferous swamp and riverine deposits (Hills 1934, 1938, 1940, 1975) so that stratigraphic ages could be derived for the volcanics. The putative dates were later confirmed by physical dating, which showed that the Older Volcanics vary in age from Late Eocene to Early Miocene (e.g. Hills 1975; Price et al. 1988; Orth et al. 1995; Fig. 9.8).

Thus, using the principles of superposition and topographic position, the lava flows permitted the indirect dating of the valleys and the adjacent surfaces into which they are incised. Though the age of basalts varies within the Eastern Uplands between Eocene and Holocene, it is surely the age of the oldest flows in any given region that is critical, for that indicates the minimum age for the dissection of the valleys and hence of the surfaces into which they are incised. Considered regionally, incision of river valleys in the Eastern Uplands began prior to the later Eocene. Hills realised this and deduced that the high plains of eastern Victoria were of earliest Tertiary or Mesozoic age and a similar rationale applies to the New South Wales uplands. Later work has both corroborated and developed such ideas (Taylor et al. 1985; Young and McDougall 1985; Wray et al. 1993). In eastern Victoria, for instance, surfaces of putative

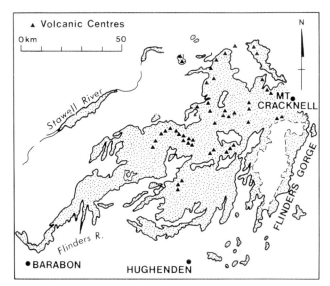

Fig. 9.10 Map of the Sturgeon volcanic province, north Queensland, showing a lava flow now inverted as an elongate flat-topped ridge north of Barabon. Also a discontinuous valley-floor remnant in the valley of the Stawell River. (After Stephenson et al. 1980)

Cretaceous, Jurassic and Triassic ages have been noted (Jenkin 1988, p. 408; Fig. 9.8b).

Tasmania typifies the rest of the Eastern Uplands in that obvious planation surfaces are faulted and are difficult to correlate. Dislocations associated with the separation of Australia and Antarctica during the later Mesozoic and earliest Tertiary caused the development of major NNW–SSE trending horsts and grabens (the Macquarie Harbour, Derwent, and Midlands grabens are examples of the latter). Faulting continued through the Cenozoic and is still active.

The landscape is broadly stepped (a fact that has been exploited by engineers in the siting of dams to generate hydro-electric power), with prominent levels preserved around 275 m, 400–430 m and 730–820 m. The landscape can readily be interpreted in terms of the principle of topographic position, with surfaces formed at lower and lower levels as streams have incised (Davies 1959).

Sheets of Jurassic dolerite underlie the 450 m high central plateau and cap some of the highest mountains; but not all, for bevelled quartzite ranges stand at similar elevations. Thus the summit surface, whether preserved on igneous rocks or other materials, is erosional, and postdates the Jurassic igneous activity. It is tempting to correlate the highest surface (Fig. 9.9), now much dissected by streams and glaciers, with the high plains of eastern Victoria and southeastern New South Wales.

Indirect evidence also points to the higher surfaces of central Tasmania being of probable Mesozoic age. Valley-floor basalt flows, such as those preserved in the Forth, Mersey and Ringarooma valleys, are of Early Tertiary age, suggesting that the valleys and the high plains into which they are incised are of earlier Tertiary age, or older. The dolerite sills and volcanic rocks are weathered, in many places producing bauxite or laterite. At one time it was thought that some bauxite, at any rate, dated from the later Mesozoic, but subsequent work suggests that the duricrusts are Tertiary, in some instances as old as Eocene, but no older. Nevertheless, as the duricrusts stand relatively low in the relief, the principle of topographic position suggests that the high planation surfaces are of considerable antiquity.

Age of rivers

A further implication arising from the occurrence of the volcanic extrusions in the Eastern Uplands is that many major valleys which carry Eocene lava flows — old valleys like those in the Shoalhaven catchment, the old Tumut, and so on — are of an antiquity comparable to those mentioned from the western cratons and associated areas. There has also been inversion with old valleys now filled with lava flows and standing high in the local relief. The former Flinders River valley, north and northeast of Barabon in northwest Queensland, provides a good example (Fig. 9.10), and the Einasleigh valley, north of Einasleigh township, is another, though in both instances the changes occurred relatively recently. The ancestral Murrindal River of eastern Victoria, however, which flowed east of the present channel, was a valley in Eocene times, as was the Sassafras, now inverted, in southeastern New South Wales.

Summary

Though some Eastern Uplands planation surfaces are locally well defined and dated, it is difficult to make general statements that are valid for the entire region. Nevertheless, it is clear that surfaces of Mesozoic age are widely and substantially preserved.

Chapter 10

SURVIVAL

Review of the problem

Though not an exhaustive summary covering every last square kilometre of the continent, the reviews presented in the preceding six chapters demonstrate that remnants of very old surfaces are widely developed and preserved. They are a common element of the cratonic and orogenic terrains of Australia.

It has been said that: 'few observations have been made of the Mesozoic age of landscapes throughout tropical Australia' (Nott 1996). As the foregoing discussion of northern Australian regions shows, the statement is surely mistaken. Remnants of very old surfaces, either of epigene-etch type, as in the Hamersley Range and Kakadu, or exhumed as at Tindal and the Isa Highlands and Einasleigh Uplands, are widely distributed and long recognised. The same comment applies to many other parts of Australia.

In summary, exhumed surfaces are commonplace in the Australian landscapes. Most are of limited area but some, like the Tindal Plain and the sub-Cretaceous–Jurassic surface located southwest of the Eromanga Basin, are of considerable though as yet undetermined extent. They range in age from latest Archaean (headwaters of Yule River in the Pilbara Craton: Twidale 1986) to Middle or Late Pleistocene (Murphy Haystacks, northwestern Eyre Peninsula: Twidale and

Campbell 1984). Many relatively minor glaciated pavements, some of various Precambrian ages, others Late Palaeozoic, are recorded from northern and northwestern Western Australia and in many parts of southeastern Australia. Also, apart from the widespread sub-Cretaceous remnants, the many exhumed surfaces of various ages that have been noted from many parts of the continent are not included. Amongst these are remnants of sub-Eocene age in the valleys marginal to the former Willochra Lake in the southern Flinders Ranges; a probable sub-Permian surface on the higher parts of Yorke Peninsula; and surfaces of various Precambrian ages, e.g. on the eastern side of Lake Gairdner in the Gawler Ranges, and numerous others.

Of the old surfaces and forms that on the evidence

Era	Period	Surface
Cenozoic		
	Tertiary Eocene	Silcrete, central Australia (South Australia, Queensland, Northern Territory)
		Flinders Ranges ridge and valley, South Australia; Macdonnell Ranges, Northern Territory; earlier/older parts of New Plateau, Western Australia
Mesozoic		
	Late Cretaceous	Horwitz Surface, Western Australia; Uluru, Kata Tjuta and Mt Conner, Northern Territory
	Early Cretaceous	Summit surface, Flinders Ranges, South Australia; Nott Surface, Gawler Ranges, South Australia
	Cretaceous *but detail uncertain*	Summit surface, Macdonnell, Musgrave-Everard ranges, Northern Territory and South Australia; Eastern Uplands
	Jurassic	Lateritic surface, Gulfs region of South Australia; Arcoona Plateau, South Australia; Old Plateau, Western Australia; Kakadu, Northern Territory; and Eastern Uplands
	?Triassic	Webb Surface, Flinders Ranges, South Australia; Beck Surface, Gawler Ranges, South Australia; ?Old Plateau, Western Australia; and Baw Baw Surface, Victoria
Palaeozoic		
	Permian	Glaciation over most of the present Australian continent.

Table 10.1   Distribution and age of Australian palaeosurfaces.

have never been covered but are of epigene or etch origin, with the latter dominant, several categories of various ages can be listed (Table 10.1).

- Eocene surfaces include many of the silcrete-capped plateaux of central Australia, the ridge and valley topographies of the Flinders and Macdonnell ranges, the earlier sectors of the New Plateau of the Yilgarn Block, and the Hamersley (etch) Surface.
- The epigene precursor of the Hamersley Surface, the Horwitz Surface, dates from the Cretaceous, as do the summit bevels of Uluru (and possibly also the summits of low domes in the Kata Tjuta complex and of Mt Conner), and the Musgrave and Everard ranges.
- The Nott (etch) Surface of the Gawler Ranges and the summit surfaces of the Flinders and Macdonnell ranges are of Early Cretaceous age, and many of the high plains of the Eastern Uplands also fall into this category.
- Surfaces of putative Triassic or Jurassic ages are preserved in the uplands bordering the South Australian Gulfs, the Arcoona Plateau, the Old Plateau of the Yilgarn, and the Baw Baw Surface of eastern Victoria. The Kakadu massif was in existence in the Early Cretaceous but the complex summit surface may be older.
- Implied Triassic surfaces are suggested by the field evidence in the Flinders and Gawler ranges (Webb and Beck surfaces respectively).

The inclusion in this listing of surfaces that are clearly implied but of which no known remnant has been identified or recognised may be adversely criticised as misleading. But they are part of the denudation chronology of the districts in which they occurred. Just as the impression of a mollusc or a dinosaur's foot constitutes evidence of a former environment, so do these ghost-like surfaces add to our understanding of the chronology and mode of development of the landscape.

Very old surfaces of one type or another occur in many parts of the continent (Twidale 1976b, 1994). The degree of confidence with which these ancient landscapes have been dated, varies. The principles of superposition, that in an undisturbed sequence of rocks the lower beds are oldest, and of topographic position, that in undisturbed landscapes older

landforms stand higher than those low in the relief, apply, but more specific evidence is available for several regions.

The geological evidence for the age of the Gawler Ranges bornhardt landscape, for example, is sound, for the erosion of the surfaces is clearly linked to stratigraphically dated genetically related deposits. Similarly, in the Eastern Uplands, valleys and the surfaces into which they are incised must be older than the numerically dated lava flows that run down the valleys. On Kangaroo Island the surface on which the lava flowed is older than the volcanics. Similarly the great age of features like Kakadu and the Arcoona Plateau is based in sound geological evidence, for they stood as islands at a time when (Cretaceous) seas inundated the surrounding areas.

The dating of certain other surfaces poses problems. The age attributed to some surfaces, e.g. the Uluru bevel and the Hamersley Surface, depends on palaeontological dating, which has changed, and probably will again (e.g. Twidale and Harris 1977; Harris and Twidale 1991). Similarly, the occurrence of primary and secondary laterite confuses the analysis of landscapes on the Yilgarn Craton and on Kangaroo Island: whether kaolinised regoliths are related to lateritic weathering has caused some concern, though on balance the evidence of antiquity seems plausible. On the other hand, and as noted, several of the very old palaeosurfaces discussed stand higher in the local landscapes than duricrusted (laterite, silcrete) surfaces of mid Tertiary (typically Miocene) age; thus corroborating the putative Early Tertiary or Mesozoic ages of the higher remnants. Dating of surfaces thought to be planed off by rivers graded to Cretaceous shorelines is less secure though not unreasonable. The same comment applies to projections such as that used to suggest an age for the crestal bevel of Uluru.

Not all landscapes include a recognisable palaeosurface. For instance, the Grampians of western Victoria is a fold mountain range developed in Middle Palaeozoic rocks. The ridge crests may have stood as low residuals on the Mesozoic planation surface evidenced to the east. The present ridge and valley forms may have developed by differential subsurface weathering at that time. But no evidence germane to the problem has yet been adduced. Similarly the Stirling and associated Porongurup ranges of the southwest of Western Australia may have evolved in relation to the lateritised land surface known as the Old Plateau, but again, evidence is lacking.

The greatest obstacle to accepting even the closely constrained dating of surface and forms like the Gawler Ranges and Kakadu, however, is an inherent disbelief in the possibility of antiquity of the scale and extent implied. For instance, and concerning the proposed age of lateritic surfaces in the Gulfs region of South Australia, great antiquity is said to be 'unreasonable' or 'unlikely' (Bourman 1989, p. 158; 1995, p. 16). In part this results from a long-standing acceptance of the conventional view that all landscapes are youthful, in part from a well-founded common sense. How can land surfaces withstand the elements for scores or even a few millions of years? Yet, if such old surfaces exist, as has been strongly suggested and even demonstrated, they must be possible.

Even if, on balance, the field evidence suggests that only half of the substantial relics of very old landscapes, remnants of Gondwana, alleged to persist in the Australian landscape, are real, the question still arises as to what factors are conducive to long-term survival (Twidale 1976b).

Global position, size and shape

Many conservative factors come together at the continental scale. Australia stands on the Australian Plate distant from plate boundaries. The latter are zones of instability where old surfaces and the evidence for their ages can readily be destroyed or rendered unrecognisable. Australia is, and long has been, tectonically stable for though faulting and warping (folding) have been, and remain, active, they are minor. The last orogeny affecting the eastern and central areas of the continent was some 250 million years ago, and the west has been tectonically stable in the sense of there having been few major disruptions, for at least 1000 million years. Tectonic stability such as is implied in such essentially undisturbed massifs as the Proterozoic quartzites of Kakadu, parts of the Kimberleys, the Arcoona Plateau and the Forster Range improves the chances of preservation by reducing the possibility of intense dissection on steep slopes.

The latitudinal position of the continent and the lack of extensive and high uplands together protected all but some southeastern areas (central Tasmania, the Kosciuszko–Buffalo region of New South Wales and Victoria) from frost and glacial effects related to cold periods of the Quaternary, so that remnants of duricrusted surfaces that predate the Cenozoic have survived.

As mentioned earlier, Australia is a large, compact, and flat country. Low elevation has several conservative advantages, for baselevel control is paramount and the effects of gravity are minimised. Though there are significant local exceptions related to reinforcement effects (see below), mountainous regions are eroded more rapidly than are plains. It might be thought that Australia has a further advantage in that about half of the continent is arid or semi-arid, areic, cryptoreic, or served by basins of interior drainage; but this is a recent situation that has only obtained for the last two million years or so.

Large continents such as Australia, with compact outlines, are insulated against the extreme effects of river rejuvenation generated by lowering of sea level. Such landscape revival, as it is called, has impacted strongly on indented continents such as Europe and peninsular and insular land masses such as West and East Malaysia, no part of which is far distant from the coast and where stream erosion appears to be ubiquitous.

Structural factors

Some rocks, either primary, such as quartzite, or secondary, such as the various duricrusts produced by weathering, are physically cohesive and/or of low chemical reactivity. When a molten magma cools, minerals crystallise out at different temperatures. Chemical weathering, which is both spatially and temporally by far the most important and widespread type of change, results from the rocks exposed at and near the Earth's surface being in an environment different from that in which they originated. 'Minerals that have formed under magmatic, hydrothermal, metamorphic or sedimentary conditions are rendered potentially unstable when exposed to the atmosphere. They are vulnerable to attack by water, oxygen and carbon dioxide. … Water penetrates through pores, cleavages and other micro openings in the minerals and dissolves the more soluble constituents' (Loughnan 1969, p. 27).

Mafic minerals, like olivine for example, react more readily than later-crystallised minerals, such as quartz. At one time this was attributed to the former being in greater disequilibrium and more unstable in the ambient conditions at and near the Earth's surface. The greater resistance to both chemical and physical attack is now linked to ionic and covalent bond strength of the minerals, though, like solution, this is not fully understood. At this stage all that can be stated with confidence is that some minerals, such as quartz, are more resistant than others in most environments.

Thus, quartzites are resistant and underlie many old ranges and plateaux, even in the humid tropics, as for example in the Kakadu Massif of northern Australia which is at least as old as the Cretaceous. Palaeosurface remnants are commonly preserved on quartzite or sandstone ridges in the Flinders and Macdonnell ranges and the Isa Highlands. Plateau massifs like Kakadu, the Kimberleys and the Forster Range and the Arcoona Plateau are underlain mainly by arenaceous formations. Resistant formations buttress weak outcrops located upstream, as for example in the central Flinders Ranges, South Australia, where quartzites situated higher in the sequence and located at the margins of a regional anticline protect the weaker shale and mudstone exposed in the core of the structure.

Though logical, this composition-based explanation of contrasted rates of weathering is an oversimplification. Basalt, rich in mafic minerals and lacking free quartz, underlies plateaux and high plains in many parts of northern and eastern Australia. In the latter region such features occur in climates ranging from hot and humid to cold. Conservation is not a function of recency for though some of the basalts of north Queensland are of latest Pleistocene age, some of those of the northwestern Northern Territory date from the Cambrian. The reason for such preservation is that though crystalline and of low permeability, basalt is pervious.

Structure influences the mode of landscape development. Weak rocks tend to be lowered, but areas underlain by flat-lying or only gently dipping resistant primary rocks or by duricrusts tend to be worn back (scarp recession). The latter mechanism (Fig. 1.1b) favours the persistence of headwater remnants of the 'initial' surface until quite late in the reduction of the older landscape, and implies a survival of some tens of millions of years in a region of continental extent. Panplanation (Crickmay 1933; Osborn and du Toit 1991), involving extensive lateral planation by rivers flowing near to baselevel, also produces a stepped topography and implies the conservation of old surfaces.

Water the destroyer

The major reason for rocks being weathered and thus rendered prone to erosion is susceptibility to invasion by, and reactivity with, water. It follows that any factor that causes water to be absent or scarce, whether at the site, local or regional scale, is conducive to survival.

In some circumstances water is a significant cause of rock disintegration. In cold lands the freeze-thaw mechanism is effective. Slaking (disintegration caused by alternations of wetting and drying, or simply by drying) induces breakdown in temperate and tropical humid areas. Water may also act either as a catalyst or as an initiator in insolation weathering. The main contribution of water to rock weathering, however, is chemical. Its molecular structure makes water the supreme solvent. Solution is essential to chemical weathering, and in addition to its direct effects it prepares crystal structures for further reactions, in particular hydration and hydrolysis. In addition, water is the medium in which various chemicals and biota are transported into and from particular sites. Water of crystallisation trapped within lattices also attracts bacteria that bore into crystals and so allow penetration of solutes. Water is ubiquitous, for it occurs not only in the oceans, in lakes and in rivers but also forms a continuous layer beneath the surface of the continents as the groundwater zone. Even in the most arid of deserts there is water at depth, particularly beneath the beds of episodic rivers. But the corollary is that any factor that protects a rock against water contact or attack is conservative. Such protective factors include physical hardness and low chemical reactivity of the country rock.

In addition, at a local scale, diversion of water by obstacles or fractures gives rise to positive relief features that tend to persist (Fig. 10.1). Thus, it has been suggested that as a scarp is worn back the area of dissected (or 'initial') surface above it is decreased. The volume of water passing over the

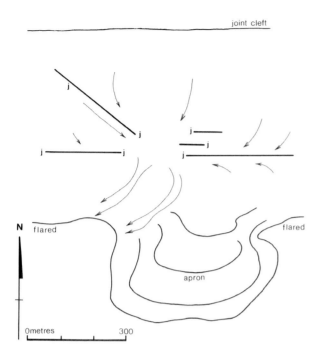

Fig. 10.1 Some local protection factors noted on Hyden Rock, Western Australia: **(a)** map of diversion of runoff along fracture resulting in preservation of rock apron (j – joint).

(b) Outstanding part of flared slope protected by presence upslope of block of rock that has diverted water flow.

(c) The original channel is now a raised rib.

scarp is diminished, and the rate of recession reduced (Twidale 1978b). Gully gravure (Bryan 1940; Twidale and Campbell 1986) has a similar effect. But these are only local and minor influences.

The importance of water partly explains the prevalence of etch forms amongst surviving palaeosurfaces. The stripping of the regolith to expose the weathering front as a bedrock surface is significant, even crucial, for whereas a regolith retains moisture a bare rock surface may dry in the sun. Hills (1975, p. 300) appreciated this when he made a critical comment which concerned the high plains of eastern Victoria but which is of general import:

> While these high surfaces of low relief clearly represent preserved relics of old surfaces which have escaped deep dissection, they have naturally suffered some reduction and modification in detail during the long periods of time to which they have been exposed to weathering and erosion, but this is relatively minor...

Regoliths retain moisture and are in this respect a destructive factor for moisture is the most potent single factor causing the alteration of rocks. In contrast, bare rock surfaces dry quickly and thus tend to be preserved. On the other hand, regoliths in which iron oxides or silica, in particular, are concentrated in horizons also have the potential to become protective, for on being relatively uplifted they drain and dry, and the mineral concentrates harden, irreversibly in the case of ferruginous compounds (Alexander and Cady 1962). This is the reason for the inverted valleys capped by silcrete in several parts of central Australia, e.g. the Grey Range between the Bulloo and Wilson creeks in southwest Queensland (see Twidale 1985, p. 144), and haematite/goethite in the Hamersley Range, northwestern Western Australia. The enduring laterite-capped plateaux and high plains of the Gulfs region of South Australia and the Darling Range and other remnants in the Yilgarn Block of Western Australia provide other examples of the protection afforded by laterite.

Rate of recession of scarps and rivers

Rivers extend their courses headwards by a combination of sapping and slumping. Such regressive erosion is favoured by joints and other structural weaknesses. Eventually headward-eroding streams breach ridges and may effect river capture. The rate at which this takes place, however,

Fig. 10.2a Shoalhaven Gorge and adjacent summit surface, southeastern New South Wales. (J. Roberts)

Fig. 10.2b Gorge cut in limestone with adjacent summit surface at Bungonia, New South Wales. (A. & R.W. Young)

may be slow. Much depends on the nature of the country rock, the depth of incision, and hence the volume of rock to be evacuated. But, in the basaltic terrain of southeastern New South Wales, the age of the volcanic country rock being physically determined and the length of the invading gorge being measurable, the rate of regression is of the order of 100 km in 60 million years (Taylor et al. 1985; Young and McDougall 1985).

Unequal activity and reinforcement effects

It has been deduced that stream systems and hence erosion extend over the entire land surface (e.g. Davis 1909, p. 267). No land surface ought to survive for very long. Some workers, however, long ago noted evidence to suggest that some areas are evidently 'out of reach of erosion' (Bliss Knopf 1924, p. 642; see also Horton 1945; Dunne and Aubry 1986). A Canadian geologist, Crickmay (1932, 1976), took the implications of the idea one step further, for he observed that unconsolidated

materials of considerable age stand close to major rivers; he argued that rivers do not accomplish marked erosion over their entire catchment. He formulated the Hypothesis of Unequal Activity (Crickmay 1976, p. 109), whereby river erosion is effective in, and close to, channels but in some instances does not affect divides. The survival of very old remnants in the cores of mountain ranges, on the watersheds between major river systems, attests such inequalities. Thus, in the Macdonnell Ranges of central Australia, duricrusted old valley floor remnants stand low in the relief but rounded and bevelled high crests, probably of Cretaceous age, are preserved on major divides.

Arenaceous rocks are pervious and many are also permeable. They are commonly subdivided by steeply dipping fractures. Thus, some rivers are more deeply incised than others, but whether developed on sedimentary, metamorphic, basaltic or granitic rocks, the landscapes consist of narrow gorges separating extensive high plains (Fig. 10.2a). Certainly such developments are facilitated by the presence of major steeply dipping fractures and pervious or permeable strata such as quartzite, sandstone or basalt (Fig. 7.2) but parallel developments are found elsewhere.

Unequal activity is also pertinent to the distribution of palaeosurface remnants. Several, such as those of Kakadu and in the Gulfs region of South Australia, are on or near the coast. They ought to be affected by sea level lowering and resultant river rejuvenation. The position of the Australian coastline did not change markedly during the Cenozoic, except during the Miocene when there was a relative rise of sea level. On the other hand, the Cretaceous witnessed widespread marine inundation, up to 40% of the continent being flooded at times (Frakes 1987; BMR Palaeogeographic Group 1992). Riverine processes are confined to the stream channels. Major rivers reaching the sea are elements of coordinated drainage systems in which headwater streams converge to form a single channel. Such rivers are widely spaced and the intervening divides commensurately broad. Thus, old landscapes have survived despite their proximity to coasts.

Inequalities in rates of erosion induce the operation of reinforcement or positive feedback mechanisms. The gist of the concept, which was recognised at least as early as 1851 (see Logan 1851; Bain 1923; see also Behrmann 1919; King 1970; Twidale et al. 1974) is that processes responsible for a landform or a landform assemblage 'induce their own continuity and acceleration and ... once developed contribute to their own perpetuation and further evolution by their own existence' (Twidale et al. 1974). Uplands shed water, so that all else being equal highlands tend to be preserved. Thus repeated uplift of some blocks, and consistent subsidence of the intervening basins, such as has been postulated for much of the Australian landscape, has been instrumental in preserving flights of palaeosurfaces on the uplands and in unconformity in the basins.

The Kimberley Block is resistant by reason of the abundance of thick dated sequences of sandstone and quartzite but, in addition, injections of volcanic diatremes dated roughly 1000 million years, 800 million years and 20 million years (Jaques et al.

1984) suggest that the region has been recurrently uplifted by swellings in the basement underlying the stack of old sediments. This would have perpetuated the domical character of the topography, the radial drainage pattern, and the tendency for water, the principal agent of weathering, to be evacuated.

Most bornhardts and other inselbergs and massifs persist initially because of structural factors, but once in relief they shed water, thus reducing possible weathering and erosion, while the adjacent plains and valleys are more degraded because of runoff, increased alteration of rocks and stream erosion. Once a site or area is standing in positive relief because of the comparative ineffectiveness of water attack, for whatever reason, that site or area tends to remain relatively upstanding.

All rivers are potentially positive feedback systems, for the deeper a river incises relative to its adjacent competitors the more runoff and shallow groundwaters it attracts at the expense of those competitors. Baselevel permitting, its potential for further incision is thus enhanced; it draws more water, which again increases its erosive potential, to the detriment of its competitors, and so on. Such persistence accounts for the demonstrated great age of some Australian rivers, and also the common development of a deep gorge incised abruptly in a featureless plateau. Rivers testify to natural selection, to inequalities in rates of weathering and erosion, the emergence of master streams, and landscapes characterised by widely spaced and deeply incised rivers (Fig. 10.2). The area out of reach of erosion may extend over most of the divides, where old palaeosurfaces may be preserved.

Summary

Several factors have contributed to the preservation of very old surfaces. Some are linked. In particular, structural factors determined by various crustal and sedimentological events have caused inequalities in the distribution of water in and on the lithosphere. These have given rise to unequal weathering and erosion, the effects of which have been maintained or enhanced by reinforcement mechanisms.

Chapter 11

PERSISTENCE AND RELIEF AMPLITUDE

Concatenation

Several of the particular conservative factors discussed (Chapter 10) are coincident, interrelated and self-enhancing. A well-fractured outcrop permits infiltration of water which increases the rate of weathering and hence erosion of the mass. On the other hand, a massive compartment of rock is not attacked with the same intensity. It then becomes upstanding in the local relief, causing it to shed water which further reduces the likelihood of weathering, and so on. As has been suggested, reinforcement or positive feedback mechanisms are of great significance in the preservation of palaeoforms, but they are genetically related to structural conditions and consequent unequal activity. Many conservative effects are causally linked, with one leading to another. Together they form a concatenation, or a series of genetically associated factors, which in turn may lead to increased relief amplitude at local and regional scales.

Uluru

Take for example Uluru, perhaps the best known of all Australian landforms (Figs 11.1 a–c). It is a steep-sided hill which stands in isolation in the desert landscape of central Australia. Visible from many kilometres away, the upland is an island mount or inselberg.

Its crest is dimpled and grooved due to the development of rock basins (gnammas) and ribbed with gutters aligned with the strike of the rocks (Figs 11.1d, e; see also Fig. 8.13a).

European discovery

Ernest Giles was the first European to sight Uluru, which he named Ayers Rock in 1872 (Giles 1889),

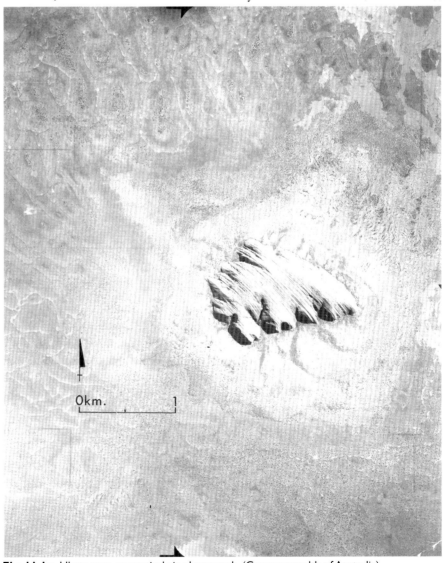

Fig. 11.1a Uluru seen on vertical air photograph. (Commonwealth of Australia)

0km.

Fig. 11.1b Uluru seen from the southeast with Kata Tjuta in the distance. O – site of deep subsurface Maastrichtian (latest Cretaceous) valley. (South Australian Government)

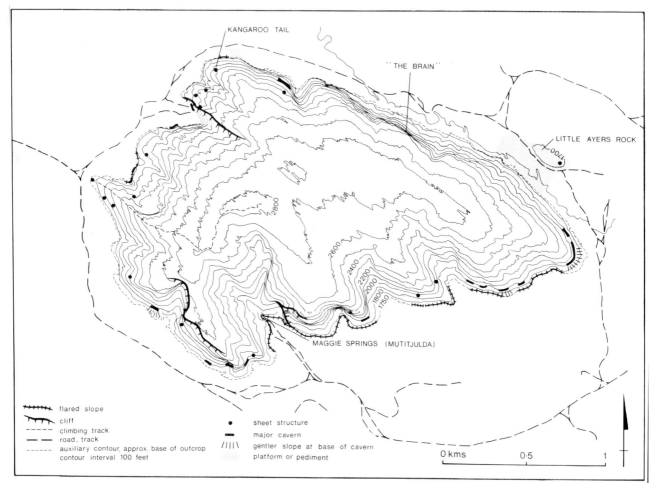

Fig. 11.1c Topographic map of Uluru.

Fig. 11.1d Bevelled and dimpled crest of Uluru, from the southeast.

Fig. 11.1e Rock basin on crest of Uluru.

Fig. 11.1f Ribbed crest of Uluru. (J. Nicol)

but he did so from afar, and W.C. Gosse was the first to examine the upland in 1873. He was impressed. He described it as one immense rock rising abruptly from the plain, climbed it (on 20 July 1873) and later confessed that 'This rock appears more wonderful every time I look at it' (Gosse 1874, p. 10), a sentiment with which many would concur. Uluru is an inselberg, or isolated steep-sided hill, with a bevelled crest, and with flanks

that are scored by gutters, with curious frettings in The Brain and elsewhere, with sheet structure in the Kangaroo Tail, gaping-mouth caves and with flared basal walls. As was early recognised, the hill is eroded in a coarse sandstone (not a granite as some have stated) of Cambrian age and stands some 877 m above sea level and 340–350 m higher than the adjacent arid plains of central Australia. The red colour is superficial and is due to a coating rich in iron and clay derived from the alteration of the arkosic sandstone (quartz with feldspar fragments). Unweathered, the sandstone is a dove-grey colour, as is seen in some cliff-foot caves and in small lightning strikes on the upper surface of the hill. The monolith has grown through time, not because it has been pushed up or upthrust (as was the Aboriginal understanding) but because of successive lowerings of the adjacent plains.

Geological setting

The inselberg is not comparable to an iceberg, for it is not the tip of an upland protruding from beneath a sea of sand. Bedrock occurs at shallow depth beneath the surrounding plains and particularly on the western, northern and eastern flanks. The sandstone is part of a NNW–SSE trending outcrop that can be traced for many kilometres to north and south. Why, then, is this particular compartment of rock upstanding and when did it form?

First, the strata in which Uluru is shaped are steeply dipping (Fig. 11.2). As they were deposited in an alluvial apron, they were originally only gently dipping, which argues that they have been tilted and folded during crustal compression. This happened in the Devonian, about 400-350 million

Fig. 11.2a Ribbed flank of Uluru with dipping strata exposed.

Fig. 11.2b The Brain: a fortuitous pattern with ends of steeply dipping strata exposed.

Fig. 11.3 Conglomeratic towers of Kata Tjuta seen **(b)** from the west, with Uluru in the distance, and (below) **(c)** in detail.

years ago. In addition, Uluru stands in roughly east–west alignment with Mt Conner to the east and Kata Tjuta to the west (Fig. 11.3). Mt Conner (Fig. 8.13b) is underlain by a sandstone basin suggesting that another phase of north–south compression may be superimposed on the Devonian folding. Thus, at Uluru the sandstone, itself physically resistant and chemically almost inert, was also

compressed. The presence of sheet fractures both exposed (Fig. 11.4a) and latent (Figs 11.4b, c) is taken by some workers as evidence of such stress and strain. The main point, however, is that water, the major agent of weathering, could not readily penetrate into a compressed rock mass. Hence it, together with other areas of cross, or interference, folding remains upstanding.

Reinforcement

Once in relief as a low hill, the early Uluru shed water, which had a further conservative function: a reinforcement or positive feedback effect. The location of the region deep in the interior of the Australian continent has rendered it immune to the effects of sea level changes. Changes in river regime during the Late Cenozoic, and in particular the dismemberment of the river systems and the formation of numerous local

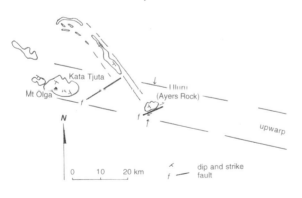

Fig. 11.3a Simplified structural map of Kata Tjuta, Uluru and Mt Conner. (After Wells et al. 1970)

Fig. 11.4a Kangaroo Tail, a sheet structure on the northwestern slope of Uluru.

Fig. 11.4b Incipient sheet fracture exposed at extreme right of cliff-foot cave in the southwestern sector of Uluru.

Fig. 11.4c Detail, showing en echelon fracture pattern (C. Wahrhaftig).

basins of enclosed drainage centred on salinas large and small, was due partly to the onset of aridity, but partly to widespread warping. The partial re-establishment of coordinated river systems flowing to Lake Eyre, such as that of the Finke, is due to the continued subsidence of the bed of the Lake and the consistent rejuvenation of the rivers flowing to it.

Age and development

As to age, the summit bevel of Uluru can be projected into and correlated with the unconformity identified beneath the plains to the west between the Cambrian arkose and Maastrichtian (uppermost Cretaceous) lignitic beds (Fig. 8.13c). The summit of Uluru is probably of latest Cretaceous age, or some 70 million years old. At that time the surface, ribbed but of low relief, and now represented by the bevel standing 190–250 m above the plains, took the form of a gentle rise carrying a regolith or soil. The regolith formed under warm humid conditions, and may have been of considerable thickness, which is not incompatible with depths of weathering reported from contemporary humid tropical regions.

The hill was left in topographic relief as the adjacent areas were eroded (Fig. 11.5). Water was shed from the initial gentle rise that was the ancestral Uluru, for being higher implies a measure of protection against water attack. The water flowed to the lower surrounding areas where weathering and erosion were accelerated and intensified. Moreover, the water accumulating in the regolith immediately adjacent to the base of the slope weathered not only vertically but also laterally, back into the compartment of intrinsically fresh sandstone. A steep slope was thus induced, characterised by minor features produced by intensive scarp-foot weathering. They include flared slopes, tafoni and breaks of slope. Elsewhere concavities or flares are exposed in the natural subsurface (e.g. Twidale 1962; Twidale and Bourne 1998b). Abrupt breaks of slope between flares and adjacent platforms are evident at many locations (Fig. 11.6a). Tafoni coexist with flared slopes on many granite hills as well as at the southern base of Uluru just to the west of Mutitjilda Waterhole (Figs 11.6b, c).

During this phase of subsurface weathering, the hill-plain junction and thus the zone of fluctuating water table stood about 35–60 m above present plain level. The intense weathering associated with that zone caused the formation of deep indentations or what are termed gaping-mouth caves, as well as breaks of slope in the bedrock surface, at that level (Figs 11.7a–c). Shallow groundwaters penetrated along the steeply inclined bedding planes and produced a fretted bedrock surface, patches of

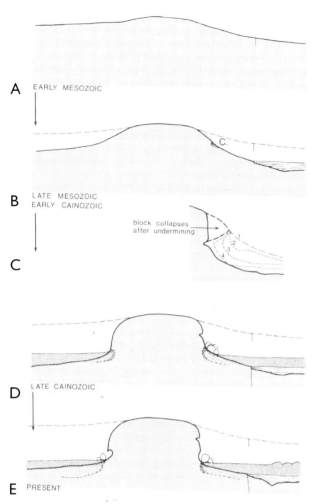

A EARLY MESOZOIC

B LATE MESOZOIC
   EARLY CAINOZOIC

   block collapses
   after undermining

C

D LATE CAINOZOIC

E PRESENT

Fig. 11.5 Diagram illustrating the age, evolution and exposure of Uluru. Episodic exposure has occurred as a result of the lowering of the surrounding plain. It is evidenced by various landforms preserved on the flanks of the inselberg. Breaks of slope and a line of gaping-mouth caves or shelters (C) suggest a phase of intense weathering 35–60 m above the present plain (B), and flared slopes and cliff-foot caves (D) indicate another when the hill-plain junction stood 4–5 m higher than at present. Slight lowering of soil level evidenced by rock platforms may be due to human activities.

Fig. 11.6a Sharp break of slope between flared slope and platform in the southern piedmont of Uluru. (C. Wahrhaftig)

Fig. 11.6b Flared slope and tafoni west of Mutitjilda Waterhole, southern piedmont of Uluru.

Fig. 11.6c Flared slope and tafoni at the base of the granitic Kokerbin Hill, Yilgarn Block, Western Australia.

which are now exposed, particularly on the eastern flank of the Rock, and most spectacularly in the fortuitously shaped feature aptly known as The Brain (Fig. 11.2b). A lowering of the plains by about 30 m caused further subsurface weathering in the scarp foot, causing the development of concave or flared slopes 4–5 m high (Fig. 11.6a). Indentations that became cliff-foot caves were also exposed at several sites around the base of the inselberg, and especially along the southern flank (Fig. 11.7d). Basal steepening has, in places, caused blocks on the slope above to become unbuttressed and to collapse or slip on to the piedmont plain (Fig. 11.7d). During the later Cenozoic (possibly the Miocene: see Otte and Shaw 1983) chalcedonic limestone accumulated on the plains adjacent to Uluru. In very general terms they corroborate the age of the residual but also suggest that processes active in the piedmont zone of the inselberg have been active recently (Fig. 11.5), while the plains proper have been subject to aeolian and riverine deposition.

Fig. 11.7a Gaping-mouth caves or tafoni located 35–60 m above plain level on the southern slope of Uluru.

Fig. 11.7b Detail of gaping mouth cave

Fig. 11.7c Break of slope in the same altitudinal range, southeastern flank of Uluru. Note also shelters at break of slope, flared base to right, steeply dipping strata and potholes on stream line.

Fig. 11.7d Gaping-mouth cave with fallen blocks at base of southwestern slope of Uluru. (South Australian Tourist Bureau)

Meanwhile the upper bevel of Uluru had been stripped of its regolith, exposing the ribbed and basined surface typical of weathering fronts. Some of the ribs are coincident with beds, others with bedding planes indurated by silica. Whatever their origin they channel runoff, and the related ribs exposed on the steep marginal slopes have been deepened by the water cascading down the flanks in waterfalls after heavy rains. Prominent potholes due to water erosion are developed in some of the channels (Fig. 11.7c). The upper surface of the residual has remained stable with only minor changes in its level and morphology. Recent lowering of the piedmont plain by some 3-40 cm is suggested by the exposure of narrow, sloping

Fig. 11.8 Rock platforms exposed at base of Uluru **(a)** northeastern corner, and (below) **(b)** some 800 m west of the residual.

Fig. 11.8c Midslope concavity on one of the Kata Tjuta domes. (Sketch by C. Wahrhaftig)

platforms in which is exposed rock of light colour not yet colonised by algae or lichens (Figs 11.8a, b).

The chronology of exposure cannot as yet be reconstructed in detail, but the midslope gaping-mouth cave episode may correlate with the deep weathering (regolith roughly 150 m thick) evidenced throughout central Australia particularly in relation to the widespread siliceous mantles of Eocene age (cf. Mabbutt 1965). Though not as well developed, similar morphological evidence of episodic exposure has been noted on the conglomeratic domes and towers of Kata Tjuta. There, basal steepening — including, though rarely, flared slopes — is common and concavities are developed at midslope on several of the higher residuals (Fig. 11.8c).

Fig. 11.9a Weathering front exposed as concavity or incipient flared slope in granite in reservoir at Yarwondutta Rock, Eyre Peninsula. Note flared slope in background — a former weathering front similar to that now seen in the reservoir, but revealed by natural erosion. (Twidale 1962)

Relief amplitude

This analysis of the evolution of Uluru suggests that for the last 70 million years there has been a hill where Uluru now stands, though it has changed in that its flanks have been steepened. It also demonstrates how a slight topographic rise can be converted into a prominent, steep-sided relief feature as a result of topographically induced differential subsurface weathering and subsequent erosion, and reinforcement or positive feedback effects.

Because of the episodic lowering of the surrounding plains during the Cenozoic, Uluru has come to stand higher and higher in the local relief. Persistent scarp-foot weathering by subsurface moisture has resulted in its flanks becoming steeper and steeper. The line of gaping-mouth caves that is prominent on the southern face of the inselberg dates from a time when the plain stood much higher than it now does and the flared slopes, again well represented on the southern face, from a time when the plain was 4–5 m higher than present. Relief amplitude has increased through time and the trend probably continues.

Other regional examples

Uluru is not an isolated example of a landform the vertical dimensions of which are due to episodic relief amplitude having increased atectonically through time, in this instance over a period of some 70 million years. Similar sequences of events

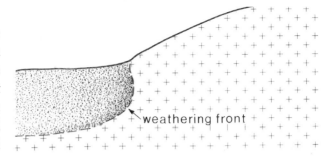

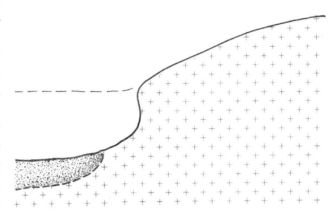

Fig. 11.9b Suggested two-stage development of flared slopes. Weathering resulting from runoff shown as shaded area. In stage one it is in place, in stage two it has been stripped to expose the concave or flared bedrock surface beneath. Repetition of this two-stage process produces stepped slopes.

leading to increased relief amplitude are evidenced in both cratonic and orogenic settings.

Consider, for instance, the granitic inselberg landscape of northwestern Eyre Peninsula which is part of the Gawler Craton (Twidale and Bourne 1975). Yarwondutta Rock provides the basic evidence. First, a concave or flared bedrock slope is exposed in an artificial excavation in the northeastern piedmont of the rock (Fig. 11.9), demonstrating conclusively that such forms can be initiated beneath the natural land surface and are etch forms (Twidale 1962, Twidale and Bourne 1998). Second, the northwestern slope of the residual is stepped (Figs 3.11c, 11.10) with treads separated by risers which are flared. Bearing

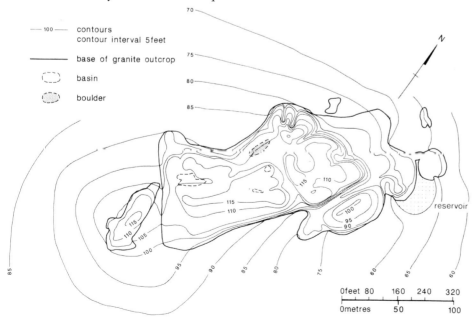

Fig. 11.10 Contour map of Yarwondutta Rock, near Minnipa, northwestern Eyre Peninsula, South Australia.

Fig. 11.11a Crest of Yarwondutta Rock, northwestern Eyre Peninsula, dimpled because of the development of numerous basins or gnammas.

Fig. 11.11b Incipient rock basins developed on a recently exposed granite platform, northwestern Eyre Peninsula, South Australia. Such occurrences show that basins are initiated below the land surface at the weathering front.

Fig. 11.12a Flared slope located on midslope, some 35 m above plain level, on western side of Mt Wudinna, northwestern Eyre Peninsula.

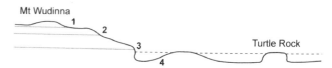

Fig. 11.12b Section (E–W) through Mt Wudinna and environs showing suggested stages from 1 (oldest) to 4 (present day) in the exposure of the hills.

Fig. 11.12c Eastern slope of Ucontitchie Hill, northwestern Eyre Peninsula, showing multiple flared zones.

in mind the origin of the flared components of the stepped slope, it is suggested that the hill has come to stand higher and higher in the local landscape as a result of alternations of stability and weathering and instability and erosion. During each stable phase piedmont weathering occurred and concave bedrock surfaces were shaped at shallow depth beneath the land surface, largely by waters running off the bare hillslopes above. During the phases of erosion the plains around the residual were lowered and the piedmont regolith was etched out to expose the flared slopes. The dimpled upper surface of Yarwondutta is probably an older etch surface (Fig. 11.11a, cf. Fig. 11.11b), which has been left relatively high and dry and remained essentially untouched during the multiple lowerings of the adjacent plains and the etching out of the piedmont zone (Twidale and Bourne 1975; Twidale 1982a, 1982b, 1982c). The rock basins or gnammas have expanded, but the surface remains basically as it was when first exposed.

Flared forms are not the only indicators of piedmont weathering. As at Uluru they are but one component of a small assemblage of forms which includes breaks of slope and tafoni and which developed in the scarp-foot zone as a result of intense chemical attack.

Mt Wudinna is one of several bornhardts the episodic exposure of which is attested by a stepped morphology. About 35 m above the present plain (the height of the base of the hill varies spatially) an incomplete ring of forms such as flared slopes (Fig. 11.12a), breaks of slope and small tafoni encircles the hill. Flared slopes up to 3-4 m high occur in many sectors of the present piedmont. Thus pauses in the erosion of the plains at stages when they stood roughly 35 m and 3–5 m higher than present are indicated. The 3–5 m level is coincident with the dimpled crest of the nearby Turtle Rock and the unnamed rock which stands between the two other residuals (Fig. 11.12b).

Other stepped inselbergs identified on northwestern Eyre Peninsula include Carappee Hill, south of Kimba, Ucontitchie and Cocata hills to the south of Wudinna, and Poondana and Tcharkuldu rocks which, like Yarwondutta Rock, are in the Minnipa district. On Carappee Hill a distinct shoulder (Figs 5.11a, b) transecting foliation, sheet fractures and jointing stand some 185 m above the base and 50 m below the crest. Basal flares are present in places. The eastern slope of Ucontitchie Hill displays evidence in the form of flared zones, of multiple alternations of weathering and erosion (Fig. 11.12c). The other residuals mentioned are stepped at the same sort of scale as the northwestern slope of Yarwondutta Rock, i.e. with steps just 2–4 m apart.

Thus, the stepped forms are widely distributed and suggest that parts of the inselberg landscape has witnessed episodic exposure and that relief amplitude has increased through time. The scarp-foot landform assemblages now perched on the side slopes of inselbergs and ridges above plain and valley floor level can be construed as indicating pauses in valley lowering or regional planation (i *in* Fig. 11.13). They can, to the contrary, be taken as evidence of phases of spasmodic etching of the piedmont zone which are not necessarily related to events on the plains proper (ii *in* Fig. 11.13): it could be argued that while the piedmont was being

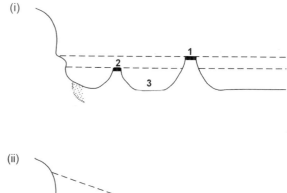

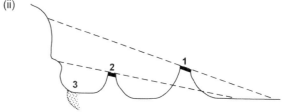

Fig. 11.13 Alternative interpretations of piedmont development: **(i)** with planation reaching base of slope, and **(ii)** etching out of piedmont zone.

reduced the plains were stable.

The period during which relief amplitude has increased is considerable, for the upper surfaces of Mt Wudinna and Ucontitchie Hill, like the shoulder located high on Carappee Hill, can be correlated with Mesozoic remnants preserved in the Gawler Ranges to the north, the Arcoona Plateau to the northeast, and the Gulfs region to the south and southeast (for summary, see Twidale 1994). The multiple steps on the higher residuals such as Mt Wudinna have been interpreted as the result of episodic exposure during a chronology linked to various of the duricrusted surfaces preserved in the area (Twidale and Bourne 1975).

Evidence of similar alternations of piedmont weathering and erosion, and implied increased relief amplitude, has been noted on many of the granitic inselbergs of the southern Yilgarn Block of Western Australia. Again the examples are widely distributed, suggesting a regional pattern. Thus a stepped morphology indicative of episodic exposure has been recorded on The Humps (Fig. 6.5) in the Hyden district, on several residuals in the Salt River district south of Kellerberrin, and on Bank and McDermid rocks west of Norseman (Twidale et al. 1999; Twidale and Bourne 1998a, 1998b; Bourne and Twidale 2000, 2002; Fig. 11.14). Here the time scale of events is similar to that of the Eyre Peninsula examples, for the Old Plateau,

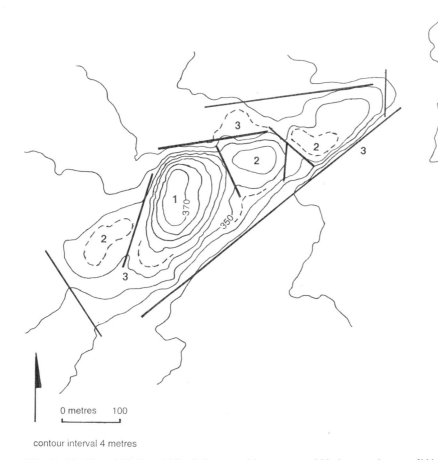

Fig. 11.14 Map of McDermid Rock, between Norseman and Hyden, southwest of Western Australia, showing contours (continuous lines) and form-lines (dashed lines), major fractures (heavy lines) and steps numbered 1–3, in descending order of elevation and age. (Adapted from map drawn by McMullen, Nolan and Partners Surveyors, W.A.).

beneath which the higher residuals were shaped, is of Mesozoic age (see Chapter 6).

The topography of orogenic belts can also be construed as implying increased relief amplitude. Upland crests have been weathered and eroded much more slowly than have the valley floors in the same locality. The general argument is that ridges and ranges shed water, the principal agent of weathering and erosion, whereas valleys are receptacles for runoff and seepage. Though it is difficult to identify specific evidence that crestal areas have been stable, in the Flinders Ranges the Woodard Surface provides a suggestive benchmark. It has been exhumed and is quite extensively preserved in the northern part of the upland. The overlying Cretaceous strata and Bopeechee regolith have been stripped but the re-exposed surface cut in various Precambrian rocks remains as a prominent summit bevel. Just as the Nott Surface of the Gawler Ranges shows little sign of dissection, so the Woodard retains its essential integrity.

The valleys of orogenic regions also show evidence of episodic exposure. In the Flinders Ranges mesas capped by blocky quartzitic debris (in places ferruginised), underlain by kaolinised bedrock and standing 5–15 m above the adjacent valley floors, are widely distributed (e.g. Figs 4.19c, d) and perched weathered remnants indicate former hill-plain junctions related to the old valley floors. The piedmonts also display flights of covered pediments as for instance in the Brachina regions (Twidale 1981b; Bourne and Twidale 1998). South of Hawker an extensive gravel-capped remnant of the old valley floor is preserved in the headwater valley of the Kanyaka Creek and in the lower Mt Arden Creek valley the extensive old valley floor included a sub-Eocene planation surface and silcreted surfaces. The valley floors were etched out, probably beginning in the Oligocene.

The valleys and piedmonts of the Macdonnell Ranges carry similar evidence of episodic deepening of valleys in the form of duricrusted mesas capped by laterite or silcrete, and various gravel-capped terraces (Mabbutt 1966; Woodburne 1967). The ferruginous duricrust is pre-Miocene in age (Woodburne 1967) so that the valley deepenings have occurred in the later Cenozoic.

To the west, in the Hamersley Range, the spectacular inverted valley floors capped by Robe River Pisolite stand 20–80 m above the adjacent plains (Fig. 6.8) and argue a post-Eocene lowering of plains by the local heights of the mesas.

Summary

Thus the field evidence points to episodic exposure of the uplands and to lowerings of plains and valley floors, the latter leading to increased relief amplitude through time. Both cratonic and orogenic terrains carry evidence of increased relief amplitude during the Cenozoic in the fold mountains but

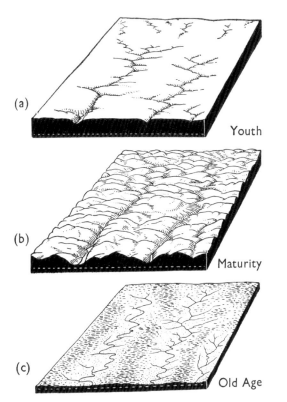

Fig. 11.15 Suggested stages in the development of a peneplain. (After Holmes 1965)

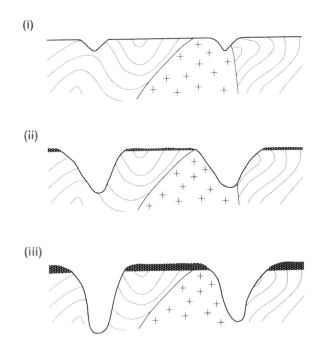

Fig. 11.16 Suggested model of landscape evolution that allows the survival of palaeoforms. Incision is limited to the stream channels and immediately adjacent areas. Reinforcement effects plus the weathering and presence or development of a protective veneer on the divides ensure that this situation is maintained. Thus, palaeosurfaces persist high in the relief.

probably over longer periods on the cratons. These are long-term trends, not phases or stages in a cyclic or sequential development. The Davisian peneplain model includes a youthful phase of stream incision and increasing relief amplitude but gives way to slower incision and lowering of divides (Fig. 11.15). In the scarp-retreat model the initial relief amplitude is maintained with very little diminution until late in the cycle. But, again, the changes occur within a temporally limited sequence of events. The increases in relief amplitude recorded in the old Australian landscapes have continued, and indeed have been reinforced, through successive phases of weathering and erosion. The evidence of weathering beneath present valley floors suggests that the trend continues. Water gravitates to plains and valleys, which are weathered and then eroded. This, taken together with a scarcity of water and low rates of weathering and erosion on the adjacent uplands, has led to long-term increases in relief amplitude. Clearly a new model that accommodates such deep incision, increases in amplitude and the preservation of divides over scores and even a few

hundreds of millions of years is required (Twidale 1991; Fig. 11.16).

It is not suggested that rock surfaces have remained unchanged through time, but rather, and as suggested in the foregoing regional accounts, that gross forms whether isolated hills, plains, or ridge and valley assemblages, have persisted over periods of scores and even a few hundreds of millions of years. Whatever their morphology they remain recognisable as relics of old landscapes. Spatial inequalities in rates of weathering and erosion have not only aided their preservation but have led also to long-term changes in relief amplitude in time.

Concatenation is real. Valleys and plains are low-lying because they are underlain by relatively weak rocks that have been exploited by groundwaters and rivers. Uplands are characterised by resistant rocks which shed waters that flow to the valleys and plains. Once standing in relief, the topographic contrasts caused by various structural factors are enhanced by uneven water distribution and reinforcement effects.

Chapter 12

OLD SURFACES AND GENERAL THEORY

Three aspects of landscape development that are incompatible with conventional geomorphological and geological thinking were identified at the beginning of this analysis: the presence of remnants of very old surfaces, most of them of etch/epigene type, in the contemporary landscape; how and why such remnants have survived; and the atectonic increase in the relief amplitude of some topographic features.

Examples of old land surfaces and evidence for their antiquity are presented in chapters 4 through 9. Even if particular pieces of evidence and argument are challenged or negated, the weight of evidence points to the widespread long-term survival of land surfaces which are of epigene-etch type, and do not owe their conservation to burial. Possible reasons for survival are discussed in Chapter 10. The evidence and arguments for increases in relief amplitude through time are presented in Chapter 11 with reference to specific regions, such areas as Uluru and environs, the Flinders Ranges, the Gawler Ranges, Eyre Peninsula, the Macdonnell Ranges and the Hamersley Range.

Several comments are in order. First, the interpretation of the Australian landscape has been facilitated not only by several factors conducive to the persistence of landforms and surfaces, but also by several that permit the age or age-range of those forms to be determined with reasonable certainty. For, in addition to the ready use of conventional geological and geomorphological methods of dating land surfaces, which has been greatly facilitated by the geological mapping and physical dating of rocks and strata, several particular circumstances have obtained:

- widespread Late Palaeozoic (Permian) glaciation has provided a temporal back marker which, with the exception of some exhumed forms, signals the beginning of the evolution of the landscape as we see it

- various marine transgressions of the Cretaceous, but particularly of the widespread Early Cretaceous (Neocomian–Aptian), have permitted the dating both of surfaces exhumed from beneath related sediments and also, though less certainly, the dating of surfaces thought to have been eroded by rivers graded to associated shorelines

- volcanicity associated with divergent plate margins during the separation of Australia from other Gondwanan elements (Tasmania, Kangaroo Island, southwest of Western Australia), and hotspot activity in parts of eastern Australia at various times in the Cenozoic, have greatly aided the dating of adjacent surfaces.

Even so, though these particular factors have applied, it is in many instances the concatenation of factors and common sense argument that have proved crucial to dating.

All this is not to suggest that all of the Australian continent is very old. The great plains and deserts of central Australia, the coasts, the volcanoes of the South East of South Australia and of western Victoria (Gill 1967, 1976; Sheard 1995), and the Great Barrier Reef are youthful, though the latter is rather older than was thought at one time. But substantial elements of the landscape are ancient.

Second, the persistence of very old etch surfaces implies the former existence of even older surfaces all with regoliths developed that have been stripped to expose the erstwhile weathering fronts as etch surfaces. Supportive evidence is to hand in the Gawler, Flinders and Hamersley ranges. Possible remnants of an equally great age are preserved, for example, in the Gulfs region of South Australia, where relics of a Triassic landscape are preserved.

Third, on the cratons and older orogens, not only have old landform assemblages persisted, but relief amplitude arguably has increased through the later

Mesozoic and the Cenozoic. High plains and ridge crests appear to have been stable and remain essentially untouched. Plains and valley floors, however, have been lowered, in part at least, because of human interference with the environment. The time scale for such changes is much greater than that implied in conventional models of landscape evolution.

Fourth, Australia is not unique in the age of its scenery, for landscapes of considerable antiquity are also recorded in Africa south of the Sahara (Wellington 1937; Dixey 1938; King 1942, 1962; Michel 1978; Partridge and Maud 1987; Partridge 1998). There, in addition to stratigraphic and topographic data, ingenious use has been made of kimberlite pipe morphology (Hawthorne 1975; Partridge 1998) for dating surfaces. In South America the Roraima Plateau is certainly very old (Briceño and Schubert 1990) and palaeosurfaces of putative antiquity have been noted elsewhere in that continent (see King 1956; Schaefer and Dalrymple 1995; Demoulin et al. 2005). Several old palaeosurfaces have been reported or inferred in North America (e.g. Wilson 1903; Rose 1955; Curtis et al. 1958; Poag and Sevon 1989) and some of the older orogens such as the Welsh Massif and the western areas of the Iberian Peninsula in Europe are also suspect in this regard (Jones 1931; Twidale and Vidal Romani 1994).

Nevertheless, these conclusions though germane to old continental regions, to the shields and cratons, and to the older (Palaeozoic and older) orogens, which are relatively quiescent in a tectonic sense, can scarcely be relevant to the analysis of landscapes developed on tectonically active regions such as the Alps and the Himalayas.

In passing, it may be noted that those areas affected by Late Cenozoic ice sheets and glaciers are not necessarily youthful. As has been pointed out (Boyé 1950; Bird 1967; Twidale 1990; Lidmar-Bergström 1997), some glaciers have acted as bulldozers and effectively stripped pre-existing regolith to expose the bedrock surface — the weathering front — beneath. Thus oldlands (Hills 1955; cf. Wilson 1903, Twidale 1999) such as the Laurentian Shield and the Baltic Shield (e.g. Fogelberg 1985) may, in large measure, be etch surfaces with a long and complex chronology. Similarly valleys of the Kosciuszko region and of central Tasmania may also be etch surfaces.

The widespread preservation of old surfaces does not imply that the Australian continent is static. It is changing, and will continue to change both with respect to its global position and its external form (Twidale and Bourne 2004). Nevertheless, several factors have together not only allowed the conservation of substantial areas of ancient Australia, but have also permitted these relic surfaces and forms to be dated. Dorothea Mackellar's (1911) poetic description of Australia as 'a sunburnt country. A land of sweeping plains' reflects reality. But, whereas most of the more extensive plains are youthful, others are of an unimaginable antiquity. This is why the arid continent is also known as the land of sweeping and ancient plains: the continent consists substantially of oldlands which are ancient landmasses consisting of a complex of surfaces of different origins and ages. They are palimpsest surfaces.

In the quotation cited on page 11, it was stated that Australia is ugly. Australia is certainly arid and flat, and it lacks the green and wooded hills, the ubiquitous evidence of human habitation, the intimate ever-varied landscapes so beloved, and rightly so, of many parts of Europe. But beauty is in the eye of the beholder, and regardless of the aesthetic feelings they induce, Australian landscapes are challenging for they are at odds with the received wisdom in several respects. This is no bad thing, for in science all advance begins with awkward evidence and silly questions leading to heretical answers. But new ideas are most frequently regarded as heresy and many are uneasy with ideas with which they are unfamiliar. Either way, the path of the nonconformist is uncomfortable.

The stark forms and ever-changing colours of the Australian scenery have inspired painters and poets, and the demonstrated great antiquity of many Australian landscapes continues to astound and attract those with the knowledge to appreciate what that implies. Many would share the sentiments expressed by the late Sir Walter Crocker (1981, p. 201) when he wrote that: 'Landscape, scenery, has always given … a peculiar degree of enjoyment and refreshment'. Certainly for anyone with a feeling for time and for the evolution of the landscape in which they live the very antiquity of many parts of the Australian landscape must add a sense of wonder to an appreciation of its grandeur.

GLOSSARY

Absolute dating: numerical dating, but not strictly 'absolute' or exact, because the figure given includes a margin of error, which though only a small percentage of the whole, nevertheless indicates a possible limited age-range rather than a specific date.

AFTT or apatite fission track thermochronology: experimental method of determining the rates of denudation. Nuclear decay of ^{238}U creates lines (tracks) of radiation (fission) damage to the crystal in which the uranium occurs. These fission tracks seal or anneal at high temperatures. However, at low temperatures, for example, when erosion brings the crystal and rock near to the land surface, a cooling surface, the fission tracks persist. The number of tracks increases with age and the fission track age is determined by the number of tracks per unit area. This indicates when the rock and mineral cooled below the annealing temperature. Making certain assumptions about the local geothermal gradient, this allows rates of uplift to be estim-ated. Given the volume of debris evacuated in time X, denudation rates can also be calculated. As with cosmogenic nuclide dating, there are many variables and potential difficulties (e.g. Goudie 1981, p. 293; also Bishop and Goldrick 2000).

Anomalous drainage pattern: drainage that is incompatible with either local structure or slope or both.

Antecedent stream: stream that preceded, and maintained its course through, an uplifted land mass and now flows across an upland and the structural and topographic grain.

Appalachian type: fold mountain region with remnants of a planation surface or surfaces located high in the relief.

Atectonic: non-tectonic, no tectonic influence.

Authigenic: developed in situ.

Backwearing: wearing back of slopes; also known as scarp retreat or recession.

Baselevel: theoretical limit toward which erosion by rivers extends.

Block: (a) craton that has always been exposed, or (b) angular mass of rock with a diameter greater than some 254 mm.

Bluff: scarp, conventionally applied to terrestrial forms, e.g. river bluff, whereas 'cliff' is used of coastal features. But 'cliff' is still frequently applied to inland forms.

Bornhardt: hemispherical or domical hill, usually granitic, but also found in arenaceous rocks and limestone. Some such 'half-oranges' are isolated as inselbergs, but others stand in ordered groups in massifs or complex uplands. Named after the German explorer Wilhelm Bornhardt (e.g. 1900).

Bracketing: procedure by which the age limits of a stratum or surface are derived from the ages of youngest rocks below it and the oldest above.

Breached snout: the nose or snout of a plunging anticline in resistant strata, typically quartzitic, across which a stream has excavated a valley or gorge.

Butte: very small plateau the critical feature being that the maximum diameter of its flat crest is less than its height above the adjacent plain.

Calcrete: calcareous duricrust or carapace; also known as caliche, kunkar, kanker.

Chemical weathering: breakdown of a rock involving alteration of one or more of the contained minerals.

Cliff-foot cave or shelter: elongate hollow or cave located at the base of a hill.

Corestone (or kernel): rounded core or kernel or

mass of fresh rock surviving after subsurface water attack causes preferential wearing of corners and edges of a joint block. In this way cubic shapes are converted to spherical. With the removal of the weathered rock the corestone is exposed and becomes a boulder.

Cosmogenic nuclide (radionuclide): neutrons such as ^{10}Be, ^{26}Al and ^{36}Cl are produced high in the atmosphere under cosmic ray bombardment. They settle on and in the surface and near-surface rocks. The rate of accumulation is known so that the concentration of such nuclides is a measure of the age of exposure of the surface and indicates rates of erosion for the period since exposure. Because of the short half-lives of the elements involved, applications of the method are limited to the recent past. There are other theoretical and methodological problems (Sharp and Birman 1963; Phillips et al. 1990; Watchman and Twidale 2002) but in ideal circumstances (e.g. a fresh fault scarp) the method is productive.

Craton: shield area with remnants of old orogens preserved within the outcrop of deformed crystalline rocks; see also Block.

Downwearing: erosional lowering of a rock mass.

Duricrust: hard crust or carapace of a particular mineral composition developed at or near the surface of the regolith and concentrated in a specific horizon by pedogenic processes. Duricrusts may be rich in iron oxides (laterite, ferricrete) silica, either crystalline or opaline (silcrete), gypsum (gypcrete) or calcium carbonate (calcrete).

Epigene, or subaerial: at the surface.

Erosion: wearing away or lowering of the surface, under gravity, by rivers, glaciers, waves or the wind.

Erosion cycle: sequence of events during which a planate surface is uplifted and then reduced to a lower surface of low relief similar to that at which the sequence started. Cyclic because the end product is similar to the original. A misnomer because more than erosion is involved.

Erosional offloading: decrease in lithostatic pressure in rocks resulting from decreased load consequent on erosion.

Erosional surface: surface shaped by erosional processes, conventionally one of low relief. As more than erosion is involved in shaping the surface (for instance, weathering, possibly mass movements of material) 'planation surface' is preferable.

Etch: to gnaw or eat into chemically.

Etch form: bedrock surface shaped by etching; see also two-stage form.

Etch plain: surface of low relief initiated by water weathering beneath the surface and exposed when the weathered mantle or regolith has been stripped away.

Etch surface: surface shaped by etching.

Exhumed surface: surface that has been buried and then re-exposed or resurrected.

Fault: fracture along which displacement has taken place and can be demonstrated. cf. Joint.

Fault scarp: exposed fault plane; a tectonic form.

Fault-line scarp: erosional scarp caused by differential weathering and erosion of contrasted rock types brought into juxtaposition by faulting: a structural form.

Ferricrete: iron-rich duricrust. Differs from a laterite in that the latter is part of a weathered profile with various horizons, whereas a ferricrete is any iron-rich encrustation.

Fission-track: see AFTT.

Flared slope: concavity cut in rock, commonly at the base of a hill (but also found on higher slopes) and on boulders and around armchair-shaped hollows.

Geomorphology: science of landforms, concerned with the understanding and explanation of the origin (where, why and when?) of scenery or landscapes, whereas physiography implies a description of topography.

Gondwana: literally, the land of the Gonds, a tribe of peninsular India. The name given by Wegener (1924) to indicate the supercontinent which 1100–2000 million years ago comprised what are now the southern continents plus peninsular India.

Groundwater: that part of underground water that is in the zone of saturation; also known as phreatic water, in contrast to vadose (or 'wandering') waters that are in the near surface zone of aeration and which migrate to the water table and the phreatic zone beneath it. Groundwaters commonly occur to depths of a kilometre but have been found at ten times that depth. 'Shallow' groundwaters are those within 700–800 m of the surface.

Grus (or gruss): literally, German for fine gravel, but used in the geological literature for a disintegrated and possibly partly altered granite. Typical grus, or soil derived from granite, consists of clay with fragments of quartz and feldspar.

Headward erosion: recession of head of stream above source; also known as regressive erosion.

High plain: surface of low relief located high in the landscape but merging with adjacent lowlands via gentle slopes; cf. Plateau.

Hotspot volcanicity: volcanic activity associated with mantle plumes many of which develop not at or near plate junctions but distant from them.

Hypothesis of Unequal Activity: suggestion that rates of weathering and erosion are not the same over the entire land surface; in particular, that whereas kinetic energy generated by rivers may cause rapid incision in and near the stream channel, agencies active on the intersecting divides or watersheds are much less effective.

Inlier: outcrop of older rocks surrounded by younger; cf. Outlier.

Inselberg: isolated steep-sided hill or mountain. German *Insel* = island, *Berg* = mountain, hence island mountain, or a rocky hill that looks like an island rising out of the sea. 'Island mount' or 'island mountain' was the name used to describe such hills by early English-speaking explorers.

Inselberg landscape: landscape consisting of extensive plains interrupted by a few isolated steep-sided hills or inselbergs.

Inversion of relief: landscape in which structural highs (anticlines, domes) are preferentially weathered and eroded to form plains, and where conversely lows (synclines, basins) come to stand high in the relief.

Isostasy: concept of equal standing implying that volume times density is a constant. Thus high mountains are underlain by less mass, plains by denser but less voluminous materials.

Isostatic adjustment: subsidence or uplift as a result of deposition or erosion of rock, inundation or withdrawal of sea, waxing or waning of ice sheet; even the construction and flooding of a major reservoir.

Joint: fracture along which there has been no demonstrable displacement.

Laterite: weathered mantle consisting of a sandy upper zone or horizon overlying an iron-rich layer containing small spheres or pisoliths of iron oxide (commonly haematite, goethite), which in turn overlies a bleached (white, but frequently mottled) clay-rich (kaolinised) zone. This merges with the fresh bedrock. This ferruginous duricrust takes its name from the Latin *later* = a brick, because in peninsular India, where it was first noted by European travellers and surveyors, the material is readily dug out and shaped with a spade or other sharp-edged tool when wet, but hardens irreversibly on drying; and it was, and is, widely used as a building material.

Law of superposition: in a normal (i.e. undisturbed) sequence of sedimentary strata age increases with depth below the surface.

Lineament: straight or gently arcuate structural feature which is several scores of kilometres in length and which finds expression in the landscape.

Lithostatic pressure: vertical and lateral pressure exerted by the weight of overlying rocks.

Long-term landscape evolution: development over a long period. In Europe (though not by all workers) a surface dating from the later Tertiary is regarded as old. In the southern hemisphere especially (and increasingly, also in North America) Mesozoic surfaces are accepted as representing long-term events.

Lowering of slope: wearing down, downwearing.

Mesa: small plateau, i.e. one of limited lateral extent; cf. Butte.

Mohorovicic discontinuity (Moho): boundary between Earth's crust and mantle; according to Skobelin (1992), the primordial Earth's surface.

Morphostratigraphic marker: specific stratum or pedogenic horizon that can be traced and correlated over considerable lateral distances.

Morphotectonics: study of the Earth's major relief features, particularly those at regional or continental scale related to tectonics or structure.

Multicyclic landscape: landscape in which remnants of planate surfaces standing at various elevations in the landscape suggest development in several phases or cycles of weathering and erosion.

Neotectonic: tectonic movements of post-Miocene age (i.e. less than 5 million years old).

Oldland: palimpsest surface comprising elements of various origins and ages.

Orogen: linear or arcuate belt of rocks that has been deformed. Dissection typically has produced ridge and valley topography, though in Appalachian or older type orogens remnants of planation surfaces are preserved high in the relief.

Orthogonal joint system: system of three sets of joints disposed roughly at right angles to each other, subdividing the rock mass into cubic or quadrangular blocks.

Outlier: isolated outcrop of younger rocks surrounded by older; cf. Inlier.

Palaeochannel: old river channel. Latin *palaeo* = old.

Palaeodrainage: old river system.

Palaeomagnetism: study of the magnetic fields of past ages.

Palaeosurface: old surface.

Palimpsest (surface): surface shaped by various agencies at various times.

Pangaea: literally, 'all Earth', the super-supercontinent comprising Laurasia, Gondwana and the shallow Tethyan sea that existed between about 300 and 200 million years ago.

Pediment: smooth, gently sloping plain developed in the piedmont and meeting the backing scarp in a sharp break of slope or piedmont angle (nick). Covered pediments carry a veneer of coarse introduced alluvial debris; mantled pediments a regolith of coarse sand and wash; while in rock pediments or rock platforms country rock is exposed over most of the surface.

Peneplain: Latin *pene* = almost; hence peneplain, almost a plain. Rolling or undulating surface of low relief that is still slowly evolving.

Peneplanation: processes of weathering, wash and stream erosion responsible for the formation of a peneplain.

Permeability: measure of the ease with which liquids pass through a rock mass.

Perviousness: measure of the ease with which liquids pass through a rock mass by way of fractures.

Piedmont angle, or piedmont nick: abrupt change of slope between scarp and pediment.

Piedmont zone: area at the base of a range of upland; cf. Scarp-foot zone.

Planation surface: erosional surface of low relief.

Plateau: high plain bounded by precipitous slopes or bluffs.

Plate tectonics: the Earth's crust is subdivided into lithospheric plates which through time have migrated laterally across the surface of the globe. The present configuration of plates is the result of a break-up of Pangaea about 200 million years ago and subsequent lateral motions of the plates. Friction and distortion at plate boundaries (junctions, sutures) is a major cause of earthquakes.

Platform: (a) region of essentially undisturbed sediments underlain by basement rocks, or (b) planate bedrock surface, usually of limited extent and of erosional origin. (cf. terrace, a planate surface, usually of limited areal extent, of depositional origin; bench, a planate surface of structural origin, e.g. one coincident with an exposed bedding plane;

and ledge, a bench in a coastal setting.)

Positive feedback: see Reinforcement effect.

Principle of topographic position: in a tectonically undisturbed landscape (and with the exception of exhumed forms, and more rarely, certain steep slope elements) the lower a surface stands in the topography the younger it is.

Recurrent tectonics: repeated dislocations along the same structural line; also known as resurgent tectonics.

Regolith: mantle of weathered rock plus any transported material covering the underlying fresh rock; see Saprolite, saprolith.

Regressive stream erosion: headward erosion of stream.

Reinforcement effect, or positive feedback mechanism: self-perpetuating and self-augmenting or enhancing mechanisms. In their development, many landforms involve reinforcement effects. Take a bornhardt: once upstanding it sheds water to the adjacent plains or valleys. It remains comparatively dry and so is weathered and eroded only very slowly. The plains, on the other hand, receive more water and are weathered and eroded. So the hills become higher, stay drier, and persist, whereas the plains are lower and tend to become still lower.

Relative dating: comparative age deduced from location in landscape or according to relationships of strata and other rock formations (see Principle of topographic position, and Law of superposition).

Relief inversion: an originally low point in the topography now stands relatively high, or a high area becomes relatively low.

Rodinia: super-supercontinent that existed some 1200–900 million years ago.

Saprolite, saprolith: refers to a mantle of chemically weathered rock; see Regolith.

Scarp-foot depression: linear depression at the base of slope caused by concentrated (chemical) weathering beneath the land surface.

Scarp-foot zone: zone immediately at the base of the scarp, as opposed to the piedmont zone that is rather broader.

Scarp retreat, or recession: backwearing of slope with maintenance of similar form and inclination throughout.

Sheet structure: slab, about one half metre or more thick, defined by sheet fractures or arcuate (usually arcuate-upward) fractures. Commonly attributed to pressure release consequent on erosional offloading, but there is considerable evidence that sheet fractures and structures are associated with compressional stress.

Shield: ancient nucleus of a continent consisting of deformed crystalline rocks.

Silcrete: duricrust rich in silica, commonly consisting of larger fragments set in a fine matrix, which is either crystalline or amorphous. Occurs as sheets in valley floors or skins on blocks and boulders.

Slope decline, or lowering: wearing down of slopes.

Slope retreat: backwearing.

Stepped inselberg, or bornhardt: hill, the slopes of which display steep sectors, steps or risers, separated by level areas, or treads. The steps may be flared, due to repeated alternations of subsurface weathering and stripping of the regolith (grus) to expose the flared slopes and platforms.

Stepped landscape: landscape that consists of flattish areas separated by steep slopes or scarps.

Stratigraphy: study of the characteristics, structures and ages of strata.

Stream persistence: capacity of a stream to maintain its course through resistant structures.

Structure (*sensu lato* or in the broad sense): any crustal characteristic that influences the shape of the land surface. Active crustal effects such as folding or faulting are tectonic, e.g. a fault scarp. The term structure (*sensu stricto* or in the narrow sense) implies passive crustal influences, such as joints, which are exploited by external agencies giving rise to differential weathering and erosion.

Survival / persistence / conservation: continued existence of a form or surface through long eons of time.

Tectonism: any crustal activity such as faulting, folding or volcanicity that affects the form of the Earth's surface.

Transverse drainage: streams that run across structural lines or trends.

Two-stage form: form that has evolved in two stages, the first being initiation by subsurface weathering, the second the erosion of the regolith so formed and the exposure of the weathering front as an etch or two-stage form. The weathering front, and hence the resultant plain, may be regular and smooth — an etch plain; or irregular with projecting hills — an inselberg landscape.

Unconformity: discontinuity in a rock sequence indicative of a break in deposition, and by inference an hiatus or break in time.

Underprinting: impression from below of older structures on an overlying sequence, and hence on weathering and erosion of the exposed younger beds.

Unequal activity: differential lowering of the surface owing to the concentration or erosion in and near stream channels. Also, and implicitly, the preservation of divides.

Valley impression: incision and maintenance of a valley by a stream imposed on resistant formations.

Water table: level of free-standing water in fissures and pores at the top of the saturated (phreatic) groundwater zone.

Weathered mantle: layer of weathered rock, the regolith.

Weathering front: lower limit of effective weathering, the junction between regolith and fresh rock. The front advances downwards. Thus the initial stages of weathering are seen near the front, and the higher in the regolith, the closer to the surface, the more advanced the weathering.

Weathering: breakdown or alteration of rocks as a result of their reaction with water (meteoric, groundwaters) or the air, and the chemicals and biota carried in these fluids. Weathering processes are mechanical, chemical or biotic, though several processes commonly combine to bring about rock disintegration and decay.

REFERENCES

Ager D. 1993. *The New Catastrophism*. Cambridge University Press, Cambridge, 231 p.

Alexander L.T., Cady J.G. 1962. Genesis and hardening of laterite in soils. *United States Department of Agriculture Technical Bulletin* 1282, 90 p.

Allen S.R., Simpson C.J., McPhie J., Daly S.J. 2003. Stratigraphy, distribution and geochemistry of widespread felsic volcanic units in the Mesoproterozoic Gawler Range Volcanics, South Australia. *Australian Journal of Earth Sciences* 50, 97–112.

Alley N.F. 1973. Landsurface development in the Mid-North of South Australia. *Transactions of the Royal Society of South Australia* 97, 1–17.

Alley N.F., Lemon N.M. 1988. Evidence of earliest (Neocomian) marine influence, northern Flinders Ranges. *Geological Survey of South Australia Quarterly Notes* 106, 2–7.

Almeida F.F.M. 1953. Botucatú, a Triassic desert of South America. *XIX International Geological Congress, Algiers (1952)* 7, 9–24.

Ashley G.H. 1931. Our youthful scenery. *Geological Society of America Bulletin* 42, 537–546.

Babington B. 1821. Remarks on the geology of the country between Tellicherry and Madras. *Transactions of the Geological Society of London* 5, 328–339.

Bain A.D.N. 1923. The formation of inselberge. *Geological Magazine* 60, 97–107.

Bagas L. 1988. Geology of Kings Canyon National Park. *Northern Territory Geological Survey Department of Mines and Energy Report* 4, 21 p.

Baker V.R. 1973. Paleohydrology and sedimentology of Lake Missoula flooding in eastern Washington. *Geological Society of America Special Paper* 144, 79 p.

Baragwanath W. 1925. The Aberfeldy district, Gippsland. *Geological Survey of Victoria Memoirs* 15, 45 p.

Bascom F. 1921. Cycles of erosion in the piedmont province of Pennsylvania. *Journal of Geology* 29, 540–559.

Behrmann W. 1919. Der Vergang der Selbstverstärkung. *Gesellschaft für Erdkunde zu Berlin*, 153–157.

Belton D.X., Brown R.W., Kohn B.P., Fink D., Farley K.A. 2004. Quantitative resolution of the debate over antiquity of the central Australian landscape: implications for the tectonic and geomorphic stability of cratonic interiors. *Earth and Planetary Science Letters* 219, 21–34.

Benbow M.C. 1990. Tertiary coastal dunes of the Eucla Basin, Australia. *Geomorphology* 3, 9–29.

Benbow M.C., Lindsay J.M., Alley N.F. 1995a. Eucla Basin and palaeodrainage, pp. 178–186 *in* Drexel J.F., Preiss W.V. (editors) The Geology of South Australia. Volume 2, The Phanerozoic. *Geological Survey of South Australia Bulletin* 54, Adelaide, 347 p.

Benbow M.C., Alley N.F., Callen R.A., Greenwood D.R. 1995b. Geological history and palaeoclimate, pp. 208–217 *in* Drexel J.F., Preiss W.V. (editors) The Geology of South Australia. Volume 2, The Phanerozoic. *Geological Survey of South Australia Bulletin* 54, Adelaide, 347 p.

Benson W.N. 1909. Petrographical notes on certain Pre-Cambrian rocks of the Mount Lofty Ranges with special reference to the geology of the Houghton district. *Transactions of the Royal Society of South Australia* 33, 101–140.

Benson W.N. 1911. A note descriptive of a stereogram of the Mt Lofty Ranges, South Australia. *Transactions of the Royal Society of South Australia* 35, 108–111.

Bierman P.R., Caffee M. 2002. Cosmogenic exposure and erosion history of Australian bedrock forms. *Geological Society of America Bulletin* 114, 787–803.

Binks P.J., Hooper G.J. 1984. Uranium in Tertiary palaeochannels, 'West Coast Area', South Australia. *Proceedings of the Australasian Institute of Mining and Metallurgy* 289, 271–275.

Bird J.B. 1967. *The Physiography of Arctic Canada*. The Johns Hopkins Press, Baltimore, Maryland, 336 p.

Bird M.L., Chivas A.R. 1988. Oxygen-isotope dating of the Australian regolith. *Nature* 331, 513–516.

Bird M.L., Chivas A.R. 1989. A stable-isotope study of laterite bauxites. *Geochimica et Cosmochimica Acta* 53, 3239–3256.

Birkenhauer J. 1991. The Great Escarpment of southern Africa and its coastal forelands: a re-appraisal. *Münchener Geographische Abhandlungen, Reihe B* 11, 419 p.

Bishop P. 1995. Drainage rearrangement by river capture, beheading and diversion. *Progress in Physical Geography* 19, 449–473.

Bishop P., Goldrick G. 2000. Geomorphological evolution of the East Australian continental margin, pp. 226–254 *in* Summerfield M.A. (editor) *Geomorphology and Global Tectonics*. John Wiley and Sons, Chichester, 367 p.

Bishop P., Young R.W. 1980. Discussion: On the Cainozoic uplift of the southeastern Australian highland. *Journal of the Geological Society of Australia* 27, 117–119.

Bliss Knopf E. 1924. Correlation of residual erosion surfaces in the eastern Appalachians. *Geological Society of America Bulletin* 35, 633–668.

Blissett A.H., Creaser R.A., Daly S.J., Flint R.B., Parker, A.J. 1993. Gawler Range Volcanics, pp.107–124 *in* Drexel J.F., Preiss W.V., Parker A.J. (editors) The Geology of South Australia. Volume 1, The Precambrian. *Geological Survey of South Australia Bulletin* 54, Adelaide, 242 p.

Bloomfield C. 1957. The possible significance of polyphenols in soil formation. *Journal of the Science of Food and Agriculture* 8, 389–392.

BMR Palaeogeographic Group 1992. *Australia: Evolution of a Continent.* Australian Government Publishing Service, Commonwealth of Australia, Canberra, 96 p.

Bornhardt, W. 1900. *Zur Oberflachungestaltung und Geologie Deutsch Ostafrikas*. Reimer, Berlin, 595 p.

Bourman R.P. 1989. 'Investigations of ferricretes and weathered zones in parts of southern and southeastern Australia: a reassessment of the "laterite" concept.' Unpublished MSc thesis, University of Adelaide, Adelaide, 495 p.

Bourman R.P. 1995. A review of laterite studies in southern South Australia. *Transactions of the Royal Society of South Australia* 119, 1–28.

Bourman R.P., Lindsay J.M. 1989. Timing, extent and character of faulting on the eastern margin of the Mt Lofty Ranges, South Australia. *Transactions of the Royal Society of South Australia* 113, 63–67.

Bourne J.A., Twidale C.R. 1998. Pediments and alluvial fans: genesis and relationships in the western piedmont of the Flinders Ranges, South Australia. *Australian Journal of Earth Sciences* 45, 123–135.

Bourne J.A., Twidale C.R. 2000. Stepped inselbergs and their significance for general theories of landscape development. *South African Journal of Geology* 103, 105–119.

Bourne J.A., Twidale C.R. 2002. Morphology and origin of three bornhardt inselbergs near Lake Johnston, Dundas Shire, Western Australia. *Journal of the Royal Society of Western Australia* 85, 83–102.

Bourne J.A., Twidale C.R. 2003. Geomorphological development of the Baxter Hills, a conglomeratic upland near Iron Knob, South Australia. *Zeitschrift für Geomorphologie* 47, 351–371.

Bourne J.A., Twidale C.R. 2005. Penecontemporary tectonic forms in basement areas: evidence derived from quarry exposures on northwestern Eyre Peninsula, South Australia. *Geodinamica Acta* 18, 101–113.

Bourne J.A., Twidale C.R., Smith D.M. 1974. The Corrobinnie Depression, Eyre Peninsula, South Australia. *Transactions of the Royal Society of South Australia* 98, 139–152.

Bowman J.R. 1992. The 1988 Tennant Creek, Northern Territory, earthquakes: a synthesis. *Australian Journal of Earth Sciences* 39, 651–669.

Boyd R. 1960. *The Australian Ugliness*. Penguin, Ringwood, Victoria, 256 p.

Boyé M. 1950. *Glaciaire et Périglaciaire de l'Ata Sund, nord-oriental Groenland.* Hermann, Paris, 176 p.

Brasier M.D., Green O.R., Jephcoat A.P., Kleppe A.K., Van Krankendonk M.J., Lindsay J.F., Steel A., Grassineau N.V. 2002. Questioning the evidence for Earth's oldest fossils. *Nature* 416, 76–81.

Bremer H. 1983. Albrecht Penck (1858–1945) and Walter Penck (1888–1923), two German geomorphologists. *Zeitschrift für Geomorphologie* 27, 129–138.

Briceño, H.O., Schubert, C., 1990. Geomorphology of the Gran Sabana, Guyana Shield, southeastern Venezuela. *Geomorphology* 3, 125–141.

Brock E.J., Twidale C.R. 1984. J.T. Jutson's contributions to geomorphological thought. *Australian Journal of Earth Sciences* 31, 107–121.

Brown D.A., Campbell K.S.W., Crook K.A.W. 1968. *The Geological Evolution of Australia and New Zealand.* Pergamon, Oxford, 409 p.

Brown E.H. 1980. Historical geomorphology: principles and practices. *Zeitschrift für Geomorphologie Supplementband* 36, 9–15.

Brown C.M. 1983. Discussion: A Cainozoic history of Australia's Southeast Highlands. *Journal of the Geological Society of Australia* 28, 483–486.

Browne W.R. 1964. Grey billy and the age of tor topography in Monaro. *Proceedings of the Linnaean Society of New South Wales* 84, 322–325.

Bryan K. 1940. Gully gravure: a method of slope retreat. *Journal of Geomorphology* 3, 89–107.

Buchanan F. 1807. *A Journey from Madras Through the Countries of Mysore, Canara and Malabar.* East India Company, London, Volume 2, pp. 436–460.

Campana B. 1958a. The Mt Lofty–Olary region and Kangaroo Island, pp. 3–27 *in* Glaessner M.F., Parkin L.W. (editors) *The Geology of South Australia.* Melbourne University Press/Geological Society of Australia, Melbourne, 163 p.

Campana B. 1958b. The Flinders Ranges, pp. 28–45 *in* Glaessner M.F., Parkin L.W. (editors) *The Geology of South Australia.* Melbourne University Press/Geological Society of Australia, Melbourne, 163 p.

Campbell E.M., Twidale C.R. 1991a. The evolution of bornhardts in silicic volcanic rocks in the Gawler Ranges, South Australia. *Australian Journal of Earth Sciences* 38, 79–93.

Campbell E.M., Twidale C.R. 1991b. Relationship of residual hills and sheet fractures in the Gawler Ranges and environs, South Australia. *Transactions of the Royal Society of South Australia* 115, 53–66.

Carter E.K. (compiler) 1959. Westmoreland — 4-mile Geological Series. Sheet E/54-5, Australian National Grid. *Bureau of Mineral Resources, Geology and Geophysics, Explanatory Notes* 14, 8 p.

Carter E.K., Öpik A.A. 1959. *Geological Map of Northwestern Queensland.* Scale 10 miles to 1 inch. Bureau of Mineral Resources, Geology and Geophysics, Canberra.

Carter E.K., Öpik A.A. 1961. Lawn Hill — 4-mile Geological Series. Sheet E/54-9, Australian National Grid. *Bureau of Mineral Resources, Geology and Geophysics, Explanatory Notes* 21, 17 p.

Christian C.S. 1952. Regional land surveys. *Journal of the Australian Institute of Agricultural Science* 18, 140–146.

Christian C.S., Stewart G.A. 1953. General report on survey of Katherine–Darwin region 1946. *CSIRO Australia Land Research Series* 1, 24 p.

Clarke J.D.A. 1994a. Geomorphology of the Kambalda region, Western Australia. *Australian Journal of Earth Sciences* 41, 229–239.

Clarke J.D.A. 1994b. Lake Lefroy, a palaeodrainage playa in Western Australia. *Australian Journal of Earth Sciences* 41, 417–427.

Commander D.P. (compiler) 1989. *Hydrogeological Map of Western Australia.* Scale 1:2,500,000. Geological Survey of Western Australia, Perth.

Craft F.A. 1932. The physiography of the Shoalhaven Valley. *Proceedings of the Linnaean Society of New South Wales* 57, 245–260.

Craft F.A. 1933. Surface history of the Monaro. *Proceedings of the Linnaean Society of New South Wales* 58, 229–244.

Crick F. 1988. *What Mad Pursuit.* Basic Books, New York, 182 p.

Crickmay C.H. 1932. The significance of the physiography of the Cypress Hills. *Canadian Field Naturalist* 46, 185–186.

Crickmay C.H. 1933. The later stages of the cycle of erosion. Some weaknesses in the theory of the cycle of erosion. *Geological Magazine* LXX, 337–347.

Crickmay C.H. 1976. The hypothesis of unequal activity, pp. 103–109 *in* Melhorn W.N., Flemal R.C. (editors) *Theories of Landform Development.* State University of New York, Binghamton, New York, 306 p.

Crocker W. 1981. *Travelling Back: The Memoirs of Sir Walter Crocker.* Macmillan, Melbourne, 222 p.

Crohn P.W. 1979. Discussion: On the Cainozoic uplift of the southeastern Australian highland. *Journal of the Geological Society of Australia* 26, 318.

Crook K.A.W., Cook P.J. 1966. Gosses Bluff – diapir,

cryptovolcanic structure or astrobleme. *Journal of the Geological Society of Australia* 13, 495–516.

Curtis G.H., Evernden J.F., Lipson J. 1958. Age determination of some granitic rocks in California by the potassium-argon method. *California Division of Mines Special Report* 54, 16 p.

Daily B., Twidale C.R., Milnes A.R. 1974. The age of the lateritized summit surface on Kangaroo Island and adjacent areas of South Australia. *Journal of the Geological Society of Australia* 21, 387–392.

Daily B., Milnes A.R., Twidale C.R, Bourne J.A. 1979. Geology and geomorphology, pp. 1–38 *in* Tyler M.J., Twidale C.R., Ling J.K. (editors) *Natural History of Kangaroo Island.* Royal Society of South Australia, Adelaide, 184 p.

Dalrymple G.B. 1991. *The Age of the Earth.* Stanford University Press, Stanford, 474 p.

Daniels J.L. 1975. Bresnahan and Mount Minnie basins, pp. 143–147 *in* Geology of Western Australia. *Geological Survey of Western Australian Memoir* 2, 541 p.

David T.W.E. 1908. Geological notes on Kosciusko, with special reference to evidences of glacial action. *Proceedings of the Linnaean Society of New South Wales* 33, 657–668.

David T.W.E., Howchin W. 1897. Notes on the glacial features of the Inman Valley, Yankalilla, and Cape Jervois district. *Transactions of the Royal Society of South Australia* 21, 61–67.

Davies J.L. 1959. High level erosion surfaces and landscape development in Tasmania *Australian Geographer* 7, 193–203.

Davis S.N. 1964. Silica in streams and groundwater. *American Journal of Science* 262, 870–891.

Davis W.M. 1899. The geographical cycle. *Geographical Journal* 14, 481–504.

Davis W.M. 1909. *Geographical Essays.* (edited D.W. Johnson). Dover, Boston, 777 p.

Davis S.N. 1964. Silica in streams and groundwater. *American Journal of Science* 262, 870–891.

Demoulin A., Zarate M., Rabassa J. 2005. Long-term landscape development: a perspective from the southern Buenos Aires ranges of east central Argentina. *Journal of South American Earth Sciences* 19, 193–204.

Derruau M. 1965. *Précis de Géomorphologie.* Masson, Paris, 415 p.

Dixey F. 1938. Some observations on the physiographical development of central and southern Africa. *Transactions of the Geological Society of South Africa* 41, 113–170.

Dixey F. 1942. Erosion cycles in central and southern Africa. *Transactions of the Geological Society of South Africa* 45, 151–167.

Douglas I. 1978. Denudation of silicate rocks in the humid

tropics, pp. 216–237 *in* Davies J.L., Williams M.A.J. (editors) *Landform Evolution in Australasia.* Australian National University Press, Canberra, 376 p.

Dunn E.J. 1908. The Buffalo Mountains. *Memoirs of the Geological Survey of Victoria* 6, 11 p.

Dunne T., Aubry B.F. 1986. Evaluation of Horton's theory of sheetwash and rill erosion on the basis of field experiments, pp. 31–53 *in* Abrahams A.D. (editor) *Hillslope Processes.* Allen and Unwin, Boston, 416 p.

Elliott C.I. 1994. 'Australian Lineament Tectonics, with an emphasis on northwestern Australia.' Unpublished PhD thesis, University of Melbourne, Melbourne, 262 pp.

Eyre E.J. 1845. *Journals of Expeditions of Discovery into Central Australia and Overland from Adelaide to King George's Sound, in the Years 1840–41.* T. and W. Boone, London, 2 volumes. [Note that Eyre included diary entries for 1839, when he explored parts of Eyre Peninsula, in this account.]

Falconer J.D. 1911. *The Geology and Geography of Northern Nigeria.* Macmillan, London, 295 p.

Fay M.F., Lledo M.D., Richardson J.E., Rye B.L., Hopper S.D. 2001. Molecular data confirm the affinities of the south-west Australian endemic *Granitites* with *Alphitonia* (*Rhamnaceae*). *Kew Bulletin* 56, 669–675.

Fenner C. 1930. The major structural and physiographic features of South Australia. *Transactions of the Royal Society of South Australia* 54, 1–36.

Firman J.B. 1974. Structural lineaments in South Australia. *Transactions of the Royal Society of South Australia* 98, 153–171.

Firman J.B. 1983. Silcrete near Chundie Swamps: the stratigraphic setting. *Geological Survey of South Australia Quarterly Geological Notes* 85, 2–5.

Fisher O. 1866. On the disintegration of a chalk cliff. *Geological Magazine* 3, 354–356.

Fleming A., Summerfield M.A., Stone J.D., Fifield L.K., Cresswell R.G. 1999. Denudation rates for the southern Drakensberg escarpment, SE Africa, derived from in-situ produced 36Cl: initial results. *Journal of the Geological Society of London* 156, 209–212.

Flint, R.B. (compiler) 1993, Mesoproterozoic, pp. 106–169 *in* Drexel, J.F., Preiss W.V., Parker A.J. (editors) *The Geology of South Australia. Volume 1. The Precambrian. Geological Survey of South Australia Bulletin* 54, Adelaide, 347 p.

Fogelberg P. (editor) 1985. Preglacial weathering and planation. *Fennia* 163, 283–383.

Frakes L.A. (coordinator: Australian Cretaceous Palaeoenvironments Group) 1987. Australian Cretaceous shorelines, stage by stage. *Palaeogeography, Palaeoclimatology, Palaeoecology* 59, 31–48.

Frakes L.A., Bolton B.R. 1984. Origin of manganese giants: sea-level change and anoxic-oxic history. *Geology* 12, 83–86.

Geological Survey of Western Australia 1975. The Geology of Western Australia. *Geological Survey of Western Australia Memoir* 2, 541 p.

Geological Survey of Western Australia 1990. Geology and Mineral Resources of Western Australia. *Geological Survey of Western Australia Memoir* 3, 827 p.

Giles E. 1889. *Australia Twice Traversed: The Romance of Exploration.* Sampson, Low, Marston, Searle and Rivington, London, 2 volumes.

Gill E.D. 1967. Evolution of the Warrnambool–Port Fairy coast, and the Tower Hill eruption, western Victoria, pp. 341–364 *in* Jennings J.N., Mabbutt J.A. (editors) *Landform Studies From Australia and New Guinea.* Australian National University Press, Canberra, 434 p.

Gill E.D. 1976. Warrnambool–Port Fairy district, pp. 299–304 *in* Douglas J.G., Ferguson J.A. (editors) *Geology of Victoria.* Geological Society of Australia Special Publication 5, Melbourne, 528 p.

Glaessner M.F., Wade M. 1958. The St Vincent Basin, pp. 115–126 *in* Glaessner M.F., Parkin L.W. (editors) *The Geology of South Australia.* Melbourne University Press / Geological Society of Australia, Melbourne, 163 p.

Gordon F.R., Lewis J.D. 1980. The Meckering and Calingiri earthquakes October 1968 and March 1970. *Geological Survey of Western Australia Bulletin* 126, 229 p.

Gosse W.C. 1874. Report and diary of Mr W.C. Gosse's central and western exploring expedition, 1873. *South Australian Parliamentary Papers* 48, 23 p.

Goudie A. 1973. *Duricrusts in Tropical and Subtropical Landscapes.* Clarendon Press, Oxford, 174 p.

Goudie A. (editor) 1981. *Geomorphological Techniques.* George Allen and Unwin, London, 395 p.

Grant C. Kerr 1956. The Adelaide earthquake of 1st March, 1954. *Transactions of the Royal Society of South Australia* 79, 177–185.

Greenhalgh S.A., Love D., Malpas K., McDougall R. 1994. South Australian earthquakes 1980–92. *Australian Journal of Earth Sciences* 41, 483–495.

Gunn P.J., Meixner A.J. 1998. The nature of the basement to the Kimberley Block, Northwestern Australia. *Exploration Geophysics* 29, 506–511.

Hack J.T. 1960. Interpretation of erosional topography in humid temperate regions. *American Journal of Science* 238A, 80–97.

Hack J.T., Goodlett J.C. 1960. Geomorphology and forest ecology of a mountain region in the central Appalachians. *United States Geological Survey Professional Paper* 347, 66 p.

Haines P.W., Bagas L., Wyche S., Simons B., Morris D.G. 1991. *Barrow Creek* SF53-6. *Explanatory Notes.* 1:250,000 Geological Map Series. Northern Territory Geological Survey Department of Mines and Energy, Darwin, 53 p.

Harris W.K. 1970. 'Palynology of Lower Tertiary sediments, south eastern Australia.' Unpublished MSc thesis, University of Adelaide, Adelaide, 181 p.

Harris W.K., Twidale C.R. 1991. Revised age for Ayers Rock and the Olgas. *Transactions of the Royal Society of South Australia* 115, 109.

Hawthorne J.B. 1975. Model of a kimberlite pipe, pp. 1–15 *in* Ahrens L.H., Dawson J.B., Erlank A.J., Duncan A.R. (editors) *Physics and Chemistry of the Earth*. Volume 9. Pergamon, Oxford.

Hays J. 1967. Land surfaces and laterites in the north of the Northern Territory, pp. 182–210 *in* Jennings J.N., Mabbutt J.A. (editors) *Landform Studies from Australia and New Guinea*. Australian National University Press, Canberra, 434 p.

Hess H.H. 1962. History of the ocean basins, pp. 599–620 *in* Engel A.E., James H.L., Leonard B.F. (editors) *Petrologic Studies: A Volume in Honor of A.F. Buddington*. Geological Society of America, New York, 660 p.

Hickman A.H. 1983. Geology of the Pilbara Block and its environs. *Western Australia Geological Survey Bulletin* 127, 268 p.

Hill D. 1989. Edwin Sherbon Hills 1906–1986. *Biographical Memoirs of Fellows of the Royal Society* 33, 291–323.

Hills E.S. 1934. Some fundamental concepts in Victorian physiography. *Proceedings of the Royal Society of Victoria* 47, 158–174.

Hills E.S. 1938. The age and physiographic relationships of the Cainozoic volcanic rocks of Victoria. *Proceedings of the Royal Society of Victoria* 51, 112–139.

Hills E.S. 1940. *Physiography of Victoria*. Whitcombe and Tombs, Melbourne, 292 p.

Hills E.S. 1946. Some aspects of the tectonics of Australia. *Journal and Proceedings of the Royal Society of New South Wales* 79, 67–91.

Hills E.S. 1955. Die Landoberfläche Australiens. *Die Erde* 7, 195–205.

Hills E.S. 1956. A contribution to the morphotectonics of Australia. *Journal of the Geological Society of Australia* 3, 1–15.

Hills E.S. 1961. Morphotectonics and the geomorphological sciences with special reference to Australia. *Quarterly Journal of the Geological Society of London* 117, 77–89.

Hills E. S. 1975. *Physiography of Victoria*. Whitcombe and Tombs, Australia, 373 p.

Hingston F.J. 1962. Activity of polyphenolic constituents of leaves of *Eucalyptus* and other species in complexing and dissolving iron oxide. *Australian Journal of Soil Research* 1, 63–73.

Hobbs W.H. 1904. Lineaments of the Atlantic border region. *Geological Society of America Bulletin* 15, 483–506.

Hobbs W.H. 1911. Repeating patterns in the relief and structure of the land. *Geological Society of America Bulletin* 22, 123–176.

Hocking R.M., Moors H.T., Van de Graaff W.J.E. 1987. Geology of the Carnarvon Basin, Western Australia. *Geological Survey of Western Australia Bulletin* 133, 289 p.

Holmes A. 1918. The Pre-Cambrian and associated rocks of the district of Mozambique. *Quarterly Journal of the Geological Society of London* 74, 31–97.

Holmes A. 1931. Radioactivity and earth movements. *Transactions of the Geological Society of Glasgow* 18, 559–606.

Holmes A. 1965. *Principles of Physical Geology*. Nelson, London, 1288 p.

Hopper S.D., Chappill J.A., Harvey M.S., George A.S. 1996. *Gondwanan Heritage. Past, Present and Future of the Western Australian Biota*. Surry Beatty and Sons, Chipping Norton, NSW, 327 p.

Horton R.E. 1945. Erosional development of streams and their drainage basins. *Geological Society of America Bulletin* 56, 275–370.

Hossfeld P.S. 1926. 'The geology of portions of the counties of Light, Eyre, Sturt and Adelaide.' Unpublished MSc thesis, University of Adelaide, Adelaide, 100 p.

Hossfeld P.S. 1950. The Late Cainozoic history of the south-east of South Australia. *Transactions of the Royal Society of South Australia* 73, 232–278.

Hou B., Frakes L.A., Alley N.F., Clarke J.D.A. 2003. Characteristics and evolution of the Tertiary palaeovalleys in the northwest Gawler Craton, South Australia. *Australian Journal of Earth Sciences* 50, 215–230.

Howchin W. 1895. New facts bearing on the glacial features of Hallett's Cove. *Transactions of the Royal Society of South Australia* 19, 61–69.

Hunt C.W. 1990. *Environment of Violence*. Polar Publishing, Calgary, 199 p.

Hutton J. 1788. Theory of the Earth; or an investigation of the laws observable in the composition, dissolution and restoration of land upon the globe. *Transactions of the Royal Society of Edinburgh* 1, 209–304.

Hutton J. 1795. *Theory of the Earth, with Illustrations*. Cadell, Junior & Davies, London, 2 volumes.

Hutton J.T., Twidale C.R., Milnes A.R., Rosser H. 1972. Composition and genesis of silcretes and silcrete skins from the Beda Valley, southern Arcoona Plateau, South Australia. *Journal of the Geological Society of Australia* 19, 31–39.

Jack R.L. 1931. Report on the geology of the region to the north and northwest of Tarcoola. *Geological Survey of South Australia Bulletin* 15, 31 p.

Jacobson G., Lau J.E. (compilers) 1987. *Hydrology of Australia*. Scale 1:5,000,000. BMR, Canberra.

Jaques A.L., Lewis J.D., Smith C.B. 1986. The kimberlites and lamproites of Western Australia. *Geological Survey of Western Australia Bulletin* 132, 268.

Jaques A.L., Webb A.W., Fanning C.M., Black L.P., Pigeon R.T., Ferguson J., Smith C.B., Gregory G.P. 1984. The age of the diamond bearing pipes and associated leucite lamproites of the West Kimberley region, Western Australia. *Bureau of Mineral Resources Journal of Australian Geology and Geophysics* 9, 1–7.

Jenkin J.J. 1988. Geomorphology, pp. 403–419 *in* Douglas J.G., Ferguson J.A. (editors) *Geology of Victoria.* Geological Society of Australia, Victorian Division, Melbourne, 663 p.

Jennings, J.N. 1972. The age of Canberra landforms. *Journal of the Geological Society of Australia* 19, 371–378.

Jennings J.N. 1979. Arnhem Land: city that never was. *Geographical Magazine* 51, 822–827.

Jerram D.A., Mountney N.P., Howell J.A., Long D., Stollhofen H. 2000. Death of a sand sea: an active aeolian erg systematically buried by the Etendeka flood basalts of NW Namibia. *Journal of the Geological Society of London* 157, 513–516.

Johns R.K. 1958. Sheet 817, zone 5, *Lincoln.* Geological Atlas of South Australia 1 Mile Series. Geological Survey of South Australia, Adelaide.

Johns R.K. 1961. Geology and mineral resources of southern Eyre Peninsula. *Geological Survey of South Australia Bulletin* 37, 102 p.

Johns R.K. 1968. Investigation of lakes Torrens and Gairdner. *Geological Survey of South Australia Report of Investigations* 31, 90 p.

Johns R.K., Hiern M.N., Nixon L.G., Forbes B.G., Olliver J.G. 1981. Sheet SH53-16, *Torrens.* Geological Atlas of South Australia 1:250,000 Series. Geological Survey of South Australia, Adelaide.

Johnson W. 1960. Exploration for coal, Springfield Basin, in the hundred of Cudla-Mudla, Gordon-Cradock district. *Geological Survey of South Australia Report of Investigations* 16, 62 p.

Jones J.G., Veevers, J.J. 1982. A Cainozoic history of Australia's Southeast Highlands. *Journal of the Geological Society of Australia* 29, 1–12.

Jones J.G., Veevers, J.J. 1983a. Mesozoic origins and antecedents of Australia's Eastern Highlands. *Journal of the Geological Society of Australia* 30, 305–322.

Jones J.G., Veevers, J.J. 1983b. Reply: A Cainozoic history of Australia's Southeast Highlands. *Journal of the Geological Society of Australia* 30, 487–488.

Jones O.T. 1931. Some episodes in the geological history of the Bristol Channel region. *Report of the British Association for the Advancement of Science* 57–82.

Jutson J.T. 1914. An outline of the physiographical geology (physiography) of Western Australia. *Geological Survey of Western Australia Bulletin* 61, 240 p.

Jutson J.T. 1934. The physiography (geomorphology) of Western Australia. *Geological Survey of Western Australia Bulletin* 95, 366 p. [Reprinted 1950].

Kahle C.F. 1974. *Plate Tectonics – Assessments and Reassessments.* American Association of Petroleum Geologists, Memoir 23, Tulsa, Oklahoma, 514 p.

Kalb H.F. de 1990. *The Twisted Earth.* Lytel Eorthe Press, Hilo, Hawaii, 156 p.

Kant I. 1791. *Critique of Pure Reason.* (Guyer P., Wood A.W. [transl., editors] 1998) Cambridge University Press, Cambridge, 785 p.

Kennedy W.Q. 1962. Some theoretical factors in geomorphological analysis. *Geological Magazine* 99, 305–312.

Kern A.M., Commander D.P. 1993. Cainozoic stratigraphy in the Roe Palaeodrainage of the Kalgoorlie region, Western Australia. *Geological Survey of Western Australia Report, Professional Papers* 34, 85–95.

Keyser F. de 1964. *Innisfail, Queensland, SE/55-6, 1:250,000 geology sheet and explanatory notes.* Bureau of Mineral Resources, Geology and Geophysics, Canberra, 30 p.

King C.A.M. 1970. Feedback relationships in geomorphology. *Geografiska Annaler* 52A, 147–159.

King L.C. 1942. *South African Scenery.* Oliver and Boyd, Edinburgh, 308 p.

King L.C. 1956. Rift valleys of Brazil. *Transactions of the Geological Society of South Africa* 59, 199–208.

King L.C. 1962. *Morphology of the Earth.* Oliver and Boyd, Edinburgh, 699 p.

Kwitco, G. 1995. Triassic intermontane basins, pp. 98–101 *in* Drexel J.F., Preiss W.V. (editors) The Geology of South Australia. Volume 2, The Phanerozoic. *Geological Survey of South Australia Bulletin* 54, Adelaide, 347 p.

Laeter J.R. de, Trendall A.F. 2002. The oldest rocks: the Western Australian connection. *Proceedings of the Royal Society of Western Australia* 85, 153–160.

Lamplugh G.W. 1902. Calcrete. *Geological Magazine* 9, 575.

Langford-Smith T. (editor) 1978. *Silcrete in Australia.* University of New England Press, Armidale, NSW, 304 p.

Larin V.N. 1993. *Hydridic Earth: The New Geology of our Primordially Hydrogen-rich Planet.* (transl. C.W. Hunt) Polar Publishing, Calgary, 247 p.

Li J.-W., Vasconcelos P. 2002. Cenozoic continental weathering and its implications for the palaeoclimate: evidence from $^{40}Ar/^{39}Ar$ geochronology of supergene K-Mn oxides in Mt Tabor, central Queensland, Australia. *Earth and Planetary Science Letters* 200, 223–239.

Lidmar-Bergström K. 1997. A long-term perspective on glacial erosion. *Earth Surface Processes and Landforms* 23, 297–306.

Linton D.L. 1957. The everlasting hills. *Advancement of Science* 14, 58–67.

Logan J.R. 1851. Notices of the geology of the straits of Singapore. *Quarterly Journal of the Geological Society of London* 7, 310–344.

Loughnan F.C. 1969. *Chemical Weathering of the Silicate Minerals*. Elsevier, New York, 154 p.

Love D.N., Preiss W.V., Belperio A.P. 1995. Seismicity, neotectonics and earthquake risk, pp. 268–273 *in* Drexel J.F., Preiss W.V. (editors) The Geology of South Australia. Volume 2, The Phanerozoic. *Geological Survey of South Australia Bulletin* 54, Adelaide, 347 p.

Lovering T.S. 1959. Significance of accumulator plants in rock weathering. *Geological Society of America Bulletin* 70, 781–800.

Lowry D.C. 1970. Geology of the Western Australian part of the Eucla Basin. *Geological Survey of Western Australia Bulletin* 122, 201 p.

Lowry D.C., Jennings J.N. 1974. The Nullarbor karst, Australia. *Zeitschrift für Geomorphologie* 18, 35–81.

Ludbrook N.H. 1980. *A Guide to the Geology and Mineral Resources of South Australia*. Department of Mines and Energy, South Australia, Adelaide, 230 p.

Mabbutt J.A. 1961a. 'Basal surface' or 'weathering front'. *Proceedings of the Geologists' Association of London* 72, 357–358.

Mabbutt J.A. 1961b. A stripped land surface in Western Australia. *Transactions of the Institute of British Geographers* 29, 101–114.

Mabbutt J.A. 1965. The weathered land surface in central Australia. *Zeitschrift für Geomorphologie* 9, 82–114.

Mabbutt J.A. 1966. Landforms of the western Macdonnell Ranges, pp. 83–119 *in* Dury G.H. (editor) *Essays in Geomorphology*. Heinemann, London, 404 p.

Mackellar D. 1911. 'My Country', first published in the London *Spectator* in 1908 as 'Core of my heart', the poem was revised and republished in its final well-known form in the collection, *Closed Door and Other Verses*. Australian Authors Agency, Melbourne, at p. 70.

Macleod W.M. 1966. The geology and iron deposits of the Hamersley Range area, Western Australia. *Geological Survey of Western Australia Bulletin* 117, 170 p.

Madigan C.T. 1931. The physiography of the western Macdonnell Ranges, central Australia. *Geographical Journal* 78, 417–433.

Madigan C.T. 1932. The geology of the western Macdonnell Ranges, central Australia. *Quarterly Journal of the Geological Society of London* 86, 672–711.

Mahard R.H. 1942. The origin and significance of intrenched meanders. *Journal of Geomorphology* 5, 32–44.

Maignien R. 1966. *Review of Research on Laterites*. Natural Resources Research IV, UNESCO, Paris, 148 p.

Maitland A.G. 1911. The geological features and mineral resources of the Pilbara Goldfield. *Geological Survey of Western Australia Bulletin* 40 (reprint, not circulated, of *Bulletins* 15, 20 and 23, 1904–1909).

McCue K. 1990. Australia's large earthquakes and recent fault scarps. *Journal of Structural Geology* 12, 761–766.

McDougall I., Wellman P. 1976. Potassium-Argon ages for some Australian Mesozoic igneous rocks. *Journal of the Geological Society of Australia* 23, 1–9.

McGowran B., Lindsay J.M., Harris W.K. 1971. Attempted reconciliation of Tertiary biostratigraphic systems, pp. 273–281 *in* Wopfner H., Douglas J.G. (editors) *The Otway Basin of southeastern Australia*. Special Bulletin Geological Surveys of South Australia and Victoria, Melbourne, 464 p.

McNally G.H., Wilson I.R. 1995. Silcretes of the Mirackina Palaeochannel, Arckaringa, South Australia. *AGSO Journal of Australian Geology and Geophysics* 16, 295–301.

Meyerhoff A.A., Meyerhoff H.A. 1974. Tests of plate tectonics, pp. 43–145 *in* Kahle C.F. (editor) *Plate Tetconics: Assessments and Reassessments*. American Association of Petroleum Geologists, Memoir 23, Tulsa, Oklahoma, 514 p.

Michel P. 1978. Cuirasses bauxitiques et ferrugineuses d'Afrique occidentale. Aperçu chronologique. *Travaux et Documents de Géographie Tropicale* 33, 11–32.

Miles K.R. 1952. Geology and underground water resources of the Adelaide Plains area. *Geological Survey of South Australia Bulletin* 27, 257 p.

Miller R.P. 1937. Drainage lines in bas-relief. *The Journal of Geology* 45, 432–438.

Milnes A.R., Hutton J.T. 1983. Calcretes in Australia, pp. 119–162 *in Soils. An Australian Viewpoint*. CSIRO, Melbourne/Academic Press, London, 928 p.

Milton B.E., Twidale C.R. 1977. Structure of the Willochra Basin, southern Flinders Ranges, South Australia. *Transactions of the Royal Society of South Australia* 102, 71–77.

Milton D.J., Sutter J.F. 1987. Revised age for the Gosse's Bluff impact structure, Northern Territory, Australia based on 40Ar/39Ar dating. *Meteoritics* 22, 281–289.

Molina Ballesteros E., Campbell E.M., Bourne J.A., Twidale C.R. 1995. Character and interpretation of the regolith exposed at Point Drummond, west coast of Eyre Peninsula, South Australia. *Transactions of the Royal Society of South Australia* 119, 83–88.

Morley L.W., LaRochelle A. 1964. Palaeomagnetism as a means of dating geological events. *Royal Society of Canada Special Publication* 8, 39–51.

Mory A.J., Beere G.M. 1988. Geology of the onshore Bonaparte and Ord Basins. *Geological Survey of Western Australia Bulletin* 134, 184 p.

Mulder C.A., Whitehead B.R. 1988. Geology of Katherine National Park. *Northern Territory Geological Survey Department of Mines and Energy Report* 3, 31 p.

Nabarro F.R.N. 1967. *Theory of Crystal Dislocations*. Clarendon Press, Oxford, 821 p.

Namier L.B. 1955. *Personalities and Powers*. Hamish Hamilton, London, 157 p.

Needham R.S. 1982. *Alligator, Northern Territory*. 1:100,000 *Geological Map Commentary*. Bureau of Mineral Resources, Geology and Geophysics, Canberra, 27 p.

Northcote K.H. 1946. A fossil soil from Kangaroo Island, South Australia. *Transactions and Papers of the Royal Society of South Australia* 70, 294–296.

Nott J.F. 1994. Long-term landscape evolution in the Darwin region and its implications for the origin of landsurfaces in the north of the Northern Territory. *Australian Journal of Earth Sciences* 41, 407–415.

Nott J.F. 1996. Long-term landscape evolution on Groote Eylandt, Northern Territory. *AGSO Journal of Australian Geology and Geophysics* 16, 303–307.

O'Driscoll E.S.T. 1986. Observations of the lineament-ore relationship. *Philosophical Transactions of the Royal Society of London* Series A, 317, 195–218.

O'Driscoll E.S.T., 1989. Edwin Hills and the lineament-ore relationship, pp. 247–267 *in* LeMaitre, R.W. (editor) *Pathways in Geology. Essays in Honour of Edwin Sherbon Hills*. Hills Memorial Volume Committee/Blackwell, Melbourne, 463 p.

O'Driscoll E.S.T., Campbell I.B. 1997. Mineral deposits related to Australian continental ring and rift structures with some terrestrial and planetary analogies. *Global Tectonics and Metallogeny* 6, 83–101.

Offe L.A., Shaw R.D. 1983. *Alice Springs Region Northern Territory*. 1:100,000 *Geological Map Commentary*. Bureau of Mineral Resources, Geology and Geophysics, Canberra, 22 p.

O'Leary D.W., Friedman J.D., Pohn H.A., 1976. Lineament, linear, lineation: some proposed new standards for old terms. *Geological Society of America Bulletin* 87, 1463–1469.

Ollier C.D. 1982a. The Great Escarpment of eastern Australia: tectonic and geomorphic significance. *Journal of the Geological Society of Australia* 29, 13–23.

Ollier C.D. 1982b. Geomorphology and tectonics of the Dorrigo Plateau, N.S.W. *Journal of the Geological Society of Australia* 29, 431–435.

Ollier C.D., Gaunt G.P.M., Jurkowski I. 1988. The Kimberley Plateau, Western Australia. *Zeitschrift für Geomorphologie* 32, 239–249.

Ollier, C.D., Pain C.F. 1994. Landscape evolution and tectonics in southeastern Australia. *AGSO Journal of Australian Geology and Geophysics* 15, 335–345.

Ollier, C.D., Pain C.F. 1996. Reply: Landscape evolution and tectonics in southeastern Australia. *AGSO Journal of Australian Geology and Geophysics* 16, 325–331.

Öpik A.A. 1958. The geology of the Canberra City District. *Bureau of Mineral Resources Geology and Geophysics Bulletin* 32, 99 p.

Öpik A.A. 1961. The geology and palaeontology of the headwaters of the Burke River, Queensland. *Bureau of Mineral Resources Geology and Geophysics Bulletin* 53, 249 p.

Öpik A.A., Carter E.K., Noakes L.C. 1961. Mount Isa — 4-mile Geological Series. Sheet F/54-1, Australian National Grid. *Bureau of Mineral Resources, Geology and Geophysics, Explanatory Notes* 20, 20 p.

Orth K., Vandenberg A.H.M., Nott R.J., Simons B.A. 1995. Murrindal 1:100,000 Geological Map Report. Department of Energy and Minerals, *Geological Survey of Victoria Report* 100, 237 p.

Osborn G., du Toit C. 1991. Lateral planation of rivers as a geomorphic agent. *Geomorphology* 4, 249–260.

Pain C.F. 1983. Geomorphology of the Barrington Tops area, New South Wales. *Journal of the Geological Society of Australia* 30, 187–194.

Palfreyman W.D. 1984. Guide to the Geology of Australia. *Bureau of Mineral Resources Bulletin* 181, 111 p.

Parker A.J. (compiler) 1993. Geological framework, pp 18–31 *in* Drexel J.F., Preiss W.V., Parker A. J. (editors) The Geology of South Australia. Volume 1. The Precambrian. *Geological Survey of South Australia Bulletin* 54, Adelaide, 242 p.

Parkin, L.W. 1953. The Leigh Creek coalfield. *Geological Survey of South Australia Bulletin* 31, 74 p.

Partridge T.C. 1998. Of diamonds, dinosaurs and diastrophism: 150 million years of landscape evolution in southern Africa. *South African Journal of Geology* 101, 167–184.

Partridge T.C., Maud R.R. 1987. Geomorphic evolution of southern Africa since the Mesozoic. *South African Geological Journal* 90, 179–208.

Paterson S.J. 1970. Geomorphology of the Ord-Victoria area, pp. 83–91 *in* Stewart G.A. (editor) Lands of the Ord–Victoria area, Western Australia and Northern Territory. *CSIRO Land Research Series* 28, 135 p.

Penck W. 1924. *Die Morphologische Analyse*. Engelhorn, Stuttgart, 283 p.

Penck W. 1953. *Morphological Analysis of Land Forms*. (transl. H. Czeck, K.C. Boswell) Macmillan, London.

Perry W.J., Roberts H.G. 1968. Late Precambrian glaciated pavements in the Kimberley region, Western Australia. *Journal of the Geological Society of Australia* 15, 51–56.

Phillips F.M., Zreda M.G., Smith S.S., Elmore D., Kubik P.W., Sharma P. 1990. Cosmogenic Chlorine-36 chronology for glacial deposits at Bloody Canyon, eastern Sierra Nevada. *Science* 248, 1529–1532.

Pickup G., Allen G., Baker V.R. 1988. History, palaeo-channels and palaeofloods of the Finke River, central Australia, pp. 172–200 *in* Warner R.F. (editor) *Fluvial Geomorphology of Australia*. Academic Press, Sydney, 373 p.

Pietsch B.A., Rawlings D.J., Haines P.W., Page M. 1997. *Groote Eylandt Region* SD53-7,8,11,12. *Explanatory Notes*. 1:250,000 Geological Map Series. Northern Territory Geological Survey Department of Mines and Energy, Darwin, 32 p.

Playford P.E., Cockburn A.E., Low G.H. 1976. Geology of the Perth Basin, Western Australia. *Geological Survey of Western Australia Bulletin* 124, 311 p.

Playford P.E., Cope R.N., Cockburn A.E. 1975. Phanerozoic, *in* Geology of Western Australia. *Geological Survey of Western Australia Memoir* 2, 451–457.

Plumb K.A., Gemuts I. 1976. Precambrian geology of the Kimberley region, pp. 6–10 *in* 25th International Geological Congress Excursion Guide 44C.

Plumb K.A., Veevers J.J. 1971. *Cambridge Gulf* SD/52-14 .1:250,000 *Geological Series Explanatory Notes*. Bureau of Mineral Resources Geology and Geophysics, Canberra, 30 p.

Poag C.W., Sevon W.D. 1989. A record of Appalachian denudation in postrift Mesozoic and Cenozoic sedimentary deposits of the U.S. Middle Atlantic continental margin, *in* Gardner T.W., Sevon W.D. (editors) Appalachian Geomorphology. *Geomorphology Special Issue* 2, 119–157.

Preiss W.V. (compiler) 1987. The Adelaide geosyncline. *Geological Survey of South Australia Bulletin* 53, 438 p.

Preiss W.V. 1995. Tectonic evolution of the Mid-North, South Australia, pp. 141–142 *in* Clare Valley Conference, Geological Society of Australia, Specialist Group in Tectonics and Structural Geology, *Abstracts* 40, 185 p.

Price R.C., Gray C.M., Nicholls I.A., Day A. 1988. Cainozoic volcanic rocks, pp. 439–451 in Douglas J.G., Ferguson J.A. (editors) *Geology of Victoria*. Geological Society of Australia, Victorian Division, Melbourne, 663 p.

Quigley M.C., Cupper M.L., Sandiford M. 2006. Quaternary faults of south-central Australia: palaeoseismicity, slip rates and origin. *Australian Journal of Earth Sciences* 53, 285–301.

Ramanaidou R.C., Morris R.C., Horwitz R.C. 2003. Channel iron deposits of the Hamersley Province, Western Australia. *Australian Journal of Earth Sciences* 50, 669–690.

Rasmussen B. 2000. Filamentous microfossils in a 3,235-million-year-old volcanogenic massive sulphide deposit. *Nature* 405, 676–678.

Read H.H. 1957. *The Granite Controversy*. Murby, London, 430 p.

Retz J.F.P. de G. (1613–1679) 1903. *Memoirs of Cardinal de Retz*. Merrill and Baker, New York, 422 p.

Reynolds M. 1953. The Cainozoic succession of Maslin and Aldinga Bays, South Australia. *Transactions of the Royal Society of South Australia* 76, 114–140.

Rice S. 2005. Vilification outs are there for a reason. Academics must speak their minds. *The Australian* 21 September 2005, p. 28.

Rose E.R. 1955. Manicouagan Lake – Mushalagan Lake area, Quebec. Scale 1:253,440. Geologic map with marginal notes. *Geological Survey of Canada, Paper* 55-2.

Russell, G.A. 1935. Crystal growth in solution under local stress. *American Mineralogist* 20, 733–737.

Rütimeyer L. 1769. *Ueber Thal- und See-Bildung. Beitrage zum Verständniss der Oberfläche der Schweize.* Carl Schultze's Universitaetsbuchdruckerei, Basel, 95 p.

Salama R.B. 1997. Geomorphology, geology and palaeohydrology of the broad alluvial valleys of the Salt River System, Western Australia. *Australian Journal of Earth Sciences* 44, 751–765.

Saul J.M. 1976. Circular structures of large scale and great age at the Earth's surface. *Nature* 271, 345–349.

Schaefer C., Dalrymple J. 1995. Landscape evolution in Roraima, North Amazonia: planation, paleosols and paleoclimates. *Zeitschrift für Geomorphologie* 39, 1–28.

Schopf J.W., Packer B.M. 1987. Early Archaean (3.3-billion to 3.5-billion-year-old) microfossils from Warrawoona Group, Australia. *Science* 237, 70–73.

Schumm S.A. 1963. Disparity between present rates of denudation and orogeny. *United States Geological Survey Professional Paper* 454, 13 p.

Selwyn A.R.C. 1860. Geological notes of a journey in South Australia from Cape Jervis to Mount Serle. *South Australian Parliamentary Papers* 20, 15 p.

Sharp R.F., Birman J.H. 1963. Additions to classical sequence of Pleistocene glaciations, Sierra Nevada, California. *Geological Society of America Bulletin* 74, 1079–1086.

Sheard M.J. 1995. Quaternary volcanic activity and volcanic hazards, pp. 264–268 *in* Drexel J.F., Preiss W.V. (editors) The Geology of South Australia. Volume 2. The Phanerozoic. *Geological Survey of South Australia Bulletin* 54, Adelaide, 347 p.

Sheard M.J. 2001. Callabonna 1:250,000 geological map released. *MESA Journal* 21, 27–29.

Sivarajasingham S., Alexander L.T., Cady J.G., Cline M.G. 1962. Laterite. *Advances in Agronomy* 14, 1–60.

Skobelin E.A. 1992. Composition of the upper geospheres and the nature of the 'Moho', pp. 32–42 *in* Hunt C.W. (editor) *Expanding Geospheres. Energy and Mass Transfers from Earth's Interior*. Polar Publishing, Calgary, 421 p.

Skwarko S.K. 1966. Cretaceous stratigraphy and palaeontology of the Northern Territory. *Bureau of Mineral Resources Geology and Geophysics Bulletin* 73, 133 p.

Sprigg R.C. 1945. Some aspects of the geomorphology of portion of the Mount Lofty Ranges. *Transactions of the Royal Society of South Australia* 69, 277–303

Sprigg R.C., Campana B., King D. 1954. Sheet I53-16, Zone 5, *Kingscote*. Geological Atlas of South Australia, 1 Mile Series. Geological Survey of South Australia, Adelaide.

Stephens C.G. 1964. Silcretes of Central Australia. *Nature* 203, 1407.

Stephenson P.J., Griffin T.J., Sutherland F.L. 1980. Cainozoic volcanism in northeastern Australia, pp. 349–374 *in* Henderson R.A., Stephenson P.J. (editors) *The Geology and Geophysics of Northeastern Australia*. Geological Society of Australia, North Queensland Division, Townsville, 468 p.

Stewart A.J., Blake D.H., Ollier C.D. 1986. Cambrian river terraces and ridgetops in central Australia: oldest persisting landforms. *Science* 233, 758–761.

Stuart-Smith P., Needham R.S., Bagas L., Wallace D.A. 1987. *Pine Creek, Northern Territory*. 1:100,000 *Geological Map Commentary*. Bureau of Mineral Resources Geology and Geophysics, Canberra, 40 p.

Sussmilch C.A. 1909. Notes on the physiography of the Southern Tableland of New South Wales. *Proceedings of the Royal Society of New South Wales* 43, 331–354.

Sutherland F.L. 1991. Cainozoic volcanism, Eastern Australia: a predictive model based on migration over multiple 'hotspot' magma sources, *in* Williams M.A.J., De Deckker P., Kershaw A.P. (editors) The Cainozoic in Australia: a re-appraisal of the evidence. *Geological Society of Australia Special Publication* 18, 15–43.

Tate R. 1879. The anniversary address of the president. *Transactions and Proceedings and Report of the Philosophical Society of Adelaide, South Australia for 1878–9*, xxxix–lxxv.

Tattam C.M. 1972. Edwin Sherbon Hills. *University Gazette (Melbourne)* (October), 8–10.

Taylor A.J.P. 1950. *Essays in English History*. Penguin, Harmondsworth, 335 p.

Taylor G.A. 1958. The 1951 eruption of Mt Lamington, Papua. *Bureau of Mineral Resources Geology and Geophysics Bulletin* 38, 117 p.

Taylor T.G. 1911. Physiography of Eastern Australia. *Commonwealth Meteorology Bureau Bulletin* 8, 18 p.

Taylor G., Eggleton R.A., Holzhauer C.C., Maconachie L.A., Gordon M., Brown M.C., McQueen K.G. 1992. Cool climate lateritic and bauxitic weathering. *Journal of Geology* 100, 669–677.

Taylor G., Taylor G.R., Bink M., Foudoulis C., Gordon I., Hedstrom J., Minello J., Whippy F. 1985. Pre-basaltic topography of the northern Monaro and its implications. *Australian Journal of Earth Sciences* 32, 65–71.

Thornbury W.D. 1954. *Principles of Geomorphology*. Wiley, New York, 618 p.

Tilley C.E. 1921. A tholeiitic basalt from eastern Kangaroo Island. *Transactions of the Royal Society of South Australia* 45, 276–277.

Toit A.L. du 1937. *Geology of South Africa*. Oliver and Boyd, Edinburgh, 611 p.

Traves D.M. 1955. The geology of the Ord-Victoria region, northern Australia. *Bureau of Mineral Resources Geology and Geophysics Bulletin* 27, 133 p.

Trendall A.F. 1990. Cratons. Introduction, pp. 11–13 *in*

Geological Survey of Western Australia. Geology and Mineral Resources of Western Australia. *Western Australia Geological Survey Memoir* 3, 827 p.

Turner F.J., Verhoogen J. 1960. *Igneous and Metamorphic Petrology*. McGraw-Hill, New York, 694 p.

Twidale C.R. 1955. Interpretation of high-level meander cut-offs. *Australian Journal of Science* 17, 157–163.

Twidale C.R. 1956. Chronology of denudation in northwest Queensland. *Geological Society of America Bulletin* 67, 867–882.

Twidale C.R. 1962. Steepened margins of inselbergs from north-western Eyre Peninsula, South Australia. *Zeitschrift für Geomorphologie* 6, 51–69.

Twidale C.R. 1964. A contribution to the general theory of domed inselbergs. Conclusions derived from observations in South Australia. *Transactions and Papers of the Institute of British Geographers* 34, 91–113.

Twidale C.R. 1966a. Chronology of denudation in the southern Flinders Ranges, South Australia. *Transactions of the Royal Society of South Australia* 90, 3–28.

Twidale C.R. 1966b. Late Cainozoic activity of the Selwyn Upwarp. *Journal of the Geological Society of Australia* 13, 491–494.

Twidale C.R. 1968a. *Geomorphology, With Special Reference to Australia*. Nelson, Melbourne, 406 p.

Twidale C.R. 1968b. Origin of Wave Rock, Hyden, Western Australia. *Transactions of the Royal Society of South Australia* 92, 115–123.

Twidale C.R. 1972. The neglected third dimension. *Zeitschrift für Geomorphologie* 16, 283–300.

Twidale C.R. 1976a. *Analysis of Landforms*. Jacaranda Wiley, Brisbane, 572 p.

Twidale C.R. 1976b. On the survival of paleoforms. *American Journal of Science* 276, 77–95.

Twidale C.R. 1978a. On the origin of Ayers Rock, central Australia. *Zeitschrift für Geomorphologie Supplementband* 31, 177–206.

Twidale C.R. 1978b. On the origin of pediments in different structural settings. *American Journal of Science* 278, 1138–1176.

Twidale C.R. 1980. The Devil's Marbles, central Australia. *Transactions of the Royal Society of South Australia* 104, 41–49.

Twidale C.R. 1981a. Granitic inselbergs: domed, block-strewn and castellated. *Geographical Journal* 147, 54–71.

Twidale C.R. 1981b. Origins and environments of pediments. *Journal of the Geological Society of Australia* 28, 423–434.

Twidale C.R. 1982a. *Granite Landforms*. Elsevier, Amsterdam, 372 p.

Twidale C.R. 1982b. The evolution of bornhardts. *American Scientist* 70, 268–276.

Twidale C.R. 1982c. Les inselbergs à gradins et leur signification: l'exemple de l'Australie. *Annales de Géographie* 91, 657–678.

Twidale C.R. 1983. Australian laterites and silcretes: ages and significance. *Revue de Géographie Physique et Géologie Dynamique* 24, 35–45.

Twidale C.R. 1984a. The Lochiel Landslip, South Australia. *Australian Geographer* 17, 35–39.

Twidale C.R. 1984b. The enigma of the Tindal Plain, Northern Territory. *Transactions of the Royal Society of South Australia* 108, 95–103.

Twidale C.R. 1985. Old land surfaces and their implications for models of landscape evolution. *Revue de Géomorphologie Dynamique* 34, 131–147.

Twidale C.R. 1986. Granite platforms and low domes: newly exposed compartments or degraded remnants? *Geografiska Annaler Series A: Physical Geography* 68, 399–411.

Twidale C.R. 1990. The origin and implications of some erosional landforms. *The Journal of Geology* 98, 343–364.

Twidale C.R. 1991. A model of landscape evolution involving increased and increasing relief amplitude. *Zeitschrift für Geomorphologie* 35, 85–109.

Twidale C.R. 1994. Gondwanan (Late Jurassic and Cretaceous) palaeosurfaces of the Australian craton. *Palaeogeography, Palaeoclimatology, Palaeoecology* 112, 157–186.

Twidale C.R. 1997. Persistent and ancient rivers: some Australian examples. *Physical Geography* 18, 215–241.

Twidale C.R. 1999. Oldlands: characteristics and implications based on the Australian experience. *Physical Geography* 20, 273–304.

Twidale C.R. 2000a. Edwin Hills: morphotectonics and other geomorphological contributions. *Proceedings of the Geologists' Association of London* 111, 71–82.

Twidale C.R. 2000b. The Lochiel Landslip, a mass movement developing in 1974 but originating 600–700 million years earlier, Vol. 3, pp. 1489–1494 *in* Bromhead E., Dixon N., Ibsen M.-L. (editors) *Landslides in Research, Theory and Practice.* Proceedings ISSMGE and BGS 8th International Symposium on Landslides, 26–30 June 2000, Cardiff, Wales. Thomas Telford Publishing, London, 1684 p.

Twidale C.R. 2000c. Early Mesozoic (?Triassic) landscapes in Australia: evidence, argument, and implications. *The Journal of Geology* 108, 537–552.

Twidale C.R., 2002. The two-stage concept of landform and landscape development involving etching: origin, development and implications of an idea. *Earth-Science Reviews* 57, 37–74.

Twidale C.R. 2004. River patterns and their meaning. *Earth-Science Reviews* 67, 159–218.

Twidale C.R. 2006. Architecture and antiquity of the shield lands, *in* Andre, M.-F. (editor) *Festschrift in Honour of Alain Godard.* Presses Universitaires Blaise Pascal, Clermont Ferrand. In press.

Twidale C.R., Bourne J.A. 1975. Episodic exposure of inselbergs. *Geological Society of America Bulletin* 86, 1473–1481.

Twidale C.R., Bourne J.A. 1978. Bornhardts developed in sedimentary rocks, central Australia. *The South African Geographer* 6, 35–51.

Twidale C.R., Bourne J.A. 1996. Development of the land surface, pp. 46–62 *in* Davies M., Twidale C.R., Tyler M.J. (editors) *Natural History of the Flinders Ranges.* Royal Society of South Australia, Adelaide, 208 p.

Twidale C.R., Bourne J.A. 1998a. Origin and age of bornhardts, southwest of Western Australia. *Australian Journal of Earth Sciences* 45, 903–914.

Twidale C.R., Bourne J.A. 1998b. Flared slopes revisited. *Physical Geography* 19, 110–133.

Twidale C.R., Bourne J.A. 1999. The use of duricrusts and topographic relationships in geomorphological correlation: conclusions based in Australian experience. *Catena* 33, 105–122.

Twidale C.R., Bourne J.A. 2000a. Rock bursts and associated neotectonic forms at Minnipa Hill, northwestern Eyre Peninsula, South Australia. *Environmental and Engineering Geoscience* 6, 129–140.

Twidale C.R., Bourne J.A. 2000b. Dolines of the Pleistocene dune calcarenite terrain of western Eyre Peninsula, South Australia: a reflection of underprinting? *Geomorphology* 33, 89–105.

Twidale C.R., Bourne J.A. 2001. *A Field Guide to Hyden Rock, Western Australia.* Wave Rock Management P/L, Hyden, 68 p.

Twidale C.R., Bourne J.A. 2004. Neotectonism in Australia: its expressions and implications. *Géomorphologie* 3, 179–194.

Twidale C.R., Bourne J.A., Smith D.M. 1974. Reinforcement and stabilisation mechanisms in landform development. *Revue de Géomorphologie Dynamique* 23, 115–125.

Twidale C.R., Bourne J.A., Smith D.M. 1976. Age and origin of palaeosurfaces on Eyre Peninsula and the southern Gawler Ranges, South Australia. *Zeitschrift für Geomorphologie* 20, 28–55.

Twidale C.R., Bourne J.A., Vidal Romaní J.R. 1999. Bornhardt inselbergs in the Salt River Valley, south of Kellerberrin, Western Australia (with notes on a tessellated pavement in granite and pinnacles in laterite). *Journal of the Royal Society of Western Australia* 82, 33–49.

Twidale C.R., Bourne J.A., Vidal Romaní J.R. 2005. Beach etching and shore platforms. *Geomorphology* 67, 47–61.

Twidale C.R., Campbell E.M. 1984. Murphy Haystacks, Eyre Peninsula, South Australia. *Transactions of the Royal Society of South Australia* 108, 175–183.

Twidale C.R., Campbell E.M. 1986. Localised inversion on steep hillslopes: gully gravure in weak and in resistant rocks. *Zeitschrift für Geomorphologie* 30, 35–46.

Twidale C.R., Harris W.K. 1977. The age of Ayers Rock and the Olgas, central Australia. *Transactions of the Royal Society of South Australia* 101, 45–50.

Twidale C.R., Horwitz R.C., Campbell E.M. 1985. Hamersley landscapes of the northwest of Western Australia. *Revue de Géologie Dynamique et de Géographie Physique* 26, 173–186.

Twidale C.R., Lindsay J.M., Bourne J.A. 1978. Age and origin of the Murray River and Gorge in South Australia. *Proceedings of the Royal Society of Victoria* 90, 27–42.

Twidale C.R., Milnes A.R. 1983. Slope processes active late in arid scarp retreat. *Zeitschrift für Geomorphologie* 27, 343–361.

Twidale C.R., Prescott J.R., Bourne J.A., Williams F.M. 2001. Age of desert dunes near Birdsville, southwest Queensland. *Quaternary Science Reviews* 20, 1355–1364.

Twidale C.R., Shepherd J.A., Thomson R.M. 1970. Geomorphology of the southern part of the Arcoona Plateau and the Tent Hill region, west and north of Port Augusta, South Australia. *Transactions of the Royal Society of South Australia* 94, 55–67.

Twidale C.R., Vidal Romaní J.R. 1994. The Pangaean inheritance. *Cuadernos Laboratorio Xeolóxico de Laxe* 19, 7–36.

Van de Graaff W.J.E., Crowe R.W.A., Bunting J.A., Jackson M.J. 1977. Relict Early Cainozoic drainages in arid Western Australia. *Zeitschrift für Geomorphologie* 21, 379–400.

Vasconcelos, P.M., 1999. K-Asr and $^{40}Ar/^{39}Ar$ geochronology of weathering processes. *Annual Reviews of Earth and Planetary Science* 27, 183–229.

Vasconcelos P.M., Conroy M. 2003. Geochronology of weathering and landscape evolution, Dugald River valley, NW Queensland, Australia. *Geochimica et Cosmochimica Acta* 67, 2913–2930.

Vening Meinesz F.A. 1947. Shear patterns in the Earth's crust. *Transactions of the American Geophysical Union* 28, 1–61.

Vine F.J., Matthews D.H. 1963. Magnetic anomalies over oceanic ridges. *Nature* 199, 947–949.

Ward L.K. 1925. Notes on the geological structure of Central Australia. *Transactions of the Royal Society of South Australia* 49, 61–84.

Watchman A.L., Twidale C.R. 2002. Relative and 'absolute' dating of land surfaces. *Earth-Science Reviews* 58, 1–49.

Waterhouse J.D., Commander D.P., Prangley C., Backhouse J. 1995. Newly recognised Eocene sediments in the Beaufort River palaeochannel. *Geological Survey of Western Australia Annual Review* 1993–1994, 82–86.

Wayland E.J. 1934. Peneplains and some erosional landforms. *Geological Survey of Uganda Annual Report (for Year Ending 31st March 1934) and Bulletin* 1, 77–79.

Wegener A. 1924. *The Origin of Continents and Oceans.* (transl. J.G.A. Skerl) Methuen, London, 212 p.

Wellington J.H. 1937. The pre-Karroo peneplain in the South-central Transvaal. *South African Journal of Science* 33, 281–295.

Wellman P.W. 1971. 'The age and palaeomagnetism of the Australian Cenozoic volcanic rocks.' Unpublished PhD thesis, Australian National University, Canberra, 388 p.

Wellman P. 1972. Early Miocene potassium-argon age for the Fitzroy lamproites of Western Australia. *Journal of the Geological Society of Australia* 19, 471–474.

Wellman P. 1979a. On the Cainozoic uplift of the southeastern Australian highland. *Journal of the Geological Society of Australia* 26, 1–9.

Wellman P. 1979b. Reply: On the Cainozoic uplift of the southeastern Australian highland. *Journal of the Geological Society of Australia* 26, 318.

Wellman P. 1980. Reply: On the Cainozoic uplift of the southeastern Australian highland. *Journal of the Geological Society of Australia* 27, 119.

Wells A.T., Forman D.J., Ranford L.C., Cook P.J. 1970. Geology of the Amadeus Basin, central Australia. *Bureau of Mineral Resources Geology and Geophysics Bulletin* 100, 222 p.

Whitehouse F.W. 1940. The lateritic soils of western Queensland, *in* Studies in the Late Geological History of Queensland. *Papers, Department of Geology, University of Queensland* 2, 2–22.

Wilde S.A., Valley J.W., Peck W.H., Graham C.M. 2001. Evidence from detrital zircons for the existence of continental crust and oceans in earth 4.4 Ga ago. *Nature* 409, 175–178.

Willis B. 1936. East African plateaus and rift valleys. *Studies in Comparative Seismology.* Washington D.C., *Carnegie Institute Publication* 470, 358 p.

Williams G.E. 1969. Characteristics and origin of a Precambrian pediment. *The Journal of Geology* 77, 183–207.

Williams G.E. 1973. Late Quaternary piedmont sedimentation, soil formation and palaeoclimates in arid South Australia. *Zeitschrift für Geomorphologie* 17, 102–125.

Williams G.E. 1994. Acraman, South Australia: Australia's largest meteorite impact structure. *Proceedings of the Royal Society of Victoria* 106, 105–127

Williams G.E., Schmidt P.W. 1997. Palaeomagnetic dating of sub-Torridon Group weathering profiles, NW

Scotland: verification of Neoproterozoic palaeosols. *Journal of the Geological Society, London* 154, 987–997.

Willmot E.P. 1987. *Australia: The Last Experiment.* Australian Broadcasting Corporation, Sydney, 61 p.

Wilson A.W.G. 1903. The Laurentian peneplain. *The Journal of Geology* 11, 615–669.

Woodall R. 1994. Empiricism and concept in successful mineral exploration. *Australian Journal of Earth Sciences* 41, 1–10.

Woodard G.D. 1955. The stratigraphic succession in the vicinity of Mt Babbage Station, South Australia. *Transactions of the Royal Society of South Australia* 78, 8–17.

Woodburne M.O. 1967. The Alcoota fauna, central Australia. *Bureau of Mineral Resources, Geology and Geophysics Bulletin* 87, 185 p.

Wooldridge S.W. 1951. The role and relations of geomorphology, pp. 19–31 *in* Stamp L.D., Wooldridge S.W. (editors) *London Essays in Geography* (Llewellyn Rodwell Jones Memorial Volume). Longmans, Green & Co., London, 351 p.

Wopfner H. 1964. Permian-Jurassic history of the western Great Artesian Basin. *Transactions of the Royal Society of South Australia* 88, 117–128.

Wopfner H. 1967. Some observations on Cainozoic land surfaces in the Officer Basin. *Geological Survey of South Australia Quarterly Geological Notes* 23, 3–8.

Wopfner H. 1968. Cretaceous sediments on the Mt Margaret Plateau and evidence for neo-tectonism. *Geological Survey of South Australia Quarterly Geological Notes* 28, 7–11.

Wopfner H. 1969. Mesozoic era, pp. 133–171 *in* Parkin L.W. (editor) *Handbook of South Australian Geology.* Geological Survey of South Australia, Adelaide, 268 p.

Wopfner H. 1978. Silcretes of northern South Australia and adjacent regions, pp. 93–141 *in* Langford-Smith T. (editor) *Silcrete in Australia.* University of New England Press, Armidale, NSW, 304 p.

Wopfner H., Callen R., Harris W.K. 1974. The Lower Tertiary Eyre Formation of the southwestern Great Artesian Basin. *Journal of the Geological Society of Australia* 21, 17–51.

Wopfner H., Freytag I.B., Heath G.R. 1970. Basal Jurassic-Cretaceous rocks of western Great Artesian Basin, South Australia: stratigraphy and environment. *American Association of Petroleum Geologists Bulletin* 54, 383–416.

Wopfner H., Twidale C.R. 1967. Geomorphological History of the Lake Eyre Basin, pp. 117–143 *in* Jennings J.N., Mabbutt J.A. (editors) *Landform Studies from Australia and New Guinea.* Australian National University Press, Canberra, 434 p.

Wray R.A.L., Young R.W., Price D.M. 1993. Cainozoic heritage in the modern landscape near Bungonia, southern New South Wales. *Australian Geographer* 24, 45–61.

Wright R.L. 1963. Deep weathering and erosion surfaces in the Daly River Basin, Northern Territory. *Journal of the Geological Society of Australia* 10, 151–164.

Wright R.L. 1964. Geomorphology of the West Kimberley area, pp. 103–118 *in* General Report on Lands of the West Kimberley Area, *CSIRO Land Research Series* 9, 220 p.

Young R.W. 1985. Silcrete distribution in eastern Australia. *Zeitschrift für Geomorphologie* 29, 21–36.

Young R.W. 1986. Tower karst in sandstone: the Bungle Bungle Massif, northwestern Australia. *Zeitschrift für Geomorphologie* 30, 189–202.

Young R.W. 1987. Sandstone landforms of the tropical East Kimberley region, northwestern Australia. *Journal of Geology* 95, 205–218.

Young R.W. 1992. Structural heritage and planation in the evolution of landforms in the East Kimberley. *Australian Journal of Earth Sciences* 39, 141–151.

Young R.W., McDougall I. 1982. Basalts and silcretes on the coast near Ulladulla, southern New South Wales. *Australian Journal of Earth Sciences* 29, 425–430.

Young R.W., McDougall I. 1985. The age, extent and geomorphological significance of the Sassafras basalt, southeastern New South Wales. *Australian Journal of Earth Sciences* 32, 323–331.

Young R.W., McDougall I. 1993. Long-term landscape evolution. Early Miocene and modern rivers in southern New South Wales. *The Journal of Geology* 101, 35–49.

Young R.W., Short S.A., Price D.M., Bryant E.A., Nanson G.C., Gardiner B.H., Wray R.A.L. 1994. Ferruginous weathering under cool temperate climates during the Late Pleistocene in southeastern Australia. *Zeitschrift für Geomorphologie* 38, 45–57.

INDEX